Björnstjern Baade/Linus Mührel/Anton O. Petrov (eds.)

International Humanitarian Law in Areas of Limited Statehood

Adaptable and Legitimate or Rigid and Unreasonable?

Nomos

The Deutsche Nationalbibliothek lists this publication in the Deutsche Nationalbibliografie; detailed bibliographic data are available on the Internet at http://dnb.d-nb.de

ISBN 978-3-8487-4807-5 (Print)
978-3-8452-8955-7 (ePDF)

British Library Cataloguing-in-Publication Data
A catalogue record for this book is available from the British Library.

ISBN 978-3-8487-4807-5 (Print)
978-3-8452-8955-7 (ePDF)

Library of Congress Cataloging-in-Publication Data
Baade, Björnstjern / Mührel, Linus / Petrov, Anton O.
International Humanitarian Law in Areas of Limited Statehood
Adaptable and Legitimate or Rigid and Unreasonable?
Björnstjern Baade / Linus Mührel / Anton O. Petrov, (eds.)
251 p.
Includes bibliographic references and index.

ISBN 978-3-8487-4807-5 (Print)
978-3-8452-8955-7 (ePDF)

1st Edition 2018

Acknowledgements

This edited volume is the outcome of a workshop for junior researchers that took place at the Collaborative Research Centre (SFB 700) 'Governance in Areas of Limited Statehood' of Freie Universität Berlin in November 2016. We would like to take this opportunity to thank the many people whose assistance, cooperation and support made both the workshop and this edited volume possible.

Professor Dr. Heike Krieger, principal investigator of Research Project C8 'Legitimacy and Law-Making in International Humanitarian Law', supported the project from its inception and raised the necessary funds for it.

Freie Universität Berlin students Valentina Chiofalo, Jan Lukas Eiken and Antonia Herzog, who supported the organisation of the workshop as well as the editing process leading up to the publication of this volume, were diligent and conscientious research assistants. Sandra Esser assisted with the English language and honed the contributions as only a native speaker can.

We thank the participants of the workshop and especially Matthias Lippold, Dorota Banaszewska and Hannah Dönges, whose interesting and well-researched talks unfortunately could not become part of this volume. However, we tried to integrate their major research findings into this volume where possible.

We are grateful for the generous support for this project provided by the Freie Universität Berlin, the SFB 700 and the German Research Foundation (DFG).

Last but not least, we would like to thank Nomos and in particular Dr. Matthias Knopik and Stefanie Meyer for their support in publishing this volume.

Björnstjern Baade, Linus Mührel, Anton O. Petrov
Berlin, March 2018

Table of Contents

List of Contributors

Dr. Björnstjern Baade is a senior research fellow at Freie Universität Berlin and a post-doc in the working group 'Towards a Proceduralization of International Law?' at the Max-Planck-Institute for Comparative Public Law and International Law, Heidelberg
contact: b.baade@fu-berlin.de

Manuel Brunner, LL.M., is a doctoral candidate at Leibniz Universität Hannover and a lawyer working for Wolter Hoppenberg Rechtsanwälte, Hamm
contact: manuelbr@web.de

Pia Hesse, LL.M., is a doctoral candidate at Universität Potsdam and a junior lawyer at Kammergericht Berlin
contact: pia.hesse@fu-berlin.de

Dr. Heike Krieger is a Professor of Public Law and International Law at Freie Universität Berlin, and among others a Max-Planck-Fellow at the Max-Planck-Institute for Comparative Public Law and International Law, Heidelberg
contact: heike.krieger@fu-berlin.de

Charlotte Lülf, LL.M., M.A., is a doctoral candidate and a research associate at the Institute for International Law of Peace and Armed Conflict (IFHV) at Ruhr-University Bochum
contact: charlotte.luelf@ruhr-uni-bochum.de

Linus Mührel is a doctoral candidate at Freie Universität Berlin and a research associate at Technische Universität Dresden
contact: l.muehrel@fu-berlin.de

Lars Müller is a doctoral candidate at Freie Universität Berlin and a junior lawyer at Kammergericht Berlin
contact: mueller.lars@me.com

Ira Ryk-Lakhman Aharonovich, LL.M., is a PhD-candidate at University College London and a lawyer working for Tadmor & Co. Yuval Levy & Co., Tel Aviv
contact: iralakhman@gmail.com

Raphael Schäfer is a doctoral candidate at Ruprecht-Karls-Universität Heidelberg and a research fellow at the Max-Planck-Institute for Comparative Public Law and International Law, Heidelberg
contact: schaefer@mpil.de

Katja Schöberl, LL.M., is a legal advisor in International Humanitarian Law working for the German Red Cross in Berlin
contact: Schoebek@drk.de

Anton O. Petrov, LL.M. (NYU), is a doctoral candidate at Freie Universität Berlin and a junior lawyer at Kammergericht Berlin
contact: antonopetrov@gmail.com

Vincent Widdig is a doctoral candidate at European-University Viadrina, Frankfurt (Oder), and a research associate at Leibniz Universität Hannover
contact: vincent.widdig@jura.uni-hannover.de

Table of Treaties and other Legal Instruments

International Treaties

African Charter on Human and Peoples' Rights (adopted 27 June 1981, entered into force 21 October 1986) CAB/LEG/67/3 rev. 5, 21 ILM 58 (ACHPR)

American Convention on Human Rights (adopted 22 January 1696, entered into force 18 July 1978) 1144 UNTS 123 (ACHR)

Charter of the United Nations (adopted 27 June 1945, entered into force 24 October 1945) 1 UNTS XVI (UN Charter)

Convention for the Protection of Human Rights and Fundamental Freedoms, as amended by Protocols Nos. 11 and 14 (adopted 4 November 1950, entered into force 1953) ETS 5 (ECHR)

Convention for the Settlement of Investment Disputes between States and Nationals of other States (opened for signature 18 March 1965, entered into force 14 October 1966) 575 UNTS 159 (ICSID Convention)

Geneva Convention for the Amelioration of the Condition of the Wounded and Sick in Armed Forces in the Field (adopted 21 August 1949, entered into force 21 October 1950) 75 UNTS 31 (GC I)

Geneva Convention for the Amelioration of the Condition of Wounded, Sick and Shipwrecked Members of Armed Forces at Sea (adopted 21 August 1949, entered into force 21 October 1950) 75 UNTS 85 (GC II)

Geneva Convention relative to the Treatment of Prisoners of War (adopted 12 August 1949, entered into force 21 October 1950) 75 UNTS 135 (GC III)

Geneva Convention Relative to the Protection of Civilian Persons in Time of War (adopted on 12 August 1949, entered into force 21 October 1950) 75 UNTS 287 (GC IV)

Hague Convention Respecting the Laws and Customs of War on Land and Its Annex: Regulations Concerning the Laws and Customs of War on Land (adopted 18 October 1907, entered into force 26 January 1910) (Hague Regulations)

International Covenant on Civil and Political Rights (adopted 16 December 1966, entered into force 23 March 1976) 999 UNTS 171 (ICCPR)

Protocol Additional to the Geneva Convention of 12 August 1949, and relating the Protection of Victims of International Armed Conflicts (adopted 8 June 1977, entered into force 7 December 1978) 1125 UNTS 3 (AP I)

Protocol Additional to the Geneva Convention of 12 August 1949, and relating the Protection of Victims of Non-International Armed Conflicts (adopted 8 June 1977, entered into force 7 December 1978) 1125 UNTS 609 (AP II)

Rome Statute of the International Criminal Court (adopted 17 July 1998, entered into force 1 July 2002) 2187 UNTS 90 (ICC-Statute)

Statute of the International Court of Justice (adopted 24 October 1945, entered into force 18 November 1946) annexed to the Charter of the United Nations (ICJ-Statute)

Vienna Convention on the Law of Treaties (adopted 23 May 1969, entered into force 27 January 1980) 1155 UNTS 331 (VCLT)

Resolutions of the United Nations General Assembly

Articles on Responsibility of States for Internationally Wrongful Acts: resolution (adopted 8 January 2008 by GA Res A/RES/62/61) (ASR)

Resolutions of the United Nations Security Council

Statute of the International Criminal Tribunal for the Former Yugoslavia (as amended on 17 May 2002) (adopted 25 October 1993 by SC Resolution 827/1993) (ICTY-Statute)

Statute of the International Criminal Tribunal for Rwanda (as last amended on 13 October 2006) (adopted 8 November 1994 by SC Resolution 955/1994) (ICTR-Statute)

List of Abbreviations

ACHPR	African Charter on Human and Peoples' Rights
ACHR	American Convention on Human Rights
AJIL	American Journal of International Law
AP I	Protocol Additional to the Geneva Conventions of 12 August 1949, and relating to the Protection of Victims of International Armed Conflicts
AP II	Protocol Additional to the Geneva Conventions of 12 August 1949, and relating to the Protection of Victims of Non-International Armed Conflicts
ASIL	American Society of International Law
ASR	Articles on State Responsibility
BIT	Bilateral Investment Treaty
BYIL	British Yearbook of International Law
CA 3	Common Article 3 of the four Geneva Conventions of 12 August 1949
Case W. R. JIL	Case Western Reserve Journal of International Law
DRC	Democratic Republic of the Congo
ECHR	European Convention on Human Rights
ECtHR	European Court of Human Rights
EJIL	European Journal of International Law
FPS	full protection and security
GC I	Geneva Convention for the Amelioration of the Condition of the Wounded and Sick in Armed Forces in the Field
GC II	Geneva Convention for the Amelioration of the Condition of Wounded, Sick and Shipwrecked Members of Armed Forces at Sea
GC III	Geneva Convention relative to the Treatment of Prisoners of War
GC IV	Geneva Convention relative to the Protection of Civilian Persons in Time of War
GOJIL	Goettingen Journal of International Law
GYIL	German Yearbook of International Law
Harv. Int'l L. J.	Harvard International Law Journal
Hague Regulations	Regulations Concerning the Laws and Customs of War on Land, Annex to the Convention Respecting the Laws and Customs of War on Land of 18 October 1907
IAC	International Armed Conflict

ICC	International Criminal Court
ICC-Statute	Rome Statute of the International Criminal Court
ICCPR	International Covenant on Civil and Political Rights
ICJ	International Court of Justice
ICJ Rep	International Court of Justice, Reports of Judgments, Orders and Advisory Opinions
ICJ-Statute	Statute of the Court of International Justice
ICLQ	International and Comparative Law Quarterly
ICRC	International Committee of the Red Cross
ICSID	International Centre for Settlement of Investment Disputes
ICSID Convention	Convention for the Settlement of Investment Disputes between States and Nationals of other States
ICTR	International Criminal Tribunal for Rwanda
ICTY	International Criminal Tribunal for the former Yugoslavia
IHL	International Humanitarian Law
IHLRI	International Humanitarian Law Research Initiative
IHRL	International Human Rights Law
IIL	International Investment Law
ILC	International Law Commission
ILM	International Legal Materials
ILR	International Law Reports
ILS	International Law Studies
IO	International Organisation
IRRC	International Review of the Red Cross
ISAF	International Security Assistance Force
ISIS	Islamic State of Iraq and Syria / Daesh
IYHR	Israel Yearbook on Human Rights
J. Int'l L. of Peace & Armed Conflict	Journal of International Law of Peace and Armed Conflict
JCSL	Journal of Conflict & Security Law
JICJ	Journal of International Criminal Justice
JILP	NYU Journal of International Law and Politics
JPR	Journal of Peace Research
JZ	Juristenzeitung
KFG	Kolleg-Forschergruppe
LJIL	Leiden Journal of International Law
LTTE	Liberation Tigers of Tamil Eelam
MPEPIL	Max Planck Encyclopedia of Public International Law
NIAC	Non-International Armed Conflict
OAG	Organised Armed Group

PCIJ	Permanent Court of International Justice
POWs	Prisoners of war
RdC	Recueil des Cours de l'Académie de Droit International de La Haye
SJZ	Süddeutsche Juristenzeitung
TDM	Transnational Dispute Management
UK	United Kingdom of Great Britain and Northern Ireland
UNCITRAL	United Nations Commission on International Trade Law
UNESCO	United Nations Educational, Scientific and Cultural Organization
UN GA	United Nations General Assembly
UN HRC	United Nations Human Rights Committee
UN SC	United Nations Security Council
UN SG	United Nations Secretary-General
UN-Charter	Charter of the United Nations
US	United States of America
VCLT	Vienna Convention on the Law of Treaties
VJIL	Virginia Journal of International Law
Yale J. Int'l L.	Yale Journal of International Law
YbIHL	Yearbook of International Humanitarian Law
ZaöRV	Zeitschrift für ausländisches öffentliches Recht und Völkerrecht / Heidelberg Journal of International Law

Introduction: International Humanitarian Law and Areas of Limited Statehood

Heike Krieger, Björnstjern Baade and Linus Mührel

IHL needs to cover increasingly diverse forms of armed conflict. While its main structural features were conceived in the 19th and 20th century against the background of a predominant narrative of war conducted on a battlefield between armies and navies of sovereign States, the effectiveness of its legal rules has been constantly challenged by recurring changes in the conduct of warfare. During the last twenty-five years, the predominance of intra-State conflicts and the militarisation of terrorism has led to a focus on asymmetrical conflicts and NIACs. In recent years, challenges stem from the increasingly blurred lines between armed conflicts and more subversive forms of the use of force, as symbolised by the concept of 'hybrid warfare'. For maintaining its effectiveness, IHL needs to respond to changing social realities and thus accommodate new phenomena. Accordingly, changing conflict paradigms as well as the development of new technologies and corresponding strategies have tested the adaptability of existing rules and pushed for new rules, mostly laid down in treaty obligations.

However, since the adoption of the 1949 Geneva Conventions and the 1977 Additional Protocols, new treaties on the conduct of warfare have not been concluded. Instead, the international community has accommodated new phenomena through customary international law, interpretation and a focus on compliance. In particular, international tribunals have developed the rules of IHL in their jurisprudence and both the ICRC and the UN SC have focused on the enforcement of and compliance with IHL. Despite these efforts, including the establishment of the ICTY, the ICTR and the ICC, there is a widespread perception of a crisis of IHL. Some observers hold that its rules cannot sufficiently direct the behaviour of relevant actors.[1] In order to counter the perception of such a trend the ICRC has

1 Cf 'Report of the Secretary-General on the protection of civilians in armed conflict' UN Doc S/2017/414 (10 May 2017) 3, 7 et seq; Ian Clark et al, 'Crisis in the laws of war? Beyond compliance and effectiveness' (2017) European Journal of International Relations <http://journals.sagepub.com/doi/pdf/10.117

changed its publicity strategy and aims to shed more light on successful cases of compliance.[2] One may assume that this policy change reflects the understanding that the effectiveness and the legitimacy of norms are mutually reinforcing.[3] While emphasising that the rules of IHL are still effective might contribute to an increase in compliance, challenges to their legitimacy also need to be addressed in order to further compliance.[4]

The interplay between effectiveness and legitimacy as an important precondition for norm-compliance in IHL can be made explicit by focusing on the challenges which stem from areas of limited statehood. The present volume considers the impact such areas have on IHL and it inquires whether IHL can be adapted to meet challenges emerging from them in a way that is perceived as legitimate.

While the term 'areas of limited statehood' (A.) as such is only seldom used in legal discourse, areas of limited statehood have had a discernable impact on various developments that affect international law.[5] Regarding IHL, various challenges stem from the territorial State's limited capabilities and the need to compensate for them through other actors, in particular other States, international organisations and NGOs. Armed non-State actors' exercise of governance functions poses the most problems in this context (B.). How has IHL responded to these challenges so far? Or has a lack of responsiveness created legitimacy problems (C.)? These and other questions were probed by the contributions to this volume (D.). As a whole, the contributions reveal the dilemma that by trying to improve legitimacy and effectiveness for some actors, the same might be reduced for others.

7/1354066117714528> accessed 13 December 2017 (hereafter Clark et al, 'Crisis in the laws of war?').

2 For further reading, see Juliane Garcia Ravel, 'Changing the narrative on international humanitarian law' (*Humanitarian Law & Policy*, 24 November 2017) <http://blogs.icrc.org/law-and-policy/2017/11/24/changing-the-narrative-on-international-humanitarian-law/> accessed 13 December 2017.

3 Heike Krieger 'Governance by armed groups: Caught in the legitimacy trap?' in Cord Schmelzle and Eric Stollenwerk (eds), *Virtuous or Vicious Circle? Governance Effectiveness and Legitimacy in Areas of Limited Statehood, Special Issue* (under review).

4 Heike Krieger (ed), *Inducing Compliance with International Humanitarian Law* (CUP 2015) (hereafter Krieger, *Inducing Compliance*).

5 For further reading, see Heike Krieger, 'International Legal Order' in Tanja Börzel, Thomas Risse and Anke Draude (eds), *The Oxford Handbook of Governance and Limited Statehood* (OUP 2018, forthcoming) (hereafter Krieger, 'International Legal Order').

A. Areas of Limited Statehood[6]

Areas of limited statehood constitute those parts of a State in which the government lacks the capability to implement and enforce rules and decisions or in which they do not command a legitimate monopoly over the means of violence.[7] The term does not imply the extinction of a State (as a whole or in a certain area). The area still *de jure* belongs to the State, but its internal sovereignty there is *de facto* tenuous.

The term 'areas of limited statehood' describes an empirical phenomenon which has to be distinguished from normative concepts such as 'unwilling and unable' or 'failed' States.[8] These concepts are closely related to the phenomenon of securitisation and may thus be understood as tools of States of the Global North to push their specific interests in law-making processes, for instance in relation to re-interpretations of the right to self-defence. In contrast, the term 'areas of limited statehood' neither implies a normative judgment that a State has failed nor suggests that State failure would be the definite result of a process.[9] It is meant as a neutral analytical tool that avoids negative connotations and opens the door for an analysis from different perspectives. These can include the questions whether and to what extent the limitedness of statehood is compensated by other actors, what kind of governance they may perform, and how effective those governance functions are.[10] The term is also broader in the sense that only certain policy

6 This part draws from Krieger, 'International Legal Order' (n 5).

7 Tanja Börzel, Thomas Risse and Anke Draude, 'Governance in Areas of Limited Statehood: Conceptual Clarifications and Major Contributions of the Handbook' in Tanja Börzel, Thomas Risse and Anke Draude (eds), *The Oxford Handbook of Governance and Limited Statehood* (OUP 2018, forthcoming) (hereafter Börzel, Risse and Draude, 'Governance in Areas of limited Statehood').

8 Ibid.

9 Note that also e.g. Görlitzer Park in Berlin Kreuzberg can be qualified as an area of limited Statehood, see Börzel, Risse and Draude, 'Governance in Areas of limited Statehood'.

10 Cf Klaus Schlichte, 'A Historical Sociological Perspective on Statehood' in Tanja Börzel, Thomas Risse and Anke Draude (eds), *The Oxford Handbook of Governance and Limited Statehood* (OUP 2018, forthcoming); Andrew Brandel and Shalini Randeria, 'Anthropological Perspectives on the Limits of the State' in Tanja Börzel, Thomas Risse and Anke Draude (eds), *The Oxford Handbook of Governance and Limited Statehood* (OUP 2018, forthcoming).

areas or parts of one or more States might be affected.[11] Another advantage is that the limitedness of statehood is empirically measurable according to certain factors, including administrative capacity and monopoly of force.[12] While the term 'areas of limited statehood', which was conceived by political scientists in the Collaborative Research Centre 700 'Governance in areas of limited Statehood', has so far only seldom been used in legal discourse, it is by now gradually adopted because of its more neutral connotations.[13]

B. Legal Issues when other Actors Step in

Areas of limited statehood generally are not simply ungoverned.[14] Other actors regularly step in to perform government functions: other States, international organisations and non-State actors, including non-State armed groups and NGOs, have the potential to, and do, exercise effective and long-term regulatory power in such areas.[15] This has raised questions concerning the international legal obligations of non-State actors, international organisations and of States acting extraterritorially. The relevance of non-State practice and the possibility of a change in the structure of the law-making process that weakens or even undermines the primacy of State consent as the traditional foundation of positive international law-making, in order to improve the law's legitimacy towards non-State actors, has also become a contentious issue.

---

11 Thomas Risse and Ursula Lehmkuhl, 'Governance in Areas of Limited Statehood – New Modes of Governance?', Research Program of the Collaborative Research Center (SFB) 700 (Berlin 2006) 9.

12 Eric Stollenwerk, 'Measuring Governance and Limited Statehood' in Tanja Börzel, Thomas Risse and Anke Draude (eds), *The Oxford Handbook of Governance and Limited Statehood* (OUP 2018, forthcoming).

13 See e.g. Leuven Centre for Global Governance Studies of KU Leuven, in particular the research projects on 'human rights, democracy and rule of law', 'peace and security', and 'non-state actors' <https://ghum.kuleuven.be/ggs> accessed 13 December 2017.

14 This part draws from Krieger, 'International Legal Order' (n 5).

15 Cf various chapters in in Tanja Börzel, Thomas Risse and Anke Draude (eds), The Oxford Handbook of Governance and Limited Statehood (OUP 2018, forthcoming), e.g. Markus Lederer, 'External State Actors'; Benedetta Berti, 'Violent and Criminal Non-State Actors'; Marianne Beisheim, Annekathrin Ellersiek, and Jasmin Lorch, 'INGOs and Multi-Stakeholder Partnerships'.

I. Other States and International Organisations

With third States and international organisations, difficulties arise in the classification of armed conflicts and the determination of the applicable human rights standards. These uncertainties endanger these actors' compliance and, more generally, the relevance of the law to the situation on the ground in areas of limited statehood, and thus its effectiveness

1) Fluidity of armed conflicts

The interventions of third States in internal armed conflicts in areas of limited statehood triggered a debate concerning the classification of those armed conflicts, which directly relates to IHL's effectiveness in these conflicts. Since the law of IAC provides a framework of detailed treaty rules as well as widely accepted customary law rules, it is *prima facie* better suited to effectively govern the conduct of States. In contrast, the law of NIAC only consists of a few treaty rules and the customary law status of several rules is contested. Intervening States will have fewer legal standards to guide their conduct if the conflict is classified as non-international. Thus, IHL becomes potentially less effective due to a lack of legal certainty which regime applies.

The debate around these so-called 'internationalised' NIACs focuses on two issues. On the one hand, it concerns the relation between the intervening State and the territorial State. On the other hand, it deals with the relation between the intervening State and the non-State armed group(s).

In cases in which the territorial State consented to the use of force of another State against a non-State armed group in its own territory, it is widely agreed that there exists a NIAC between the extraterritorially acting State and the non-State armed group. Thus, only the law of NIAC is applicable to this situation. In case of a lack of consent by the territorial State, however, it is highly controversial whether in addition to the NIAC between the intervening State and the non-State armed group(s) there exists a parallel IAC between the territorial State and the intervening State. In this case then also the law of IAC would apply between the territorial State and the extraterritorially acting State, i.e. the conduct of the extraterritorially acting State could underlie the law of IAC, too. This debate gained much attention after the US-led coalition and Turkey *inter alia* started to carry out air-strikes against ISIS and other Islamic terrorist groups in Syria and to support other non-State armed groups fighting ISIS in the absence of Syria's consent.[16]

While some emphasise that the extraterritorial use of force affects the local population and the territorial State's infrastructure to argue for the existence of a parallel IAC,[17] others mention the lack of practicality of the application of the rules of IAC.[18]

In addition, the debate concerning the extent of control that a State must have over a non-State armed group to render a NIAC between the non-State armed group and the territorial State into an IAC between the intervening State and the territorial State is still ongoing with no end in sight.[19] Whereas the ICJ upholds its more restrictive effective control test,[20] the ICTY follows its broader overall control test.[21]

---

16 See the various blog-posts on this issue eg Adil Ahmad Haque, 'The United States is at War with Syria (according to the ICRC's New Geneva Convention Commentary)' (*EJIL Talk!*, 8 April 2016) <https://www.ejiltalk.org/the-united-states-is-at-war-with-syria-according-to-the-icrcs-new-geneva-convention-commentary/> accessed 17 November 2017; Ryan Goodman, 'Is the United States Already in an "International Armed Conflict" with Syria?' (*Just Security*, 11 October 2016) <https://www.justsecurity.org/33477/united-states-international-armed-conflict-syria/> accessed 17 November 2017; Ryan Goodman, 'International Armed Conflict in Syria and the (Lack of) Official Immunity for War Crimes' (*Just Security*, 18 October 2016) <https://www.justsecurity.org/33670/international-armed-conflict-syria-lack-of-official-immunity-war-crimes/> accessed 17 November 2017.

17 Tristan Ferraro and Lindsey Cameron, 'Article 2: Application of the Convention' in ICRC (ed), Commentary on the First Geneva Convention: Convention (I) for the Amelioration of the Condition of the Wounded and Sick in Armed Forces in the Field (2nd edn, CUP 2016) paras 257 et seq (hereafter Ferraro and Cameron, 'Article 2').

18 For further reading, see Terry D. Gill, 'Classifying the Conflict in Syria' (2016) 92 ILS 353; Claus Kreß, 'Some Reflections on the International Legal Framework Governing Transnational Armed Conflicts' (2010) 15 JCSL 245, 255 et seq.

19 Ferraro and Cameron, 'Article 2' (n 17) paras 265 et seq.

20 Application of the Convention on the Prevention and Punishment of Genocide (*Bosnia and Herzegovina v Serbia and Montenegro*) (Judgment) [2007] ICJ Rep 43, paras 392–393; Military and Paramilitary Activities in and against Nicaragua (*Nicaragua v United States of America*) (Judgment) [1986] ICJ Rep 14, para 115.

21 *Prosecutor v Tadic* (Judgment) IT-94-1-A (15 July 1999) paras 120 et seq.

2) Human rights in areas of limited statehood

The lack of legal certainty surrounding the question if and to what extent IHRL applies to State and non-State actors is exacerbated by all actors' potential incapacity to fully comply with their legal obligations. In areas of limited statehood, the States concerned are often incapable to protect (certain) human rights, in particular in unstable security situations. If other States, international organisations or non-State actors step in and take over government functions, the question arises by which (international) legal obligations other than IHL they are bound, and how those obligations interplay with IHL obligations. In that manner, legal uncertainty and factual obstacles to compliance challenge the legitimacy, and in turn the effectivity, of international law in areas of limited statehood.

In the last 15 years, extensive debates on the extraterritorial application of intervening States' human rights obligations have been held.[22] Starting with the *Bankovic* decision,[23] the ECtHR has, in a long line of jurisprudence, developed criteria to establish the extraterritorial application of the ECHR.[24] The approach basically still focuses on the question of how to define the degree of control which a State must exercise abroad so as to justify the application of the international or regional human rights obligations it has contracted.[25] While the extraterritorial application of human rights may in principle arise for all State activities in an

22 UN HRC, 'Concluding observations on the fourth periodic report of the United States of America' (23 April 2014) UN Doc CCPR/C/USA/CO/4; Marco Milanovic, 'Harold Koh's Legal Opinions on the US Position on the Extraterritorial Application of Human Rights Treaties' (*EJIL: Talk*, 7 March 2014) referring to Harold H. Koh, US Department of State, 'Memorandum Opinion on the Geographic Scope of the International Covenant on Civil and Political Rights' (19 October 2010) <https://www.justsecurity.org/wp-content/up-loads/2014/03/state-department-iccpr-memo.pdf> accessed 19 October 2017.

23 *Bankovic and others v Belgium and others* [GC], App no 52207/99, 12 December 2001, paras 54 et seq.

24 See in particular, summarizing the case law, *Al-Skeini and others v the United Kingdom* [GC], App no 55721/07, 7 July 2011, paras 130-142 (hereafter: *Al-Skeini*). For further reading see Marco Milanovic, *Extraterritorial Application of Human Rights Treaties* (OUP 2011).

25 *Al-Skeini*; see also: Christoph Grabenwarter, *European Convention on Human Rights* (Beck et al 2014), Article 1, paras 13-17; Heike Krieger, 'Die Verantwortlichkeit Deutschlands nach der EMRK für seine Streitkräfte im Auslandseinsatz' (2002) 62 ZaöRV 669.

interconnected and globalised world, most decisions concerned military missions in areas of limited statehood, either in a state of armed conflict, situations of occupation, or other activities involving the deployment of military forces, such as in counter-piracy operations.[26]

This extension of human rights treaties has forced States to adapt their extraterritorial conduct to human rights standards. Furthermore, it has raised questions concerning the relationship of IHRL to other law regimes, in particular IHL,[27] and even the very foundations of international law.[28] The discussions on the legality of detention in NIACs[29] or the legality of targeted killings[30] including drone strikes[31] demonstrate the depth of these questions.

26 Eg *Loizidou v Turkey*, App no 15318/89, 23 March 1995; *Markovic and others v Italy*, App no 1298/03, 14 December 2006; *Medvedyev and Others v France*, App no 3394/03, 29 March 2010; *Al-Skeini and Others v the United Kingdom*, App no 55721/07, 7 July 2011; *Pisari v the Republic of Moldova and Russia*, App no 42139/12, 21 April 2015.

27 Heike Krieger, 'A Conflict of Norms: The Relationship between Humanitarian Law and Human Rights Law in the ICRC Customary Law Study' (2006) Journal of Conflict and Security Law 265, reprinted in: Robert Cryer and Christian Henderson (eds), *Law on the Use of Force and Armed Conflict, Cheltenham*, vol. III (Edward Elgar Publishing 2007).

28 Katja Schöberl and Linus Mührel, 'Sunken Vessel or Blooming Flower? Lotus, Permissions and Restrictions within International Humanitarian Law' in this volume 59 (hereafter Schöberl and Mührel, 'Sunken Vessel or Blooming Flower?'); Manuel Brunner, 'Security Detention by the Armed Forces of a State in Situations of Non-International Armed Conflict: The Search for a Legal Basis' in this volume 89 (hereafter Brunner, 'Security Detention by the Armed Forces of a State in Situations of NIAC').

29 Ibid; Vincent Widdig, 'Detention by Organised Armed Groups in Non-International Armed Conflicts: the Role of Non-State Actors in a State Centred International Legal System' in this volume 124 (hereafter Widdig, 'Detention by Organised Armed Groups in Non-International Armed Conflicts'); Pia Hesse, 'Comment: neither Sunken Vessel nor Blooming Flower! The Lotus Principle and International Humanitarian Law' in this volume 80 (hereafter Hesse, 'Neither Sunken Vessel nor Blooming Flower!'); Anton O. Petrov, 'Comment: Detention in Non-International Armed Conflict by States – Just a Matter of Perspective on Areas of Limited Statehood?' in this volume 118 (hereafter Petrov, 'Detention in Non-International Armed Conflict by States').

30 Luise Doswald-Beck, 'The right to life in armed conflict: does international humanitarian law provide all the answers?' (2006) 88 IRRC 881.

31 Christof Heyns, Dapo Akande, Lawrence Hill-Cawthorne and Thompson Chengeta, 'The International Law Framework Regulating the Use of Armed Drones' (2016) 65 ICLQ 791.

More profoundly, while the extraterritorial application of human rights may contribute to the effectiveness of IHRL, it also calls into question the legitimacy of human rights law and its judicial institutions. The extraterritorial application of human rights challenges the whole concept that human rights are primarily meant to regulate the relationship between a State and the persons on its territory. As governance becomes disconnected from the territorially based political community, so do human rights. This, in turn, casts doubt on how regional human rights law can be transferred to certain situations, particularly armed conflicts, in which the State exercises governance in the territory of another State. As a result, human rights obligations need to be applied very flexibly to a very specific context, and the basic indeterminacy of human rights law is exacerbated.[32] Moreover, it is argued that the disconnect of human rights from the territorial political sovereign, and therefore from a specific national political discourse, does not improve the situation in areas of limited statehood.[33] In fact, the extraterritorial application of human rights in areas of limited statehood may affect the societies in which the (human rights) courts are based to a much greater extent than the people subject to an extraterritorial exercise of jurisdiction.

II. Armed Non-State Actors

Regarding non-State actors taking over government functions in areas of limited statehood, the questions arise under which conditions these actors are bound by international legal obligations and whether these obligations may effectively govern non-State actors' conduct. Up until now, international law has addressed these issues mainly in the context of obligations of armed groups in NIACs under IHL in general.[34] But, in its

---

32 Nehal Bhuta, 'The Frontiers of Extraterritoriality – Human Rights Law as Global Law' in Nehal Bhuta (ed), *The Frontiers of Human Rights* (OUP 2016) 17.

33 Ibid, 17 et seq.

34 For discussions on obligations under IHRL, see Andrew Clapham, *Human Rights Obligations of Non-State Actors* (OUP 2010); Sandesh Sivakumaran, *The Law of Non-international Armed Conflict* (OUP 2012) (hereafter Sivakumaran, *The Law of NIAC*); Sassoli and Shany, 'Should the Obligations of States and Armed Groups under International Humanitarian Law Really Be Equal?' (2012) 93 IRRC 425; Daragh Murray, *Human Rights Obligations of Non-state Armed Groups* (Hart Publishing 2016).

purpose to establish and effectively enforce binding rules that strike an appropriate balance between military necessity and humanity, IHL is even more directly challenged in areas of limited statehood. The example of the terrorist organisation ISIS has given renewed emphasis to the fact that armed non-State actors exist which totally reject international legal obligations.[35]

However, not only the rejection of international legal obligations, total or in part, i.e. deliberate non-compliance, challenges IHL in areas of limited statehood.[36] The limited capability of some non-State armed groups to comply with certain IHL rules casts doubt on the 'governance'-function of IHL in such areas and may thwart the humanitarian purpose of IHL.[37] For example, non-State armed groups might not be able to detain enemy fighters either on a factual level or legally, as well as in a manner that meets basic rule-of-law requirements.[38] As a consequence, the non-State armed group might be left with no option but to either release or to kill the enemy fighter. Since the release of a fighter would contradict the military advantage of the armed group and is therefore unrealistic, the killing of the fighter, while constituting a war crime (cf Art. 8 (2) (e) (x) Rome Statute), might seem to be an option for the group.[39] This example of detention in NIACs demonstrates that IHL's failure to address a phenomenon that is *de facto* part of areas of limited statehood may lead to non-compliance even if non-compliance is repressively sanctioned.

---

35 Annyssa Bellal, 'Beyond the Pale? Engaging the Islamic State on International Humanitarian Law' (2015) YbIHL 18, 123.

36 For further reading, see Reed M. Wood, 'Understanding strategic motives for violence against civilians during civil conflict' in Krieger, *Inducing Compliance* (n 4) 13; Zachariah Mampilly, 'Insurgent governance in the Democratic Republic of the Congo' in Krieger, *Inducing Compliance* (n 4) 44.

37 For a different perspective, see e.g. Jan Willms, 'Courts of armed groups – a tool for inducing higher compliance with international humanitarian law?' in Krieger, *Inducing Compliance* (n 4) 149.

38 Widdig, 'Detention by Organised Armed Groups in Non-International Armed Conflicts' (n 29); Marco Sassòli, 'The Convergence of the International Humanitarian Law of Non-International and International Armed Conflicts - The Dark Side of a Good Idea' in Giovanni Biaggini, Oliver Diggelmann and Christine Kaufmann (eds), *Polis und Kosmopolis - Festschrift für Daniel Thürer* (Dike/Nomos 2015) 679, 682 et seq (hereafter Sassòli, 'The Dark Side of a Good Idea').

39 Sassòli, 'The Dark Side of a Good Idea' (n 38) 683 et seq.

The increase in NIACs after 1990 has caused numerous legal debates on how to best deal with armed groups and make IHL more effective. Continuing efforts exist to fill legal gaps in the applicable law of NIAC, e.g. the Customary International Humanitarian Law Study of the ICRC,[40] other expert studies and the work of the NGO Geneva Call, which convinces non-state armed groups to sign so-called Deeds of Commitment, aiming to enhance substantive standards in NIACs.[41] These efforts have raised questions on whether and to what extent this approach by NGOs on the one side, and the practice of non-State armed groups on the other side should be included in the law-making processes.

While some aspects of these questions are still controversially debated (e.g. the relevance of agreements between the parties to a NIAC under CA 3 (3),[42] other attempts, such as the inclusion of the practice of non-State actors – *inter alia* in areas of limited statehood – in the formation of customary law, have been entirely rejected by States and forums representing a State-centric positivist approach.[43] States have become aware of a looming shift in power to non-State actors and are now seeking to minimise these actors' influence in international law-making and development. Reactions of that kind can, for example, be observed in international conferences where States emphasise that the respective process is 'State-driven'.[44] The ILC in its recent works on the Identification

40 Jean-Marie Henckaerts and Luise Doswald-Beck, *Customary International Humanitarian Law* (CUP 2005) (hereafter Henckaerts and Doswald-Beck, *Customary IHL*

41 For further reading, see Sivakumaran, *The Law of NIAC* (n 34); Sandesh Sivakumaran, 'Implementing humanitarian norms through non-State armed groups' in Krieger, *Inducing Compliance* (n 4) 125; Heike Krieger, 'Conclusion: where States fail, non-State actors rise? Inducing compliance with international humanitarian law in areas of limited statehood' in Krieger, *Inducing Compliance* (n 4) 504.

42 Lars Müller, 'Comment: Detention by Armed Groups' in this volume 163 (hereafter Müller, 'Detention by Armed Groups').

43 See eg the reaction to the methodology underlying the *Customary International Humanitarian Law Study* of the ICRC (n 40) XLI by the US government, John B. Bellinger and William J. Haynes, 'A US government response to the International Committee of the Red Cross study *Customary International Humanitarian Law*' (2007) 89 IRRC 443, 444 et seq.

44 Eg Resolution 2 of the 32nd International Conference of the Red Cross and Red Crescent (2016) 97 IRRC 1393 stating '1. ... *recalls* the guiding principles of the consultation process: the State-driven and consensus-based character of the process and the need for the consultations to be based on applicable principles

of Customary International Law or Subsequent Agreements and Subsequent Practice also rejects the relevance of non-State actors' conduct in law-making and development.[45]

The maintenance of the State consent-based law paradigm may go at the expense of legitimacy of and consequently also compliance with IHL and international law in general by non-State armed groups. On the other hand, the dangers of giving non-State armed groups a role in the law-making process should not be underestimated either. Many of these groups have a proven track record of gross violations of the laws of war, and their preferences for the development of IHL might not emphasise the protection of the individual nor respect for the rule of law at all. Non-State actors might also overemphasise their limited capabilities to comply with IHL.

Examining the question of the inclusion/exclusion of non-State actors from a more abstract angle, an opening of the law-making process towards non-State actors as well as a denial of participation may challenge international law fundamentally. Both approaches may question the simplicity, precision, universality and impartiality of international law. While the exclusion of non-State actors ignores reality, an inclusion of non-State actors may lead to a stand-still of the law-making process due to the difficulties of determining and identifying e.g. the relevant actors and their practice. Both approaches may challenge the legitimacy and the governance function of international law in general and IHL in particular.[46]

This volume, *inter alia*, further discusses the efforts to include non-State actors in the law-making process for specific topics and elaborates on further approaches that seek to accommodate non-State armed groups in the

---

of international law … 2. *recommends* the continuation of an inclusive, State-driven intergovernmental process based on the principle of consensus after the 32nd International Conference …'.

45 ILC, 'Second report on identification of customary international law by Special Rapporteur Michael Wood' (22 May 2014) UN Doc 1/CN.4/672, para 45; ILC, 'Third report on identification of customary international law by Special Rapporteur Michael Wood' (27 March 2015) UN Doc A/CN.4/682, para 79; ILC, 'Subsequent agreements and subsequent practice in relation to the interpretation of treaties: Text of the draft conclusions provisionally adopted by the Drafting Committee on first reading' (6 June 2016) UN Doc A/CN.4/L.874, Draft conclusion 5(2); ILC, 'Report on the work of the sixty-eighth session (2016)' UN Doc A/71/10, Chapter VI, 233, paras 9 et seq.

46 For further reading, see eg Joost Pauwelyn, 'Is it International Law Or Not, And Does It Even Matter?' in Joost Pauwelyn, Ramses Wessel and Jan Wouters (eds), *Informal International Lawmaking* (OUP 2012) 125.

international legal system, in order to improve the law's legitimacy and effectiveness.

C. International Humanitarian Law's Lack of Responsiveness

Ignoring changes that exist on an empirical level could also be an option for IHL. While this may preserve the integrity of the law, it would probably lead to negative consequences for its legitimacy, effectiveness, and thus the functioning of the international legal system as a whole in areas of limited statehood.[47]

In IHL, empirical phenomena have traditionally been ignored when attempts to regulate NIACs were made. The drafting history of CA 3[48] and AP II,[49] as well as the brevity of and the high threshold for AP II to apply,[50] demonstrate the general unwillingness of States to regulate internal armed conflicts by international law. Attempts by the ICRC to attach some legal importance to these conflicts prior to the 1949 Geneva Conventions were entirely rejected.[51]

A more recent example is the outcome of the 32nd International Conference of the Red Cross and Red Crescent Movement with regard to the ICRC proposals on the strengthening of compliance with IHL[52] and the

47 Heike Krieger and Georg Nolte, 'The International Rule of Law – Rise or Decline? Points of Departure' (2016) 1 KFG Working Paper, 15 et seq <http://www.kfg-intlaw.de/PDF-ftp-Ordner/KFG%20Working%20Paper%20No.%201.pdf> accessed 16 October 2017.

48 For further reading, see Jean S. Pictet (ed), *The Geneva Conventions of 12 August 1949: Commentary*, vol. I (ICRC 1952), 38 et seq (hereafter Pictet, *Commentary*); David A. Elder, 'The Historical Background of Common Article 3 of The Geneva Convention of 1949' (1979) 11 Case W. R. JIL 37.

49 Michael Bothe, Karl J. Partsch and Waldemar A. Solf, *New Rules for Victims of Armed Conflicts: Commentary on the Two 1977 Protocols Additional to the Geneva Conventions of 1949* (2nd edn, Martinus Nijhoff Publishers 2013) 693 et seq; David P. Forsythe, 'Legal Management of Internal War: The 1977 Protocol on Non-International Armed Conflicts' (1978) 72 AJIL 273.

50 Cf Art. 1 AP II.

51 Pictet, *Commentary* (n 43) 39-41.

52 ICRC, 'No agreement by States on mechanism to strengthen compliance with rules of war' (10 December 2015) <https://www.icrc.org/en/document/no-agreement-states-mechanism-strengthen-compliance-rules-war> accessed 16 October 2017; Resolution 2 of the 32nd International Conference of the Red Cross and Red Crescent (2016) 97 IRRC 1393.

dealing with detentions in NIACs.[53] It exemplifies that the international community finds it difficult to agree on how to effectively address these new phenomena. The already softened ICRC proposals, elaborated previously in years of expert meetings under the participation of States, were rejected and the process was adjourned. Academic proposals to incentivise armed non-State actors to comply with IHL by granting them combatant immunity or amnesties have likewise not attracted much support.[54]

On the other hand, Art. 17 (1) (a) ICC-Statute,[55] can be understood as a response to the challenges of investigating and prosecuting genocide, war crimes and crimes against humanity committed in areas of limited statehood. According to this article, a case before the ICC is admissible if the State having jurisdiction over it is 'unwilling or unable genuinely to carry out the investigation or prosecution'.

In sum, areas of limited statehood create a dilemma for the legitimacy and effectiveness of IHL. They pose difficulties for the application and implementation of IHL on many different levels. But while taking into account the factual particularities of these areas might render the law more legitimate and thus effective for some actors, it might simultaneously imperil its legitimacy for others. Accommodating non-State actors in the law-making process might improve the law's legitimacy for them, but it would simultaneously jeopardise its legitimacy among States. Considering actors' capabilities in the application of rules might improve compliance in the short run, but might also water down legal stadards for all actors and make the law generally less legitimate.

53 Resolution 1 of the 32nd International Conference of the Red Cross and Red Crescent (2016) 97 IRRC 1390.

54 See eg the rejection by the Diplomatic Conference of the proposals made by the ICRC regarding restrictions of the prosecution of those who participated in NIACs in Art. 10 of Draft Protocol II, Draft Additional Protocols to the Geneva Conventions of August 12, 1949, ICRC (June 1973). For a further reading, see Ives Sandoz et al (eds), *Commentary on the Additional Protocols of 8 June 1977 to the Geneva Conventions of 12 August 1949* (ICRC 1987) 4397; Jann K. Kleffner, 'From "Belligerents" to "Fighters" and Civilians Directly Participating in Hostilities' (2007) 54 Netherlands International Law Review 315, 322 et seq; Marco Sassòli, 'Taking Armed Groups Seriously: Ways to Improve their Compliance with International Humanitarian Law' (2010) 1 Journal of International Humanitarian Legal Studies 5.

55 2187 UNTS 3.

In how far can and should the law draw consequences from the challenges posed by areas of limited statehood, in order to remain relevant to the situation on the ground? At what point is it necessary to draw a line that sets standards which may remain counterfactual in the foreseeable future? Whether adaptations are necessary – and can be brought about lawfully without actually endangering IHL's overall legitimacy and effectiveness –[56] is explored from various perspectives in the contributions to this volume.

D. About this Volume

This volume further examines the implications of areas of limited statehood for IHL and inquires whether and to what extent the existing norms of IHL are capable of regulating today's armed conflicts in such areas. Can the law be interpreted in a way that is perceived by relevant actors to be legitimate, hence inspiring compliance,[57] and in how far does the law needs to adapt?

To appropriately answer these fundamental questions, the first chapter of this volume deals with the fundamentals of IHL, and examines its history and nature to lay the groundwork for the further debate. Against this theoretical background, the following two chapters focus on concrete and pressing challenges for IHL in areas of limited statehood, namely the legal basis for detention by States as well as non-State actors, and the protection of foreign investment.

Different from *Grewe's* political history (*Ereignisgeschichte*), which divides international law into different epochs, each ending with a peace treaty,[58] *Raphael Schäfer* argues that it is worthwhile to apply a different approach to the history of international law. Instead of focusing on the development of international law in its entirety, he examines the connecting (i.e. comparable) elements throughout the centuries, beyond any alleged epochal boundaries. International law is simply too old for the assumption that a problem is completely new and was never seen before. From this history-of-ideas approach, *Raphael Schäfer* analyses the history of IHL,

56 For a further reading on the interplay of effectiveness, legitimacy and compliance in IHL, see Clark et al, 'Crisis in the laws of war?' (n 1).

57 For a further reading on compliance with IHL, see the various perspectives in Krieger, *Inducing Compliance* (n 4).

58 Wilhelm G. Grewe, *Epochen der Völkerrechtsgeschichte* (Nomos 1984).

particularly how non-State actors were (legally) treated in the past and how today's discourse can be informed by previous ones.[59]

Whereas in current debates on the legal basis for detention in NIACs it is commonly argued that legal orders cannot be treated in isolation and that the focus must be laid on the interplay between the different branches of international law as well as domestic law, *Katja Schöberl* and *Linus Mührel* reason that analysing the relationship between legal regimes should not occur at the expense of studying each field on its own terms. After all, resolving potential conflicts between different legal regimes primarily depends on their respective contents. Therefore, *Katja Schöberl* and *Linus Mührel* inquire whether the norms of IHL were designed to be permissive or restrictive and how this understanding evolved over time. They discuss the relevance of the *Lotus*-principle for modern-day IHL and expose the influence general public international law's conception of 'implied' authority may have on IHL in case an explicit legal basis is missing.[60]

Pia Hesse, in her comment, enriches the theoretical discussion by broadening the perspective to the creation and development of norms in international law. *Pia Hesse* critically reviews the *Lotus*-case of the Permanent Court of International Justice and today's predominant reading of the decision, i.e. the *Lotus*-principle.[61]

The controversial debate on the legal basis for detention in NIACs gained ever more pace after States increasingly engaged in extraterritorial military action in areas of limited statehood and with the development of the extraterritorial application of human rights by the ECtHR.

Manuel Brunner takes up this debate and, in a first step, along with the recent *Serdar Mohammed v Ministry of Defense* case series before British courts,[62] scrutinises the different law regimes applicable in areas of limited statehoods regarding restrictions and potential legal bases for security detentions by States' armed forces. He not only examines IHL and IHRL, but also domestic legal frameworks in States with longstanding NIACs, like Sri Lanka and Nepal, and discusses the interplay between these regimes.

---

59 Raphael Schäfer, 'A History of Division(s): A Critical Assessment of the Law of Non-International Armed Conflict' in this volume 43.

60 Schöberl and Mührel, 'Sunken Vessel or Blooming Flower?' (n 28).

61 Hesse, 'Neither Sunken Vessel nor Blooming Flower' (n 29).

62 *Serdar Mohammed v Ministry of Defence* [2014] EWHC 1369 (QB); [2014] CN 1019; *Serdar Mohammed v Ministry of Defence* [2015] EWCA Civ 843; [2015] WLR (D) 354 [30]; and *Serdar Mohammed v Ministry of Defence* [2017] UKSC 2.

Manuel Brunner completes his analysis by pointing out the potential and weaknesses of each regime and asks whether and to what extent Security Council resolutions or Rules of Engagement could provide authorisations for security detentions by States' armed forces.[63]

In his comment, *Anton O. Petrov* supplements *Manuel Brunner's* analysis of the relationship of the different legal regimes on a meta-level. He traces the historical development of human rights law and IHL and, thus, sheds light on the clash of the underlying values of the different regimes. *Anton O. Petrov* illustrates the problem of legal uncertainty in areas of limited statehood with a view to the question which nation's life must be threatened to allow for a derogation under the derogation clauses of human rights treaties.[64]

Since non-State armed groups are major actors in areas of limited statehood, but their activities are only cursorily covered by IHL, *Vincent Widdig* reviews how and to what extent non-State armed groups might be bound *de lege lata* to IHL and human rights within the context of detention in order to gain some legal clarity. Subsequently, he addresses the questions of whether the existing regime of IHL is (still) capable of regulating non-State armed groups conduct, whether there can be a discussion outside of CA 3 GC and AP II, and how non-State armed groups' conduct may affect treaty or customary IHL. Finally, *Vincent Widdig* argues that, when talking about applicable international law, the role of domestic law within the debate over the conduct of non-State armed groups should not be forgotten. The application of domestic law in the respective State in which the conflict occurs might already be a sufficient tool to legally bind non-State armed groups to a certain legal standard.[65]

In his comment to *Vincent Widdig's* analysis, *Lars Müller* examines agreements made between the parties to a NIAC and what they provide, for example for detention. He argues that IHL effectively accepts attempts by non-State armed groups within areas of limited statehood to adjust the existing rules to the specific conflict and to expand the protection provided by these rules and, thus, already allows non-State armed groups to influence the law as it applies to their specific context. Moreover, *Lars Müller* highlights the benefits of such agreements for areas of limited statehood, as

63 Brunner, 'Security Detention by the Armed Forces of a State in Situations of NIAC' (n 28).

64 Petrov, 'Detention in Non-International Armed Conflict by States' (n 29)

65 Widdig, 'Detention by Organised Armed Groups' (n 29).

they can raise awareness for IHL, allow to translate the law into the specific context and provide a higher degree of legitimacy.[66]

The protection of foreign investments in areas of limited statehood has still not gained much attention within the international academic legal discourse, although it challenges the application and interaction of the pertinent fields of law and has caused the initiation of several legal procedures. Especially the growing number of pending arbitrations against States for compensation for losses sustained by foreign investors in armed conflicts in areas of limited statehood demonstrates the need to readdress the question of which legal regimes apply to protect foreign investments in such situations and to what extent they might coincide.

To adequately respond to these questions, *Ira Ryk-Lakhman Aharonovich* clarifies the prerequisites for the classification of commercial objects under both IIL and, based on the principle of distinction in Art. 48 AP I, IHL, which differentiates between protected civilian objects and permissible military targets. She further elaborates on under which conditions foreign investments may be classified as dual-use targets and revenue-generating targets. Finally, *Ira Ryk-Lakhman Aharonovich* examines the consequences of the classification of foreign investments as civilian objects under IHL and points out specific norm conflicts between IHL and IIL to be further dealt with.[67]

With regard to the protection of foreign investment, *Charlotte Lülf* demonstrates that challenges for IHL in areas of limited statehood occur not only in situations of NIACs, but also in IACs and in times of occupation, i.e. a situation in which the sovereign State has lost control over its own territory and hence can no longer guarantee treaty performance and perform protective functions. She hypothesises that, although IHL governs conduct during times of occupation, investment law provides more specialised norms for the matter at hand. Based on contemporary examples of occupation, such as in Ukraine or Iraq, *Charlotte Lülf* analyses the protection of foreign investment during times of occupation under IHL before turning to the specific regime of bilateral investment treaties, their

66 Müller, 'Detention by Armed Groups' (n 42).

67 Ira Ryk-Lakhman Aharonovich, 'Foreign Investments as Non-Human Targets' in this volume 171.

applicability during armed conflict and their interaction with the law of occupation.[68]

This volume provides some observations of and ideas for the formation and development of IHL in response to the challenges of areas of limited statehood. It shows possible ways to react to an empirical phenomenon, which probably was not considered during the genesis of most of the today's applicable treaties to such areas of limited statehood. Furthermore, this volume critically discusses recent case law, such as the *Serdar Mohammed v Ministry of Defence* case series before British Courts, as well as influential case law from the past, such as the *Lotus*-decision, and gives recommendations on how to understand the interplay of different law regimes including IHL, IIL, IHRL and domestic law in areas of limited statehood.

As for the long term, it is still too soon to finally conclude whether the implications on the development of international law as observed in this volume will prove to be true and how IHL as well as the other law regimes concerned will (in an interplay) respond to the challenges caused by areas of limited statehood. By contrast, however, what may be finally concluded from the perspective of this volume is that IHL is not rigid and unreasonable, but legitimate and adaptable to the challenges in areas of limited statehood.

---

68 Charlotte Lülf, 'The Protection of (Foreign) Investment during Belligerent Occupation – Considerations on International Humanitarian and International Investment Law' in this volume 194.

Part I: Fundamental Considerations

A History of Division(s): a Critical Assessment of the Law of Non-International Armed Conflict

Raphael Schäfer

A. Introduction

In recent times, the internal division of IHL into the law applicable to IACs and NIACs respectively has come into criticism: authors commented on this division using descriptions such as 'artificial', 'arbitrary', 'undesirable', or 'difficult to justify'.[1] Research projects have been initiated due to the 'difficulties arising from the application of this bifurcated system'[2] and the ICTY in its *Tadic* decision simply ignored the division with regard to the existence of a conflict when it stated:

> we find that an armed conflict exists whenever there is a resort to armed force between States or protracted armed violence between governmental authorities and organized armed groups or between such groups within a State.[3]

Drawing on this much-cited paragraph of the ICTY, one may ask why international law sees itself compelled to distinguish between these two types of conflicts, especially as the law of NIAC had been developed

---

1 Rogier Bartels, 'Timelines, Borderlines and Conflicts' (2009) 91 IRRC 35, 40.

2 Columbia Law School (Human Rights Institute), Harmonizing Standards for Armed Conflict <http://www.law.columbia.edu/human-rights-institute/counter-terrorism/harmonizing-standards-armed-conflict> accessed 19 November 2017. See, on this, Sarah Cleveland, 'Harmonizing Standards in Armed Conflict' (EJIL: *Talk!* 8 September 2014) <https://www.ejiltalk.org/harmonizing-standards-in-armed-conflict/> accessed 19 November 2017.

3 *Prosecutor v Tadic* (Decision on the Defence Motion for Interlocutory Appeal on Jurisdiction) IT-94-1 (2 October 1995) para 70. See also James G. Stewart, 'Towards a Single Definition of Armed Conflict in International Humanitarian Law: A Critique of Internationalized Armed Conflict' (2003) 85 IRRC 313; Emily Crawford, 'Unequal before the Law: The Case for the Elimination of the Distinction between International and Non-International Armed Conflicts' (2007) 20 LJIL 441.

analogously to the rules governing the law of IAC.[4] *Antony Anghie* famously argued that

> the formulation and operation of the dynamic of difference ... generates the concepts and dichotomies – for example, between private and public, between sovereign and non-sovereign – which are traditionally seen as the foundations of the international legal order.[5]

And, indeed, it seems to be true that this division can also be distinguished in IHL with its concept of IACs between sovereigns on the one hand and NIACs between a sovereign and an organised armed group on the other. If we broaden our view and look at international law more generally, it can even be read as a history of division: a division between 'us and them', or, as *Anne Orford* put it, a division of international law and its others.[6] To a certain extent, the term 'international law' still hints at its infamous imperial past.[7] The value of critical legal scholars' analyses identifying not only the imperial past of today's international law, but also its still inherent imperial structures cannot be overestimated in order to create a truly 'global' law.[8]

The (hi)stories in the textbooks concerning international law's past often only serve to legitimise present-day law and, for this reason, only seldom contain footnotes: 'one assumes that the story presented is so obvious or well known that [it] speaks itself and requires no proof.'[9] This is what one may call a narrative or a foundational myth – 'a benchmark ... that is no longer called into question.'[10] International law is full of these foundational myths – just remember the reoccurring declaration of 'Hugo Grotius as Father of International Law' or the 'Westphalian Origins of International Law' to name but a few.[11] These narratives have indeed been important, as

4 Sandesh Sivakumaran, 'Re-envisaging the International Law of Internal Armed Conflict' (2011) 22 EJIL 219, 221.

5 Antony Anghie, *Imperialism, Sovereignty and the Making of International Law* (CUP 2004) 9.

6 Anne Orford (ed), *International Law and Its Others* (CUP 2006).

7 Martti Koskenniemi, Walter Rech and Manuel Jiménez Fonseca (eds), *International Law and Empire. Historical Explorations* (OUP 2017).

8 For more on global law, see Rafael Domingo, *The New Global Law* (CUP 2006).

9 Thomas Skouteris, 'Engaging History in International Law' in José M. Beneyto, David Kennedy (eds), *New Approaches to International Law – The European and the American Experiences* (TMC Asser Press 2012) 99, 105.

10 Andrea Bianchi, *International Law Theories: An Inquiry into Different Ways of Thinking* (OUP 2016) 293 (hereafter Bianchi, *International Law Theories*).

11 See more generally Matthew Windsor, 'Narrative Kill or Capture: Unreliable Narration in International Law' (2015) 28 LJIL 743, 748 et seq.

they safeguarded the functioning of the international legal system because of their terminating effect: if a convenient and comprehensible explanation for the present is provided,[12] why should we then bother with the fact that *Alberico Gentili* was anticipating *Grotius*[13] or that the Holy Roman Empire of German Nation was a non-'Westphalian' entity up to its dissolution in 1806?[14] Narratives or founding myths work, as long as they can explain the present.[15] As soon as this is no longer the case, however, inconvenient questions will be asked that do not fit into the system.[16]

In this contribution, I follow the recently emerging critical reading of IHL and argue that today's IHL also follows a negative distinction. It shall be shown that what used to be called 'laws of war' is still present in IHL and that the overall legal corpus – contrary to what its denomination 'international humanitarian law' might suggest – does not stand in a (purely) humanitarian tradition: If IHL were truly humanitarian, why is there a need to alter the level of protection depending on the nature of the conflict in question?[17] Or, to put it even more bluntly: do dum-dum bullets cause less atrocious effects in non-international armed conflicts than they do in international ones?[18] This division, however, is of course no new

---

12 Cf Amanda Alexander, 'A Short History of International Humanitarian Law' (2015) 26 EJIL 109: 'These histories help to inform the current understanding of the nature and purpose of international humanitarian law.'

13 See eg Peter Haggenmacher, 'Grotius and Gentili: A Reassessment of Thomas E. Holland's Inaugural Lecture' in Hedley Bull, Benedict Kingsbury, Adam Roberts (eds), *Hugo Grotius and International Relations* (OUP 1992) 133.

14 See eg José-Manuel Barreto, 'Cerberus: Rethinking Grotius and the Westphalian System' in Martti Koskenniemi, Walter Rech, Manuel Jiménez Fonseca (eds), *International Law and Empire. Historical Explorations* (OUP 2016) 149, 159 et seq; Michael Axworthy and Patrick Milton, 'The Myth of Westphalia' (*Foreign Affairs* 22 December 2016) <https://www.foreignaffairs.com/articles/europe/2016-12-22/myth-westphalia> accessed 19 November 2017.

15 Bianchi, *International Law Theories* (n 10) 292.

16 Peer Zumbansen, 'Die vergangene Zukunft des Völkerrechts' (2001) 34 Kritische Justiz 46.

17 For the discussion during the conference, see Michael Bothe, Karl Josef Partsch and Waldemar A. Solf, *New Rules for Victims of Armed Conflicts: Commentary on the Two 1977 Protocols Additional to the Geneva Conventions of 1949* (Martinus Nijhoff 1982) 605 et seq; Anthony Cullen, *The Concept of Non-International Armed Conflict in International Humanitarian Law* (CUP 2010) 88.

18 Deidre Willmott, 'Removing the Distinction between International and Non-International Armed Conflict in the Rome Statute of the International Criminal Court' (2004) 5 Melbourne Journal of International Law 196, 197.

finding, as the debate accompanying the codification of the Additional Protocols even witnessed the accusation of engaging in 'selective humanitarianism'.[19]

The contribution's key argument is that the subject protected by the laws governing the NIAC is not primarily the human being as such, but the state's integrity. A finding, which is well hidden by the traditional humanitarian reading of the discipline. By applying a conceptual history approach, however, the contribution aims at showing that the laws-of-war thinking is especially predominant in the context of a NIAC.

B. What's in a Name? The Different Denominations of the Jus in Bello

The Prussian military theorist *Carl von Clausewitz* famously called war 'a true chameleon, because it changes its nature in some degree in each particular case.'[20] The same might be true for the legal regime which is supposed to govern the conduct of belligerents: the *jus in bello*. Traditionally known as the laws of war, this terminus went out of use after the Second World War in favour of the terms 'Law of Armed Conflict' and 'International Humanitarian Law'. Although war as such has *de jure* been abolished, its very concept proves to be unimpressed and *de facto* keeps preoccupying mankind as previously.

The term 'International Humanitarian Law' initially referred to the 1949 Geneva Conventions,[21] but obtained, as *Peter Haggenmacher* argues, 'quasi-official status' through the Diplomatic Conference on the Reaffirmation and Development of International Humanitarian Law Applicable in Armed Conflicts (1974 to 1977).[22] But it was not until the 1981 Conventional Weapons Convention that a reference to IHL could be

19 David P. Forsythe, 'Legal Management of Internal War: The 1977 Protocol on Non-International Armed Conflicts' (1978) 72 AJIL 279 (hereafter Forsythe, 'Legal Management of Internal War').

20 Carl von Clausewitz, *On War* (1873) Book 1, Chapter 1: 'What is War?'.

21 Theodor Meron, 'The Humanization of Humanitarian Law' (200) 94 AJIL 239 (hereafter Meron, The Humanization of Humanitarian Law').

22 Peter Haggenmacher, 'On the Doctrinal Origins of *Ius in Bello*: From Rights of War to the Laws of War' in Thilo Marauhn and Heinhard Steiger (eds), *Universality and Continuity in International Law* (Eleven International 2011) 325 (hereafter Haggenmacher, 'On the Doctrinal Origins of *Ius in Bello*').

found in an international treaty[23] – and then only in a remarkably blurry construction of an 'international humanitarian law applicable in armed conflict' (Art. 2).

Although the terms are often used interchangeably, each of them conveys a different message. *Haggenmacher* uses the ICJ's Advisory Opinion on the *Legality of the Threat or Use of Nuclear Weapons* to illustrate this assumption. When the Court refers to 'the protection of the civilian population', it speaks of 'international humanitarian law.'[24] When referring to the 'deprivation of life', however, it uses the term 'law applicable in armed conflict.'[25] This is remarkable in so far as it reminds us of the very essence of war (or 'armed conflict'):

> the right for both [belligerent parties] to proceed to mutual destructions of life and property, until one is overpowered by the other. This hostile relationship is the central fact of war, and it should be mentioned first in all its radicality. Humanitarian restrictions, eminently desirable as they are, logically come afterwards. To be sure, the general idea of restrictions, be they humanitarian or otherwise, is inherent in the very idea of a *law* applying to war.[26]

This example should underline that the terms we use also have a strong influence on our idea of reality: there is a big difference if one speaks about the *jus in bello* as 'international humanitarian law' or as 'law of armed conflict'. As much as the general call for 'humanised warfare' is to be welcomed, it must never detract from the fact that even an ideal IHL will always remain at most only the second-best solution. We must not forget that the application of IHL always follows on a previous failure and entails the loss of life – however humanely it may be conducted. Additionally, it is often neglected that 'international law consists of a family of professions' and does not exclusively belong to the realm of international legal scholars.[27] International law, understood in this sense, consists of 'a group

23 Cf Page Wilson, 'The Myth of International Humanitarian Law' (2017) 93 International Affairs 563, 564 (hereafter Wilson, 'The Myth of International Humanitarian Law')

24 Legality of the Threat or Use of Nuclear Weapons (Advisory Opinion) [1996] ICJ Rep 226, 257, para 78.

25 Ibid, 240, para 25.

26 Haggenmacher, 'On the Doctrinal Origins of *Ius in Bello*' (n 22) 326.

27 Jean d'Aspremont, Tarcisio Gazzini, André Nollkaemper and Wouter Werner, 'Introduction' in Jean Jean d'Aspremont, Tarcisio Gazzini, André Nollkaemper and Wouter Werner (eds), *International Law as a Profession* (CUP 2017) 1.

of people pursuing projects in a common professional language'.[28] This point prominently gained momentum through a letter to *Jakob Kellenberger*, then President of the ICRC, by US Department of State Legal Advisors *John Bellinger* and *William Haynes*.[29]

As the current competition between 'international humanitarian law' on the one hand and 'law of armed conflict' or 'laws of war' on the other shows, the language of international law can also be used to pursue a political agenda by its respective stakeholders.[30]

C. The Current Jus in Bello: Its Humanitarian Present and Military Past

In order to better understand the current conception of the *jus in bello*, it is worthwhile to take a critical look at the structural path it followed. The historical analysis of international law, as conducted in the course of the 'turn to history', aims at challenging the master narratives and unveiling ideology beyond the norms, thereby explaining 'why' (in contrast to 'how') international law is the way it is today.[31] 'Tradition' proves to be of crucial importance in this regard, as it furthers the perception of progress in

---

28 David Kennedy, 'One, Two, Three Many Legal Orders: Legal Pluralism and the Cosmopolitan Dream' (2007) 31 NYU Review of Law & Social Change 641, 650.

29 John Bellinger III and William J. Haynes II, 'A US government response to the International Committee of the Red Cross study *Customary International Humanitarian Law*' (2007) 89 IRRC 443 (hereafter Bellinger and Haynes, 'A US government response to the ICRC').

30 Wilson, 'The Myth of International Humanitarian Law' (n 23) 568 et seq. With regard to the 'war' against terrorism, see Frédéric Mégret, '"War"? Legal Semantics and the Move to Violence' (2002) 13 EJIL 361, 363 (hereafter Mégret 'Legal Semantics and the Move to Violence'). More generally on international law and language with the example of self-determination, see Christopher J. Borgen, 'The Language of Law and the Practice of Politics: Great Powers and the Rhetoric of Self-Determination in the Cases of Kosovo and South Ossetia' (2009) 10 Chicago Journal of International Law 1.

31 For this approach, see eg Olivier Corten, 'Les Aspects Idéologiques de la Codification du Droit International' in Régine Beauthier and Isabelle Rorive (eds), *Le Code Napoléon, un ancêtre vénéré? Mélanges offerts à Jacques Vanderlinden* (Bruylant 2004) 495.

international law.[32] From this viewpoint, tradition is, to a certain extent, always an artificial construct,[33] if not even an invention.[34]

Martti Koskenniemi, following up on the Kunzian Pendulum,[35] famously argued that international law would develop between two extremes – apology and utopia.[36] If we look at IHL and its determining elements from this perspective, we see the principles of 'military necessity' and 'considerations of humanity' as two corresponding poles. While the former is committed to the classical understanding of state sovereignty, the latter strives for the final perfection of humanity's ideal. Even IHL's two main sections[37] are roughly attributed accordingly: whereas the 'law of the Hague' supposedly stands for the military past, the 'law of Geneva' promises the glorious humanitarian future. Even if 'Geneva' seems to have displaced 'the Hague' in conceptual terms during the narrative efforts to put IHL into a humanitarian tradition,[38] we (still) see its underlying laws-of-

---

32 Cf Russell A. Miller and Rebecca M. Bratspies (eds), *Progress in International Law* (Brill 2008); Tilmann Altwicker and Oliver Diggelmann, 'How is Progress Constructed in International Legal Scholarship?' (2014) 25 EJIL (2014) 427; Thomas Skouteris, 'The Idea of Progress' in Anne Orford and Florian Hoffmann (eds), *The Oxford Handbook on the Theory of International Law* (OUP 2016) 939.

33 Thomas Kleinlein, 'International Legal Thought: Creation of a Tradition and the Potential of Disciplinary Self-Reflection' in Giuliana Ziccardi Capaldo (ed), *The Global Community Yearbook of International Law and Jurisprudence 2016* (OUP 2017); for an example of tradition building see Georg Schwarzenberger, 'A Forerunner of Nuremberg: The Breisach War Crime Trial of 1474' *The Manchester Guardian* (28 September 1946) and Gregory S. Gordon, 'The Trial of Peter von Hagenbach. Reconciling History, Historiography and International Criminal Law' in Kevin J. Heller and Gerry Simpson (eds), *The Hidden History of War Crime Trials* (OUP 2013) 13.

34 Jean d'Aspremont, 'The International Law of Statehood and Recognition: A Post-Colonial Invention' in Thierry Garcia (ed), *La Reconnaissance du Statut d'Etat à des Entités Contestées* (Pedone 2018, forthcoming).

35 Josef L. Kunz, 'The Swing of the Pendulum: From Overestimation to Underestimation of International Law' (1950) 44 AJIL 135.

36 Martti Koskenniemi, *From Apology to Utopia* (CUP 2006).

37 Jean Pictet, *The Principles of International Humanitarian Law* (ICCR 1967) 10 et seq.

38 Meron, The Humanization of Humanitarian Law' (n 21); Thilo Rensmann, 'Die Humanisierung des Völkerrechts durch das Ius in Bello – Von der Martens'schen Klausel zur "Responsibility to Protect"' (2008) 68 ZaöRV 111; Marco Sassòli, Antoine A. Bouvier and Anne Quintin, *How Does Law Protect in War? Cases, Documents and Teaching Materials on Contemporary Practice in International Humanitarian Law* (3rd edn, ICRC 2011). For a general

war-driven thinking.[39] This disparity, however, may lead to severe discrepancies between the stakeholders: the above mentioned letter of US legal advisors is a luminous example of this matter, as they saw themselves obliged to raise their voice in a discourse which had become detached from their position and remind the more progressive scholars that also customary IHL – be it focused on the principle of humanity as much as it may – still indisputably has to rely on state practice and *opinio juris* as a source of international law.[40] This is exactly where the special difficulty of law regimes operating between extremes lies: to provide a satisfactory and feasible solution for both sides, as the most utopian rules will never prevail if its apologetic element fails.

Were this not already difficult enough, the task is further complicated by another, temporal division: little scrutiny is needed to realise that IHL was made in 'and' for different times.[41] It is not without reason that the joke arose concerning the law which always comes one war late into existence. Even if it is not any longer visible in its denomination, IHL was designed on the 19th century prototype of conflict: the war between two sovereign nation States in a classical Westphalian sense. The 1859 Battle of Solferino, famously built up to IHL's founding myth by *Henry Dunant*,[42] is an early example of the ensuing industrialised warfare.[43] However, this conflict, which served as the blueprint for the developing IHL, has always been more the exception than the rule.[44]

From today's point of view, it can be seen as the product of a time which had significant and clear distinctions like the ones between a State and a non-State, a combatant and a civilian, or an international conflict and an

---

perspective cf Eric J. Hobsbawm and Terrence O. Ranger (eds), *The Invention of Tradition* (CUP 1983).

39 Scott Horton, 'Kriegsraison or Military Necessity? The Bush Administration's Wilhelmine Attitude towards the Conduct of War' (2006) 30 Fordham International Law Journal 576.

40 Bellinger and Haynes, 'A US government response to the ICRC' (n 29) 443 et seq.

41 With regard to the Geneva Conventions of 1949, see Rosa Brooks, 'The Politics of the Geneva Conventions: Avoiding Formalist Traps' (2005) 46 VJIL 197 (hereafter Brooks, 'The Politics of the Geneva Conventions').

42 Henry Dunant, *Un Souvenir de Solférino* (1862).

43 Michael Howard, *War in European History* (OUP 2009) 97 et seq (hereafter Howard, *War in European History*).

44 Arthur van Coller, 'The History and Development of the Law of Armed Conflict (Part 1)' (2014) 17 African Yearbook of International Humanitarian Law 44.

internal one,[45] all of which are being questioned today.[46] IHL, despite the reforms of 1949 and 1977, is still operating on this basis. Especially when it comes to the regulation of NIACs, States are reluctant to grant too many concessions, as the principle of reciprocity known from IACs will most probably not function. *Antonio Cassese* explains this in the following:

> On the contrary, Governments are much less, if at all, interested in having rebellions within their territory governed by international law. Their main concern is to retain enough freedom to crush promptly any form of insurrection. Their sovereignty and territorial integrity cannot but oppose any sweeping encroachment by international law. This is why so few international rules govern internal conflicts.[47]

It is therefore not surprising that the ICRC's first attempt to also extend IHL to civil wars on occasion of the 1949 conferences led only to CA 3 as a minimum yardstick.[48] The accompanying controversy also left its traces in the wording of this 'convention in miniature' as its very last sentence contains, what Cassese calls, a 'legal enigma':

> The application of the preceding provisions shall not affect the legal status of the Parties to the conflict.

It seems to be rather obvious from a political perspective that

> international law-makers wanted to dispel the fear expressed by States that such a norm on civil wars would give more power, and to some extent a promotion, to the rebels by having them gain international legitimacy.[49]

However, this is diametrically opposed to the fact that CA 3 established certain obligations with corresponding rights of the rebels, thereby declaring them – very limited – subjects of international law.[50]

---

45 Jed Odermatt, 'Between Law and Reality: "New Wars" and Internationalised Armed Conflict' (2013) 5 Amsterdam Law Forum 19.

46 Rosa E. Brooks, 'War Everywhere: Rights, National Security Law, and the Law of Armed Conflict in the Age of Terror' (2004) 153 University of Pennsylvania Law Review 675, especially 711 et seq.

47 Antonio Cassese, 'Current Trends in the Development of the Law of Armed Conflict' in Paolo Gaeta and Salvatore Zappalà (eds), *The Human Dimension of International Law* (OUP 2008) 3, 6 (hereafter Cassese, 'Current Trends in the Development of the Law of Armed Conflict').

48 Antonio Cassese, 'Civil War and International Law' in Paolo Gaeta and Salvatore Zappalà (eds), *The Human Dimension of International Law* (OUP 2008) 110, 116 et seq.

49 Ibid, 119.

50 Ibid.

From this perspective, IHL can even be seen – from a highly nonconformist and controversial point of view – as a means to support warfare, as it provides an ever-adapting regime to what seems to be inseparable from mankind:

> International humanitarian law in particular has this universal vocation, since it applies to all men and countries. In formulating and perfecting this law, to which it gave birth and of which it encourages the promotion and dissemination, the International Committee of the Red Cross has sought precisely this common ground and put forward rules acceptable to all because they are fully consistent with human nature. This is, moreover, what has ensured the strength and durability of these rules.[51]

'Formulating and perfecting this law' has been one of the central concerns of IHL since the famous Martens Clause stated: 'until a more recent code of the laws of war is issued.'[52] Amounting to an already 'theological-like' promise[53] of IHL, it mainly makes us endure the cruelties of warfare instead of questioning them. 'International humanitarian law as an accomplice of warfare' and 'the Geneva Conventions as the Magna Charta of the war time criminal' are suspicions which are hard to endure.

Interestingly and somewhat tellingly, however, a reality in which there would be no need for this legal corpus anymore – as utopian as it might seem – is never considered in the progress-influenced accounts of IHL.[54] What is regularly omitted in the standard founding myth is that the 1864 Geneva Convention's (unintentional) side effect on warfare is, in a certain sense, comparable to the usage of the railway: According to *Michael Howard*, the Battle of Solferino was the 'first war in Europe to demonstrate

---

51 Jean Pictet, 'Humanitarian Ideas Shared by Different Schools of Thought and Cultural Traditions' in Henry Dunant Institute (ed), *International Dimensions Humanitarian Law* (Martinus Nijhoff 1988) 3.

52 Regarding the controversy of the meaning of the Martens Clause, cf Rupert Ticehurst, 'The Martens Clause and the Laws of Armed Conflict' (1997) 37 IRRC 125; Antonio Cassese, 'The Martens Clause: Half a Loaf or Simply Pie in the Sky?' (2000) 11 EJIL 187.

53 On this concept, see further Martti Koskenniemi, 'International Law as Political Theology: How to Read *Der Nomos der Erde*?' (2004) 11 Constellations 492.

54 The only exception this author was able to find is Yves Sandoz and Jérôme Massé, 'Values Worth Fighting for: The Additional Protocols at 40' (*Humanitarian Law & Policy*, 8 July 2017), <http://blogs.icrc.org/law-and-policy/2017/06/08/values-worth-fighting-additional-protocols-40/> accessed 19 November 2017: 'It is indeed only when the promise of world peace has been reached – and therefore the Geneva Conventions and their Additional Protocols cease to be relevant – that we can all truly celebrate'.

the value of railways', which had the advantage that the 'forces could be maintained in good condition: the sick and wounded could be evacuated to base hospitals and replaced by fit men.'[55] This is one of the examples which strongly further the argument that the laws of war 'have been formulated, and in fact have served, to legitimate ever more destructive methods of combat.[56] IHL, 'with its soothing, almost effete touch,'[57] is only easing our conscience.

With this reading, it is comprehensible, although still lamentable, why IHL proves to be weakest when it comes to NIACs, which is where it is needed the most. AP II, which was supposed to confirm and clarify CA 3,[58] is the outcome of an intense diplomatic struggle and therefore necessarily a compromise.[59] Accordingly, the scholarly assessment was rather critical:

> Protocol II, as it emerged from the Diplomatic Conference in 1977, is a markedly debilitated instrument. Sovereignty and the fragility of many new States cast a blight over this embryonic development in humanitarian law in an area where it was particularly needed.[60]

The above mentioned very restricted international legal character of rebels in the end emerges as a false friend, as rebels, in contrast to peoples

> fighting against colonial domination and alien occupation and against racist régimes in the exercise of their right of self-determination ... [are] not confer[red] any special status ... [and] therefore retain, even from the standpoint of international law, the legal qualification impressed on them by municipal law – that of criminals.[61]

In doing so, IHL *de facto* condemns the rebels to victory and maybe even forces them to apply all means they deem necessary.

---

55 Howard, *War in European History* (n 43) 97 et seq.

56 Chris af Jochnik and Roger Normand, 'The Legitimation of Violence: A Critical History of the Laws of War' (1994) 35 Harv. Int'l L. J. 49, 51 (hereafter Jochnik and Normand, 'The Legitimation of Violence').

57 Mégret 'Legal Semantics and the Move to Violence' (n 30) 363.

58 Yves Sandoz et al, *Commentary on the Additional Protocols* (ICRC 1987) 1326 para 4365.

59 Forsythe, 'Legal Management of Internal War' (n 19).

60 Gerald I. A. D. Draper, 'The Implementation of the Geneva Conventions of 1949 and the Additional Protocols of 1977' in Michael A. Meyer and Hilaire McCoubrey (eds), *Reflections on Law and Armed Conflicts. The Selected Works on the Laws of War by the Late Professor Colonel G.I.A.D. Draper, OBE* (Kluwer 1998) 102, 109.

61 Cassese, 'Current Trends in the Development of the Law of Armed Conflict' (n 47) 6.

Although the strict separation between the application of *jus in bello* and the underlying reasons of the conflict is one of the fundamental principles of IHL,[62] the suspicion arises that IHL distinguishes between IACs and NIACs in two protocols not only because of the formal different nature of those conflicts, but also because of the different material assessment when it comes to the 'legitimacy' of the conflict. Of course, an IAC is only legal under the very strict requirements of the UN-Charter. However, the traditional thinking in terms of State sovereignty involuntarily leads to a different evaluation: whereas wars between States have always been a legal reality in international affairs, internal conflicts have long been considered to fall within the very core of a State's black box, shielding it from international law's influences and leaving it to the sole discretion of the nation State – which, of course, is keen to secure its internal stability. This sovereignty-conditioned tension between the classification of a conflict as a 'mere' riot or a NIAC proper is perceptible in Art. 3 (1) AP II, which reads:

> Nothing in this Protocol shall be invoked for the purpose of affecting the sovereignty of a State or the responsibility of the government, by all legitimate means, to maintain or re-establish law and order in the State or to defend the national unity and territorial integrity of the State.

It is hardly surprising, consequently, that States are regularly eager to classify a conflict as a domestic one below the threshold of a NIAC.[63] In sum, this is another example of the focus on sovereignty of an allegedly humanised international legal system. In a sense, therefore, the NIAC is a *jus in bello* counterpart to the illegal secessionist movement in general international law. This, together with the (of course to be welcomed) absorption of 'fighting against colonial domination and alien occupation and against racist régimes in the exercise of their right of self-determination' by AP I, leads to the somehow outlandish outcome that a proper application of AP II is only possible when several powers are fighting for the predominance in a country with a government incapable of acting (i.e. a failed state). CA 3, which was framed under the lasting impressions of the Russian, Spanish, and Greek Civil Wars (which are also examples of the aforementioned type of conflicts which AP II can address

---

62 François Bugnion, 'Jus ad Bellum, Jus in Bello and Non-International Armed Conflicts' (2003) 6 YbIHL 167, 188 (hereafter Bugnion, 'Jus ad Bellum').

63 Benjamin Zawacki, 'Politically Inconvenient, Legally Correct: A Non-International Armed Conflict in Southern Thailand' (2013) 18 JCSL 151.

properly),[64] therefore remains 'the sole source of humanitarian regulation of internecine strife.'[65]

Bearing in mind the findings of this part, it is fair to second *Rotem Giladi* in touching the sore spot and showing quite plainly the dangers of the inherent problem of the very existence of IHL and its canonical history and narratives:

> Rather than deny that legal moderation of war does in fact lend it legitimacy, entrench the divorce between the projects to humanise war and to eliminate it, or theorise the service the former renders to the latter, proponents of humanity must constantly question the very legitimacy, the very morality and efficacy, of their own enterprise. Rather than celebrate the law's humanity – In its nomenclature and institutions, interpretation and theory – they must be committed to a sober, and sobering, accounting of its history, its effect, the costs it exacts and its inhumanity. To do that, IHL professionals need to turn to history that tells of errors, roads not travelled, and tasks yet to be accomplished.[66]

D. In Lieu of a Conclusion: Thoughts on the Global War on Terror and the Search for a New Concept

The importance of giving something a name can be seen in the context of the tremendous problems concerning the legal scope of the so-called 'Global War on Terror'. What seems to be common ground is that 'the formal framework of the Geneva Conventions does not fit the struggle against terrorism well', as too many of its threshold distinctions, *inter alia* the one between IACs and NIACs, 'are premised on the continued existence of a rapidly vanishing world.'[67]

But how do we then deal with a situation that is, allegedly, neither nor'?[68] Many efforts have been made in international legal scholarship to give it

64 Bugnion, 'Jus ad Bellum' (n 62) 182.

65 David A. Elder, 'The Historical Background of Common Article 3 of the Geneva Convention of 1949' (1979) 11 Case W. R. JIL 37, 69.

66 Rotem Giladi, 'Rites of Affirmation: Progress and Immanence in International Humanitarian Law Historiography' (unpublished manuscript; the paper can be requested from rotem.giladi@helsinki.fi). See also Jochnik and Normand, 'The Legitimation of Violence' (n 56) 51.

67 Brooks, 'The Politics of the Geneva Conventions' (n 41) 199.

68 Kevin J. Heller, 'The Use and Abuse of Analogy in IHL' in Jens D. Ohlin (ed), *Theoretical Boundaries of Armed Conflict and Human Rights* (CUP 2016) 232 (hereafter Heller, 'Analogy in IHL').

some kind of name: 'Global Armed Conflict',[69] 'Global Civil War',[70] 'Transnational NIAC',[71] or 'Extraterritorial Armed Conflict'[72] are but only a few examples of a long list. What is common to all the suggested denominations is that they do not explain what their added value is to the law as it stands. This author has much sympathy for *Tawia Asnah's* conclusion that the newly (re)emerging 'language of war shapes and creates the international legal norms governing the use of force'[73] and believes the same phenomenon to be operating in the *jus in bello*. They all aim at creating a convenient legal concept for a reality which, allegedly, cannot be grasped therefore remains outside the existing legal language. However, a 'legal acceptance' – *ex factis jus oritur* – of a global armed conflict would yield to the attempt of the 'transnational terrorist' to destabilise the international legal order[74] and the US-led response of creating 'legal black holes' in the fight against terrorism.[75] Detaching international law from the ordering function its spatial limitation[76] provides can pose a severe risk, as *Carl Schmitt* already pointed out with regard to the partisans:

> [The 1949 Geneva Conventions'] foundations remain the conduct of war based on the state and consequently a bracketing of war, with its clear distinctions between

69 Jonathan Horowitz, 'Reaffirming the Role of Human Rights in a Time of "Global" Armed Conflict' (2015) 30 Emory International Law Review 2041.

70 Nehal Buta, 'States of Exception: Regulating Targeted Killing in a "Global Civil War"' in Philip Alston and Euan Macdonald (eds), *Human Rights, Intervention, and the Use of Force* (OUP 2008) 243 (hereafter Buta, 'States of Exception').

71 Heller, 'Analogy in IHL' (n 68) 245 et seq.

72 Sasha Radin, 'Global Armed Conflict? The Threshold of Extraterritorial Non-International Armed Conflicts' (2013) 89 ILS 696.

73 Tawia Asnah, 'War: Rhetoric & Norm-Creation in Response to Terror' (2003) 43 VJIL 797, 851.

74 Antonio Cassese, 'Terrorism is Also Disrupting Some Crucial Legal Categories of International Law' (2001) 12 EJIL 993.

75 S. Borelli, 'Casting Light on the Legal Black Hole: International Law and Detentions Abroad in the "War on Terror"' (2005) IRRC 39, referring *inter alia* to the English Court of Appeal in R (on the application of Ferroz Abbasi and another) v Secretary of State for Foreign and Commonwealth Affairs [2002] EWCA Civ. 1598, which expressed its concern (at para 64) as to the manner in which the applicant was detained at Guantánamo Bay, noting that 'in apparent contravention of fundamental principles recognised by [US and English] jurisdictions and by international law, Mr. Abbasi is at present arbitrarily detained in a "legal black-hole"'.

76 On the territorial question, see further Noam Lubell and Nathan Derejko, 'A Global Battlefield? Drones and the Geographical Scope of Armed Conflict' (2013) 11 JICJ 65.

> war and peace, military and civilian, enemy and criminal, war between states and civil war. When these essential distinctions fade or are even challenged, they create the premises for a type of war that deliberately destroys these clear distinctions. Then, many cautiously stylized compromise norms appear only as the narrow bridge over an abyss, which conceals a profound modification of the concepts of war, enemy and partisan – a modification full of consequences ...[77]

Attempts such as the recent decision of the ICC's Prosecutor, *Fatou Bensouda*, to 'request judicial authorisation to commence an investigation into the Situation in the Islamic Republic of Afghanistan,'[78] reminding the conflict parties of the existing – and applicable – law, can therefore only be strongly welcomed.[79]

IHL is a legal discipline which heavily operates on the basis of divisions. These divisions regularly aim at a positive effect like the 'positive discrimination' between combatants and civilians, but also open loopholes as the so-called 'War on Terror' has shown. Moreover, IHL can be addressed with several pre-assumptions, causing it to appear in a slightly different light – the competing denominations of 'international humanitarian law' and 'law of armed conflict' being the most distinctly recognisable example.

However, these different understandings also lead to disparate histories of IHL, creating differing traditions and narratives as well as aiming at another future for the legal system. The divisions going through IHL, not only in terms of legal principles, but also on a meta-level, presumably play a decisive role in explaining why there is a 'persistent violation' of IHL

---

77 Carl Schmitt, *The Theory of the Partisan – Intermediate Commentary on the Concept of the Political* (1963), translated and published in Telos (2005) 11, 32, cited by Buta, 'States of Exception' (n 70) 243.

78 Statement of ICC Prosecutor, *Fatou Bensouda*, regarding her decision to request judicial authorisation to commence an investigation into the Situation in the Islamic Republic of Afghanistan (3 November 2017) <https://www.icc-cpi.int/Pages/item.aspx?name=171103_OTP_Statement> accessed 19 November 2017.

79 For further information, see Kevin J. Heller, 'Initial Thoughts on the ICC's Decision to Investigate Afghanistan' (*Opinio Juris*, 3 November 2017) <http://opiniojuris.org/2017/11/03/otp-decides-to-investigate-the-situation-in-afghanistan/> accessed 19 November 2017; Elvina Pothelet, 'War Crimes in Afghanistan and Beyond: Will the ICC Weigh in on the "Global Battlefield" Debate?' (*EJIL: Talk!*, 9 November 2017) <https://www.ejiltalk.org/war-crimes-in-afghanistan-and-beyond-will-the-icc-weigh-in-on-the-global-battlefield-debate/> accessed 19 November 2017.

despite its ‘remarkable development’.[80] It is tempting to demand a new codification in situations like these,[81] but the fate of AP II and the unbroken, overarching significance of CA 3 have shown that this will always result in new disappointment as long as the pre-existing distortions have not been eliminated.

Placing the entire debate about the future of IHL in a historical context reminds us of the fact that we are currently observing a realignment of an entire branch of international law. International law has so far witnessed only a few, if any, true ‘Grotian Moments’ – change is normally an insidious development. It is the task of the legal historian to detect such changes and to analyse the accompanying hidden forces. International legal scholarship should be reminded once more that the turn to the better has never been a given, as the comforting narrative of progress in international law can too easily be unveiled as what it is: a tale created to safeguard the power interests in maintaining the *status quo*.

80 Dietrich Schindler, ‘International Humanitarian Law: Its Remarkable Development and Its Persistent Violation’ (2003) 5 Journal of the History of International Law (2003) 165.

81 Bugnion, ‘Jus ad Bellum’ (n 62) 191.

Sunken Vessel or Blooming Flower? Lotus, Permissions and Restrictions within International Humanitarian Law

Katja Schöberl and Linus Mührel

A. Introduction

The permissive or restrictive 'nature' of IHL is currently receiving considerable attention, in particular in debates surrounding the legal basis for detention in NIACs.[1]

Unlike the law of IAC,[2] which provides for explicit legal bases on which to deprive both POWs and civilians of their liberty,[3] treaty law governing NIAC stipulates no such basis. CA 3 and AP II regulate the treatment of persons who have been placed *hors de combat* by detention, among other reasons, and hence seem to presume that persons may at least factually be detained in NIAC.[4] The awareness that 'deprivation of liberty is an ordinary

1 See generally Sandesh Sivakumaran, *The Law of Non-International Armed Conflict* (OUP 2012) 301; Els Debuf, *Captured in War: Lawful Internment in Armed Conflict* (Editions Pedone/Hart 2013) or Lawrence Hill-Cawthorne, *Detention in Non-International Armed Conflict* (OUP 2016).

2 See especially *Hassan v The United Kingdom*, App no. 29750/09, 16 September 2014; and commentary, such as Diane Webber, 'Hassan v United Kingdom: A New Approach to Security Detention in Armed Conflict?' (*ASIL Insight*, 2015) <https://www.asil.org/insights/volume/19/issue/7/hassan-v-united-kingdom-new-approach-security-detention-armed-conflict> accessed 30 October 2017.

3 See Art. 21 GC III, Art. 42 / Art. 78 GC IV and 68 GC IV. Note that while GC III is generally considered a sufficient legal basis for interning POWs, some controversy exists as to whether GC IV, on its own, suffices for the internment of civilians or whether an additional domestic legal basis must provide for it. The ICRC maintains that no distinction between GC III and GC IV should be made in this regard and that GC IV constitutes a sufficient legal basis without additional domestic law, see ICRC, 'Internment in Armed Conflict: Basic Rules and Challenges' (Opinion Paper, November 2014) 5 <https://www.icrc.org/en/document/internment-armed-conflict-basic-rules-and-challenges> accessed 30 October 2017 (hereafter ICRC, 'Internment in Armed Conflict').

4 See CA 3, Art. 2 (1) AP II, Art. 4 AP II, Art. 5 AP II and Art. 6 AP II.

and expected occurrence in armed conflict',[5] both international and non-international, is shared by many in the meantime.[6] However, it only assists in the quest for a legal basis for detention if its 'ordinariness' constitutes 'a general practice accepted as law'[7] to form an international customary legal rule. The ICRC has indeed concluded that both customary and treaty IHL contain an inherent power to detain in NIAC.[8] With respect to customary international law, it bases its position on the fact that 'internment is a form of deprivation of liberty which is a common occurrence in armed conflict'.[9]

This position has been challenged, most recently in the *Serdar Mohammed* case before British courts.[10] The case, which has been frequently commented on,[11] addresses the detention of an assumed Taliban

---

5 32nd International Conference of the Red Cross and Red Crescent, Resolution 1 'Strengthening International Humanitarian Law Protecting Persons Deprived of their Liberty' (December 2015) preamble, para 1.

6 See also The Copenhagen Process on the Handling of Detainees in International Military Operations (The Process): Principles and Guidelines (19 October 2012) preamble, para III, which formulates that '[participants] recognised that detention is a necessary, lawful and legitimate means of achieving the objectives of international military operations' while explaining that the Guidelines themselves cannot constitute a legal basis for such detention, Principle 16 and Chairman's Commentary 16.2.

7 Art. 38 (1) (b) ICJ-Statute.

8 Jean-Marie Henckaerts et al, 'Article 3: Conflicts not of an International Character' in ICRC (ed), *Commentary on the First Geneva Convention: Convention (I) for the Amelioration of the Condition of the Wounded and Sick in Armed Forces in the Field* (2nd edn, CUP 2016) para 671.

9 ICRC, 'Internment in Armed Conflict' (n 3) 7. Rule 99 of the ICRC's Customary International Humanitarian Law Study merely states that 'arbitrary deprivation of liberty is prohibited' without positioning itself on the existence of any 'non-arbitrary' grounds of detention under IHL, see Jean-Marie Henckaerts and Luise Doswald-Beck, *Customary International Humanitarian Law*, vol. I: Rules (CUP 2005) (hereafter Henckaerts and Doswald-Beck, *Customary IHL*).

10 *Serdar Mohammed v Ministry of Defence* [2014] EWHC 1369 (QB); [2014] CN 1019 (hereafter *Serdar Mohammed v Ministry of Defence* [2014]); *Serdar Mohammed v Ministry of Defence* [2015] EWCA Civ 843; [2015] WLR (D) 354 [30] (hereafter *Serdar Mohammed v Ministry of Defence* [2015]), and *Serdar Mohammed v Ministry of Defence* [2017] UKSC 2 (hereafter *Serdar Mohammed v Ministry of Defence* [2017]).

11 See for each decision eg Marko Milanovic, 'High Court Rules that the UK Lacks IHL Detention Authority in Afghanistan' (*EJIL: Talk!*, 3 May 2014) <http://www.ejiltalk.org/high-court-rules-that-the-uk-lacks-ihl-detention-authority-in-afghanistan> accessed 30 October 2017; Sean Aughey and Aurel Sari, 'The Authority to Detain in NIACs Revisted: Serdar Mohammed in the Court of

leader by British armed forces in Afghanistan in 2010 and raises various issues, such as the scope of application of the ECHR, its relationship with IHL, and, most relevantly, the power to detain under IHL, UN SC resolutions and domestic law.[12] The courts have denied the existence of a power to detain under customary IHL for lack of uniformity of State practice and evidence of *opinio juris*[13]; the lack thereof is explained, *inter alia*, by the difficulties and uncertainties in identifying the scope of such power, i.e. 'who may be detained, on what grounds, subject to what procedures and for how long'.[14] More importantly, the courts have engaged in the ongoing discussion about 'inherent'/'implied' IHL treaty powers.[15]

The position taken by the ICRC and others is that treaty IHL contains an inherent power to detain in NIAC, as internment is a form of deprivation of

---

Appeal' (*EJIL: Talk!*, 5 August 2015) <http://www.ejiltalk.org/the-authority-to-detain-in-niacs-revisited-serdar-mohammed-in-the-court-of-appeal> accessed 30 October 2017; and Marko Milanovic, 'A Trio of Blockbuster Judgments from the UK Supreme Court' (*EJIL: Talk!*, 17 January 2017) <http://www.ejiltalk.org/a-trio-of-blockbuster-judgments-from-the-uk-supreme-court> accessed 30 October 2017.

12 The possibility of domestic law, IHRL or UN SC Resolutions to provide such authority (and their relationships) is disregarded for the purpose of this analysis. Note, however, that the debate regarding a legal basis to detain under IHL is prevalent mostly with respect to internationalised NIACS or NIACs with an extraterritorial element, in which the detaining power's ability to rely on own domestic law, informed by IHRL, cannot easily be assumed.

13 *Serdar Mohammed v Ministry of Defence* [2014] (n 10) [254]; *Serdar Mohammed v Ministry of Defence* [2015] (n 10) [241]. The Supreme Court majority deemed it unnecessary to express a concluding view while expressing a preference for rejecting the current existence of a customary legal basis, see: *Serdar Mohammed v Ministry of Defence* [2017] (n 10) [14]. For an analysis of customary IHL arguments to which the majority refers, see the dissenting opinion of Supreme Court Judge Lord Reed, *Serdar Mohammed v Ministry of Defence* [2014] (n 10) [271]. The Supreme Court's hesitance to contribute to emerging customary IHL has been described as a possible 'form of deliberate judicial conservatism', see Fionnuala Ní Aoláin, 'To Detain Lawfully or Not to Detain: Reflections on UK Supreme Court Decision in Serdar Mohammed' (*Just Security*, 2 February 2017) <https://www.justsecurity.org/37013/detain-lawfully-detain-question-reflection-uk-supreme-court-decision-serdar-mohammed> accessed 30 October 2017.

14 *Serdar Mohammed v Ministry of Defence* [2014] (n 10) [258].

15 For an in-depth analysis of the Mohammed-cases see Manuel Brunner, 'Detention for Security Reseons by Armed Forces of a State in Situations of Non-International Armed Conflict: the Quest for a Legal Basis' in this volume 89.

liberty which is not prohibited, but regulated by CA 3 and referred to explicitly in AP II.[16] It is supported by authors who have commented on the *Serdar Mohammed* case specifically or on the legal basis for detention in NIAC more generally.[17] However, the arguments opposing this position are manifold and currently seem to cumulatively be considered more persuasive by most.[18] The extent of these arguments exceeds the scope of this analysis; nonetheless, they can be succinctly summarised as follows:[19] (1) if the drafters of the Geneva Conventions and Additional Protocols had intended to provide a power to detain in NIAC, they could have done so similar to IAC; (2) CA 3 and AP II should be understood as only referring to a factual reality; (3) their mere purpose is to provide minimum standards of treatment; (4) regulation and authorisation need to be legally distinguished; i.e. to argue that, as IHL requires the humane treatment of detainees, it authorises their detention, rests on a *non sequitur*;[20] (5) States which have been and continue to be unwilling to provide non-State armed groups, to which CA 3 and AP II apply reciprocally, authority and hence power to

16 See especially ICRC, 'Internment in Armed Conflict' (n 3) 7. For comment on the Internment Opinion Paper, see Kevin Jon Heller, 'What Exactly Is the ICRC's Position on Detention in NIAC' (*Opinio Juris*, 6 February 2015) <http://opiniojuris.org/2015/02/06/exactly-icrcs-position-detention-niac> accessed 30 October 2017.

17 See for example, Jann K. Kleffner, 'Operational Detention and the Treatment of Detainees' in Terry Gill and Dieter Fleck (eds), *The Handbook of the International Law of Military Operations* (OUP 2010) 465, 471; Ryan Goodman, 'The Detention of Civilians in Armed Conflict' (2009) 103 AJIL 48; Sean Aughey and Aurel Sari, 'IHL Does Authorise Detention in NIAC: What the Sceptics Get Wrong' (*EJIL: Talk!*, 11 February 2015) <http://www.ejiltalk.org/ihl-does-authorise-detention-in-niac-what-the-sceptics-get-wrong> accessed 30 October 2017.

18 See also *Serdar Mohammed v Ministry of Defence* [2017] (n 10) [274].

19 The following summary is based on the courts' analyses in the *Serdar Mohammed*-case, supplemented by additional considerations especially in the footnotes; see *Serdar Mohammed v Ministry of Defence* [2014] (n 10) [241], *Serdar Mohammed v Ministry of Defence* [2015] (n 10) [178], *Serdar Mohammed v Ministry of Defence* [2017] (n 10) [258].

20 Commentators have added that the distinction between regulation of conduct and authorisation of conduct is of particular importance to IHL, which regulates the use of force without providing legal grounds for it (*jus ad bellum*), Lawrence Hill-Cawthorne and Dapo Akande, 'Does IHL Provide a Legal Basis for Detention in Non-International Armed Conflicts?' (*EJIL: Talk!*, 7 May 2014) <http://www.ejiltalk.org/does-ihl-provide-a-legal-basis-for-detention-in-non-international-armed-conflicts> accessed 30 October 2017.

detain cannot rely on any implied powers of detention themselves; (6) a legal basis for detention cannot be implied without specification of the scope of the power; (7) the prohibition of 'arbitrary deprivation of liberty' requires that any legal basis authorising detention must define the circumstances to which it applies with sufficient precision;[21] (8) an authorisation, or absence of prohibition,[22] to use lethal force against certain individuals does not imply a power to detain, at least because the categories of people who may be lawfully killed or detained arguably differ.

Finally, and most relevantly to this analysis, (9) the ICRC's proposition that treaty law contains an inherent power to detain because internment is 'not prohibited by Common Article 3'[23] has been rejected as an obsolete application of the *Lotus* principle.[24] The UK Court of Appeals not only observes that 'in this statement, the ICRC derives a positive power to intern from an absence of prohibition',[25] but the court supports a view of the nature of modern international law according to which the 'absence of prohibition equals authority' approach is criticised and considered to be outdated.[26]

21 To counter this specific (sub-)argument, the ICRC suggests that, in case of internationalised NIACs, either an international agreement between the international, detaining forces and the host State or the domestic law of the host State should address the scope of the detention power as 'additional authority', see ICRC, 'Internment in Armed Conflict' (n 3) 8. The ICRC has furthermore indicated that it considers 'imperative reasons of security' to be the minimum legal standard that should inform internment decisions in NIAC, see ICRC, 'Internment in Armed Conflict' (n 3) Annex I; Jelena Pejic, 'Procedural Principles and Safeguards for Internment / Administrative Detention in Armed Conflict and Other Situations of Violence' (2005) 87 IRRC 375.

22 On the similar, related debate regarding whether IHL provides a legal basis to use lethal force (including whether a lack of prohibition to kill combatants or 'fighters' implies a permission to do so), see for example Ryan Goodman, 'The Power to Kill or Capture Enemy Combatants' (2013) 24 EJIL 819 and Michael N. Schmitt, 'Wound, Capture, or Kill: A Reply to Ryan Goodman' (2013) 24 EJIL 855.

23 ICRC, 'Internment in Armed Conflict' (n 3) 7.

24 See generally Ryan Goodman, 'Authorization versus Regulation of Detention in Non-International Armed Conflicts' (2015) ILS 155; Matthias Lippold, 'Between Humanization and Humanitarization? Detention in Armed Conflicts and the European Convention on Human Rights' (2016) 76 ZaöRV 53.

25 *Serdar Mohammed v Ministry of Defence* [2015] (n 10) [202].

26 Ibid, [197]. For support of the Court's conclusion regarding this aspect, see Alex Conte, 'The UK Court of Appeal in Serdar Mohammed: Treaty and Customary IHL Provides No Authority for Detention in Non-International Armed Conflicts' (*EJIL: Talk!*, 6 August 2015) <http://www.ejiltalk.org/the-uk-court-of-appeal-

On the contrary, the court considers and rejects the possibility of IHL having 'reached the stage' where it provides for a legal basis for detention in NIAC,[27] hence thereby requiring an explicit legal authority.

This contribution aims to both analyse the current relevance of the *Lotus* principle to IHL and expose the influence of the conception of public international law on IHL's 'implied' authorities in cases of missing explicit legal bases.[28]

B. Theoretical Background

In the first section, a brief overview of the most relevant theories of international law is given in order to embed the following discussion in the appropriate context.

Since the very beginning of international law, a broad range of theories of international law has existed, all of which seek to explain the nature of international legal rules.[29] Concepts such as realism, sociological theories or critical theories have offered insights into the political and sociological factors contributing to the development of international law.[30] However, the main debate in both public international law and IHL in particular remains between proponents of a positivist and a natural law approach, both advocating for the dominance of each theory in interpreting the

---

in-serdar-mohammed-treaty-and-customary-ihl-provides-no-authority-for-detention-in-non-international-armed-conflicts> accessed 30 October 2017, who not only notes that the Court was correct in rejecting an 'absence of prohibition equals authority' approach, but who rather unapologetically remarks that '[n]o credible lawyer could genuinely assert that lack of an express prohibition constitutes authority to deprive persons of their liberty'.

27 *Serdar Mohammed v Ministry of Defence* [2015] (n 10) [9].

28 A recent *EJIL: Debate!* demonstrates the importance of a deeper reflection on the theories of international law. See (2017) 28 EJIL No. 1.

29 For an inspiring insight into the theories of international law, see Andrea Bianchi, *International Law Theories: An Inquiry into different Ways of Thinking* (OUP 2016).

30 See eg Ingo Venzke, 'Contemporary Theories and International Law-Making' (2013) 59 Amsterdam Law School Research Paper 12 <https://papers.ssrn.com/sol3/papers.cfm?abstract_id=2342175#> accessed 30 October 2017; Steven Ratner, 'Legal Realism School' in MPEPIL (online edn, OUP July 2007); Anthony Carty, 'Sociological Theories of International Law' in MPEPIL (online edn, OUP March 2008); Günter Frankenberg, 'Critical Theory' in MPEPIL (online edn, OUP October 2010).

international legal system. This appears to be the case despite the ostensible recognition that none of the theories can convincingly explain all aspects of the existing order.[31]

I. Positivism

Positivism is a generic term that describes a legal theory and covers a wide spectrum of partially competing positions which have been developed since the 19th century.[32] In a traditional positivist understanding, international law is defined as law laid down through the consent and agreement of sovereign States that are equally entitled to create norms.[33] Accordingly, law-making in international law requires two complementary elements: a 'voluntarist'- and a 'unity of sources'-element.[34] Whereas the former is needed to express that law originates from States' will,[35] the latter recognises as law only those norms that can be traced back to one ultimate source[36] and that are generated

31 See generally: Martti Koskenniemi, 'International Legal Theory and Doctrine' in MPEPIL (online edn, OUP November 2007) para 17; and specifically, Andreas von Arnauld, *Völkerrecht* (3rd edn, C.F. Müller 2016) 6, who cites the *Münchhausen Trilemma* according to which each theory leads to a circular argument, a regressive argument, or an axiomatic argument.

32 For further reading on positivism, see Jörg Kammerhofer and Jean d'Aspremont (eds), *International Legal Positivism in a Post-Modern World* (CUP 2014) or Robert Kolb, *Theories of International Law* (Bloomsbury Publishing 2016) 105-10 (hereafter Kolb, *Theories of International Law*).

33 James Crawford, *Brownlie's Principles of Public International Law* (8th edn, OUP 2012) 9 (hereafter Crawford, *Brownlie's Principles*). Note that some modern positivist approaches are open for the possibility of including non-State actors as 'law-makers', eg Bruno Simma and Andreas Paulus, 'The Responsibility of Individuals for Human Rights Abuses in Internal Conflicts: A Positivist View' (1999) 93 AJIL 302, 306 (hereafter Simma and Paulus, 'Responsibility of Individuals'); Jörg Kammerhofer, 'Non-state actors from the perspective of the Pure Theory of Law' in Jean d'Aspremont (ed), *Participants in the International Legal System: Multiple Perspectives on Non-State Actors in International Law* (Routledge 2011) 54, 59-60.

34 Frauke Lachenmann, 'Legal Positivism' in MPEPIL (online edn, OUP July 2011) para 3 (hereafter Lachenmann, 'Legal Positivism').

35 Ibid.

36 Depending on the branch of positivism, the ultimate source is to be found in State consent (consensualism) or notions such as *pacta sunt servanda* (neo-positivism) or a rule of recognition. See eg Hans Kelsen, *Reine Rechtslehre* (Deuticke, 1934) 129, who describes the ultimate source as 'Grundnorm'.

by a pre-set legal procedure.[37] Consequently, international law is not described as law above States, but as law between States and can be differentiated from 'non-law' as well as national law by its sources, procedures, and doctrine.[38]

The *Lotus* principle has been considered to reflect a traditional positivist approach towards international law. According to the *Lotus* principle, States are free in their decisions unless acts or omissions are prohibited by international law.[39] Thus, international law is seen to possess a prohibitive character.[40] Positivism, as reflected in the *Lotus* principle, has been criticised especially with regard to the 'undesired' consequences which may result from the absence of prohibitive rules[41] and for its inability to provide adequate answers to contemporary challenges.[42] The adherence to State sovereignty and State will has raised questions concerning the sources of

---

37 Lachenmann, 'Legal Positivism' (n 34) para 3.

38 Crawford, *Brownlie's Principles* (n 33) 9; Jutta Brunnée, 'Consent' in MPEPIL (online edn, OUP October 2010) para 3; Lachenmann, 'Legal Positivism' (n 34) para 30.

39 The *Lotus* principle was developed from the so-called *Lotus* decision of the PCIJ, see The Case of the S.S. "Lotus" *(France v Turkey)* [1927] PCIJ Series A No 10, in particular the Court's statement at 8: 'International law governs relations between independent States. The rules of law binding upon States therefore emanate from their own free will as expressed in conventions or by usages generally accepted as expressing principles of law and established in order to regulate the relations between these co-existing independent communities or with a view to the achievement of common aims. Restrictions upon the independence of States cannot therefore be presumed.'

40 For an alternative interpretation of the *Lotus* decision, see eg Jörg Kammerhofer, 'Gaps, the Nuclear Weapons Advisory Opinion and the Structure of International Legal Argument between Theory and Practice' (2010) 80 BYIL 333, 341-43; Pia Hesse, 'Comment: neither Sunken Vessel nor Blooming Flower! The Lotus Principle and International Humanitarian Law' in this volume 80 (hereafter Hesse, 'Neither Sunken Vesserl nor Blooming Flower!').

41 With respect to domestic (German) law, see Gustav Radbruch, 'Gesetzliches Unrecht und übergesetzliches Recht' (1946) 1 SJZ 105 (hereafter Radbruch, 'Gesetzliches Unrecht'); regarding international law, see especially Martti Koskenniemi, *From Apology to Utopia: The Structure of International Legal Argument* (2nd edn, CUP 2006).

42 Jörg Kammerhofer and Jean d'Aspremont, 'Introduction: the future of international legal positivism' in Jörg Kammerhofer and Jean d'Aspremont (eds), *International Legal Positivism in a Post-Modern World* (CUP 2014) 1, 4-7.

international law[43] and the permissibility of analogies to fill perceived 'gaps' in international law.[44] Regardless of the criticism, positivism seems to currently remain the dominant theory of international law[45] since it, *inter alia*, offers coherence and predictability.[46] This continued reliance on positivism hence suggests a generally restrictive nature of international (humanitarian) law.

II. Natural Law

The concept of natural law refers to norms and principles deduced from god, nature, reason, the idea of justice, or some social or historical necessity, i.e. from something not laid down by any human authority.[47] According to natural law theory, international law is law above States and may not be superseded by law made by States or other actors.[48] While natural law does not exclude the possible creation of positive norms through State consent,[49] it foresees the prerogative to 'correct' positive law where needed.[50] Despite a resurgence of natural law theory in public international law,[51] one of natural law's most important challenges remains the lack of an acknowledged methodology for the identification and verification of natural

---

43 With regard to customary international law, the general principles of international law and *jus cogens*, see eg Lachenmann, 'Legal Positivism' (n 34) paras 35-37, 44, 47.

44 See Silja Vöneky, 'Analogy in International Law' in MPEPIL (online edn, OUP February 2008) paras 13-14, 24.

45 See generally Steven Ratner and Anne-Marie Slaughter, 'Appraising the Methods of International Law: A Prospectus for Readers' (1999) 93 AJIL 291, 293; and specifically on human rights issues Simma and Paulus, 'Responsibility of Individuals' (n 33) 302, who note that 'in reflecting on our day-to-day legal work, we realized that, for better or for worse, we indeed employ the tools developed by the "positivist" tradition'.

46 Mary Ellen O'Connell, 'Legal Process School' in MPEPIL (online edn, OUP November 2006) para 22.

47 Alexander Orakhelashvili, 'Natural Law and Justice' in MPEPIL (online edn, OUP August 2007) para 1.

48 Alan Boyle and Christine Chinkin, *The Making of International Law* (OUP 2007) 11.

49 Kolb, *Theories of International Law* (n 32) 117.

50 See eg Radbruch, 'Gesetzliches Unrecht' (n 41).

51 Kolb, *Theories of International Law* (n 32) 116-18.

law norms,[52] which would allow international legal actors to authoritatively rely on them.[53] Natural law theory neither follows a *Lotus* approach towards international law nor does it abstractly determine whether it is generally permissive or restrictive in nature. Instead, it follows a case-by-case approach and balances different norms and principles to reach a legal conclusion[54] which may be permissive or restrictive in character, e.g. allowing or prohibiting/limiting detention in armed conflict.

C. Existence of an International Humanitarian Law-Specific Approach?

IHL is a branch of public international law governing armed conflicts by protecting those who are not or no longer participating in hostilities and by restricting the means and methods of warfare. Whereas it must, as such, be interpreted in accordance with general public international law, it constitutes a distinct body of law with several specificities.[55] This section hence considers the possible existence of an IHL-specific approach towards permissiveness and restriction based on a positivist approach, also due to lack of accepted natural law methodology. It not only assesses the *Lotus* principle's perception within IHL, but also examines its norm structure, including the significance and meaning of the principle of military necessity and the Martens Clause.

I. Perception of the *Lotus* Principle within International Humanitarian Law

The extent to which the *Lotus* principle applies to IHL has been debated predominately in the context of the ICJ's *Nuclear Weapons* Advisory

---

52 Martti Koskenniemi, 'Methodology of International Law' in MPEPIL (online edn, OUP November 2007) para 6. A prominent example which has been discussed as a possible natural law norm is the 'inherent right' to self-defence.

53 International courts as the ICJ and PCIJ have rarely based their judgments and opinions on norms or principles attributable to natural law, but reinforce their findings by invoking such notions by way of *obiter dicta*, see Lachenmann, 'Legal Positivism' (n 34) para 56.

54 See eg Gustav Radbruch, *Rechtsphilosophie: Studienausgabe* (2nd edn, C.F. Müller 2003). Radbruch describes a pyramid of natural law principles with the principle of justice on top.

55 Note for example the legally uncontested binding nature of IHL for non-State actors in NIAC.

Opinion.[56] Given that the Court was asked if 'the threat or use of nuclear weapons [is] in any circumstances permitted under international law',[57] intervening States argued over the necessity of an authorisation under international law permitting the threat or use of nuclear weapons. Some States criticised that the formulation of the question was incompatible with international law, which protects States' sovereignty and freedom to act that is only restricted by prohibitive rules under international customary or treaty law. If the Court were to answer the question, the word 'permitted' should be replaced by 'prohibited'.[58] Other States asserted that the invocation of the *Lotus* principle was inappropriate under contemporary international law and in the circumstances of the present case.[59] The Court, however, simply noted that

> ... the nuclear-weapons States appearing before it either accepted, or did not dispute, that their independence to act was indeed restricted by the principles and rules of international law, more particularly humanitarian law ..., as did the other States which took part in the proceedings.[60]

It hence concluded that 'the argument concerning the legal conclusions to be drawn from the use of the word "permitted" [is] without particular significance for the disposition of the issues before the Court'.[61] The Court thereby 'brushed aside'[62] any meaningful debate about the *Lotus* principle's application within IHL and diverted it to the judges' Separate and Dissenting Opinions.

The Opinions primarily reveal a dissent regarding the continued relevance of the *Lotus* principle for today's international legal order in general. Critics of a permissive approach to international law (1) stress the

---

56 Legality of the Threat or Use of Nuclear Weapons (Advisory Opinion) [1996] ICJ Rep 226 (hereafter *Nuclear Weapons*).

57 The question upon which the Advisory Opinion had been requested was set forth in UN GA Res UN Doc A/RES/49/75K (15 December 1994). The French text equally reads as follows: 'Est-il permis en droit international de recourir à la menace ou à l'emploi d'armes nucléaires en toute circonstance?'.

58 *Nuclear Weapons* (n 56) 238-39, paras 21 et seq.

59 Ibid, para 21.

60 Ibid, 239, para 22.

61 Ibid.

62 Christopher Greenwood, 'The Advisory Opinion on Nuclear Weapons and the Contribution of the International Court to International Humanitarian Law' (1997) IRRC 66, 67, who also demonstrates that the Court, in its subsequent analysis, considered if certain rules prohibit the use of nuclear weapons, and not whether they authorise such use.

evolution of the international legal system from co-existence to community,[63] (2) emphasise the specific context of the *Lotus* decision, i.e. the delimitation of criminal jurisdiction,[64] and (3) support natural law approaches instead of, or in addition to, legal positivism.[65] In relation to a later Advisory Opinion, the continued endorsement of the *Lotus* principle was additionally criticised for ignoring 'the possible degrees of non-prohibition, ranging from "tolerated" to "permissible" to "desirable"'[66] and for failing to explore 'whether international law can be deliberately neutral or silent on a certain issue.'[67]

Regarding the application of the *Lotus* principle to IHL specifically, dissenting judges have distinguished the context of the *Lotus* decision (i.e. the collision of two vessels on the high seas in peacetime) from situations to which IHL applies (e.g. the use of nuclear weapons in armed conflict) in order to argue that IHL was already a well-established concept at the time of the decision, but simply not relevant to it. The PCIJ's decision should thus not be used to negate IHL and to override its basic principles, such as the Martens Clause.[68] In other, more drastic, words: a case dealing with the delimitation of criminal jurisdiction, being 'scarcely an earth-shaking issue',[69] should not be seen as governing 'any act which could bring civilization to an end and annihilate mankind'.[70] More fundamentally, it is contended that the *Lotus* principle does not apply to acts or omissions which 'by reason of their essential nature, cannot form the subject of a right', as these threaten the international community's very own existence and, thus, the international legal order protecting State sovereignty.[71]

Despite individual judges' doubts about the continued relevance of the *Lotus* principle in international law and concerns about the appropriateness of its application to IHL, the ICJ has so far not decided to abandon its mainly

---

63 Declaration of President Bedjaoui in *Nuclear Weapons* (n 56) 48, para 12.

64 Ibid. On this aspect, see also Hesse, 'Neither Sunken Vessel nor Blooming Flower!' (n 40).

65 Dissenting Opinion of Judge Weeramantry in *Nuclear Weapons* (n 56) 494.

66 Declaration of Judge Simma in Accordance with International Law of the Unilateral Declaration of Independence in Respect of Kosovo (Advisory Opinion) [2010] ICJ Rep 403, 480, para 8.

67 Ibid, 480-481, para 9.

68 Dissenting Opinion of Judge Weeramantry in *Nuclear Weapons* (n 56) 495.

69 Dissenting Opinion Judge Shahabuddeen in *Nuclear Weapons* (n 56) 395.

70 Ibid, 394.

71 Ibid, 392. For an analysis of the *Lotus* principle's compatibility with the UN Charter and the law of neutrality, see also 391.

positivist view. An analysis of the norm structure of IHL might therefore complement the judges' considerations.

II. Norm Structure of International Humanitarian Law

As far as the first codifications of IHL – such as the Paris Declaration of 1856,[72] the Lieber Code of 1863,[73] the Saint Petersburg Declaration of 1868,[74] and the Oxford Manual of 1880[75] – are informative, IHL initially served to limit the belligerents' exercise of power and to generate restrictive effects by relying on certain overarching principles based on natural law.[76] As codification progressed, the formulation of and relationship between such principles was framed in positive legal rules,[77] making IHL one of the first branches of public international law to be comprehensively codified.

The norm structure of modern treaty IHL as well as its drafting history suggests that States primarily agreed on restrictive rules. The current rules of IHL treaties are generally prohibitory in wording and manner.[78] Only a few rules use permissive wording, e.g. Art. 21 GC III on the restriction of liberty of movement of prisoners of war and Art. 43 (2) AP I which grants '[m]embers of the armed forces of a Party to a conflict … the right to

---

72 Declaration Respecting Maritime Law (entered into force 16 April 1856) in British State Papers vol. LXI (1856), 155.

73 Instructions for the Government of Armies of the United States in the Field (24 April 1863) in Dietrich Schindler and Jiri Toman, *The Laws of Armed Conflicts* (3rd edn, Martinus Nijhoff Publisher 1988) 3 (hereafter Lieber Code).

74 Declaration Renouncing the Use, in Time of War, of Explosive Projectiles Under 400 Grammes Weight (entered into force 11 December 1868) in Dietrich Schindler and Jiri Toman, *The Laws of Armed Conflicts* (3rd edn, Martinus Nijhoff Publisher 1988) 102.

75 The Laws of War on Land (Oxford, 9 September 1880) in Dietrich Schindler and Jiri Toman (eds), *The Laws of Armed Conflicts* (3rd edn, Martinus Nijhoff Publisher 1988) 36.

76 Martti Koskenniemi, *The Gentle Civilizer of Nations* (CUP 2001) 70-88.

77 See Michael N. Schmitt, 'Military Necessity and Humanity in International Humanitarian Law: Preserving the Delicate Balance' (2010) 50 VJIL 796, 796 (hereafter Schmitt, 'Military Necessity'); Yoram Dinstein, 'Military Necessity' in MPEPIL (online edn, OUP September 2015) para 7 (hereafter Dinstein, 'Military Necessity').

78 This contribution perceives rules expressing obligations in IHL such as Art. 10 (2) GC I or Art. 12 (1) AP I as restrictive rules as they prohibit any behaviour which is not in compliance with the obligation.

participate directly in hostilities'. Taking into account the *travaux préparatoires*, commentators argue that the permissive wording was chosen only for reasons of clarification.[79] According to them, the prerequisite of a permissive norm for belligerents' conduct was not intended.[80] As conventional IHL is expanding, in particular with respect to limitations and prohibitions of means of warfare,[81] it may well be argued that these treaties demonstrate a continued intention of States to regulate warfare by imposing restrictions, which is equally reflected in their practice contributing to the formation of customary IHL. An examination of the rules of customary IHL, as formulated in the ICRC's Customary International Humanitarian Law Study,[82] reveals that they too have been phrased in a mostly prohibitory way with only few rules formulated in permissive wording.[83] However, according to the context of and the commentaries to the rules, these permissions either constitute exceptions to general prohibitions or provide clarifications.[84]

For a more thorough analysis of the norm structure of IHL, the following subsections discuss the contemporary significance and meaning of the principle of military necessity and of the Martens Clause for the permission or restriction of conduct in IHL.

---

79 Jean S. Pictet (ed), *The Geneva Conventions of 12 August 1949: Commentary*, vol. III (Geneva 1960) 178 (hereafter Pictet, *Commentary*); Yves Sandoz et al (eds), *Commentary on the Additional Protocols of 8 June 1977 to the Geneva Conventions of 12 August 1949* (Martinus Nijhoff Publishers 1987) 515-16 (hereafter Sandoz et al, *Commentary*).

80 Pictet, *Commentary* (n 79) 178; Sandoz et al, *Commentary* (n 79) 515-16.

81 See eg the recently adopted Treaty on the Prohibition of Nuclear Weapons (adopted 7 July 2017) UN GA A/RES/71/258 (Treaty on the Prohibition of Nuclear Weapons).

82 Henckaerts and Doswald-Beck, *Customary IHL* (n 9).

83 Ibid, Rules 1, 49, 51, 66, 68 and 128.

84 Ibid, Rule 1 which, in the first sentence, obliges parties to a conflict to distinguish between civilians and combatants. In the second and third sentence, the rule clarifies that thus, '[attacks] may only be directed against combatants', but 'must not be directed against civilians.'

1. Principle of military necessity

When the principle of military necessity was first codified in the Lieber Code in 1863,[85] it drew in part upon morality and a responsibility 'to one another and to God' in conducting warfare.[86] However, it also established the weakening of enemy forces as the only legitimate purpose of the conduct of warfare and linked the necessity of measures 'indispensable for securing the ends of the war' to their legality according to 'the modern law and usages of war'. Whereas the principle has since been understood as only permitting measures 'in accordance with law', its permissive or restrictive nature remains controversial.[87]

Concerning the principle's relation to treaty and customary rules of positive law, States, academia and jurisprudence such as the Nuremberg Tribunal's *Hostage* case have rejected the German nineteenth century doctrine of *Kriegsraison geht vor Kriegsmanier* ('the necessities of war take

---

85 See Art. 14-16 Lieber Code (n 73): 'Art. 14: Military necessity, as understood by modern civilized nations, consists in the necessity of those measures which are indispensable for securing the ends of the war, and which are lawful according to the modern law and usages of war'; 'Art. 15: Military necessity admits of all direct destruction of life or limb of armed enemies, and of other persons whose destruction is incidentally unavoidable in the armed contests of the war ... Men who take up arms against one another in public war do not cease on this account to be moral beings, responsible to one another and to God.' and 'Art. 16: Military necessity does not admit of cruelty – that is, the infliction of suffering for the sake of suffering or for revenge ... and, in general, military necessity does not include any act of hostility which makes the return to peace unnecessarily difficult.'

86 The principle of military necessity and the Martens Clause are therefore often-cited examples of concepts containing notions of natural law; see Rupert Ticehorst, 'The Martens Clause and the Laws of Armed Conflict' (1997) 37 IRRC 125, 132-33 (hereafter Ticehorst, 'Martens Clause'); Michael Salter, 'Reinterpreting Competing Interpretations of the Scope and Potential of the Martens Clause' (2012) 17 JCSL 403, 433-34 (hereafter Salter, 'Reinterpreting Competing Interpretations'); David Turns, 'Military Necessity' (*Oxford Bibliographies*, 2012) <http://www.oxfordbibliographies.com/> accessed 30 October 2017; David Luban, 'Military Necessity and the Cultures of Military Law' (2013) 26 LJIL 315, 340 (hereafter Luban, 'Military Necessity'). This analysis considers them from a positivist perspective only.

87 See, among others, Burrus M. Carnahan, 'Lincoln, Lieber and the Laws of War: The Origins and Limits of the Principle of Military Necessity' (1998) 92 AJIL 213; Schmitt, 'Military Necessity' (n 77); and Nils Melzer, 'Targeted Killing or Less Harmful Means? – Israel's High Court Judgment on Targeted Killing and the Restrictive Function of Military Necessity' (2006) 9 YbIHL 87.

precedence over the rules of war'[88]). The Tribunal provided that '[m]ilitary necessity or expediency do not justify a violation of positive rules'[89] and that the prohibitions contained in the Hague Regulations 'control and are superior to military necessities of the most urgent nature except where the Regulations themselves specifically provide the contrary'.[90] Examples of contemporary rules providing for the possibility to invoke military necessity in exceptional circumstances include Art. 8 GC I and GC II, Art. 53 GC IV, Art. 52 (2) AP I, Art. 62 (1) AP I and Art. 71 (3) AP I as well as Rules 38 (B), 39, 43 (B), 50, 51, 56 and 156 of the ICRC's Customary International Humanitarian Law Study.[91] These articles support the conclusion that the principle of military necessity only permits departure from prohibitive rules if the rules foresee such a possibility.[92]

The role of the principle of military necessity in situations not explicitly covered by rules of positive IHL remains a subject of debate[93] and practical relevance, e.g. with respect to the legal basis for detention in NIAC, as illustrated above. Some argue that the principle is not limited to rules of positive law specifically foreseeing its application, but may serve as an independent rule – either as customary law or as a general principle of law within the meaning of Art. 38 (1) (c) ICJ-Statute – in the absence of explicit rules of positive law (i.e. providing a basis for detention).[94] Others maintain

88 Luban, 'Military Necessity' (n 86) 341.

89 *The United States of America v Wilhelm List, et al* (1948) Law Reports of Trials of War Criminals selected and prepared by the United Nations War Crimes Commission, vol. VIII, 66 (hereafter *US v Wilhelm List, et al*).

90 Ibid, 69.

91 Henckaerts and Doswald-Beck, *Customary IHL* (n 9). For an example of domestic regulation reflecting this position, see Office of General Counsel, Department of Defence, Law of War Manual, (Washington 2016) paras 1.3.3.2, 2.1.2.3 and 2.2. (hereafter DoD Manual), which defines military necessity as 'the principle that justifies the use of all measures needed to defeat the enemy as quickly and efficiently as possible that are not prohibited by the law of war'.

92 On the IHL-specific approach towards State responsibility (i.e. necessity as a possible circumstance precluding wrongfulness according to Art. 25 (2) (a) ASR), see eg Marco Sassòli, 'State Responsibility for Violations of International Humanitarian Law' (2002) 84 IRRC 401.

93 For an early discussion, see *US v Wilhelm List, et al* (n 89) 63-64, in which the Tribunal discussed under which circumstances violations of rules derived from fundamental concepts of justice, humanity and the rights of individuals may be justified (which were, however, not met in the case).

94 See eg DoD Manual (n 91) 2.2.1.

that the principle may never be invoked as an independent rule, but only if a norm explicitly foresees its application.[95]

Ultimately, the existence or non-existence of the principle of military necessity as an independent rule of IHL seems to be of only limited significance for the purpose of this analysis. If the principle was an independent rule of IHL, its existence would only be relevant for the examination of an IHL-specific approach towards the *Lotus* principle if its nature was permissive. Such an independent permissive rule would imply that States are not free in their belligerent conduct, but are dependent on permission and are obliged to act at least within the limits of the principle of military necessity's scope of permission. Otherwise (i.e. if the principle of military necessity was restrictive in nature), it would in principle reinforce the application of the *Lotus* principle within IHL, but serve to restrict belligerents' freedom to conduct that is militarily necessary.

Currently, there seems yet to be insufficient support for the existence of an independent rule of the principle of military necessity, either permissive or restrictive in nature, within positive IHL. Therefore, it seems unjustified to, firstly, conclude that the principle of military necessity affirms or constrains the application of the *Lotus* principle within IHL or to, secondly, derive a humanitarian law-specific approach from it.

2. Martens Clause

Due to its uncommonly broad wording and drafting history, the Martens Clause has been subject to a variety of interpretations. In general, four main approaches for the interpretation of the Clause can be identified. These consider it as: (1) irrelevant/inapplicable, (2) a reminder that customary and conventional international law apply in parallel, (3) an affirmation of the existence of a separate source of international law to be distinguished from customary and conventional international law, and (4) a prevention of an *a contrario* argument based on the *Lotus* principle.[96]

---

95 See eg Dinstein, 'Military Necessity' (n 77) paras 8-10, who refers to war crime trials after World War II; Nobuo Hayashi, 'Requirements of Military Necessity in International Humanitarian Law and International Criminal Law' (2010) 28 Boston University International Law Journal 39.

96 See generally Jochen von Bernstoff, 'Martens Clause' in MPEPIL (online edn, OUP December 2009); Ticehorst, 'Martens Clause' (n 86); Salter, 'Reinterpreting Competing Interpretations' (n 86).

Whereas some have argued that the Martens Clause has lacked normative status since its inception, others have put forward that the Clause has lost legal significance over time. The former position is based on the Clause's (historical) context. It stresses that the inclusion of the Clause, proposed by Russian diplomat *Fyodor Fyodorovich Martens*, into the legally non-binding preamble of the 1899 Hague Convention II[97] was a compromise between the great powers and smaller States over a dispute on the inclusion of rules of the 1874 Brussels Declaration dealing with combatant status for resistance fighters during belligerent occupation, and therefore only constituted a 'diplomatic ploy'.[98] The latter position submits that the wording of the Martens Clause ('until a more complete code of the laws of war is issued') implied a temporary restriction to the Clause's scope of application which was triggered when 'a more complete code of the laws of war' was issued with the adoption of the 1949 Geneva Conventions and their Additional Protocols of 1977.[99] Both arguments, considered in isolation, ignore that the Martens Clause has not only been reaffirmed in subsequent conventions, but legally revalued when included in the substantive provisions of the Geneva Conventions and AP I.[100]

---

97 Convention (II) with Respect to the Laws and Customs of War on Land (adopted 29 July 1899, entered into force 04 September 1900) in Dietrich Schindler and Jiri Toman (eds), The Laws of Armed Conflicts (3rd edn, Martinus Nijhoff Publisher 1988) 69-93. The Preamble notes that '[until] a more complete code of the laws of war is issued, the High Contracting Parties think it right to declare that in cases not included in the Regulations adopted by them, populations and belligerents remain under the protection and empire of the principles of international law, as they result from the usages established between civilized nations, from the laws of humanity, and the requirements of the public conscience'.

98 Antonio Cassese, 'The Martens Clause: Half a Loaf or Simply Pie in the Sky?' (2000) 11 EJIL 187, 193-94 and 197 (hereafter Cassese, 'The Martens Clause').

99 See especially the position of the Russian Federation in *Nuclear Weapons* (n 56), 'Written Statement and Comments of the Russian Federation on the Issue of the Legality of the Threat or Use of Nuclear Weapons' (19 June 1995) 13 <http://www.icj-cij.org/files/case-related/95/8796.pdf> accessed 30 October 2017.

100 See common Art. 63/62/142/158 GC, Art. 1 (2) AP I, the preamble to AP II and compare the wording of Art. 1 (2) AP I: 'In cases not covered by this Protocol or by other international agreements, civilians and combatants remain under the protection and authority of the principles of international law derived from established custom, from the principles of humanity and from the dictates of public conscience.'

The submissions of the UK and the US to the ICJ in the *Nuclear Weapons* Advisory Opinion reflect a second interpretative approach, according to which the Martens Clause only serves as a reminder that customary international law continues to apply after the adoption of a treaty norm, but has no normative content of its own.[101] Yet, it is not apparent why a reminder (legally binding or not) should be necessary, given that international law knows no hierarchy in the sources of legal obligations. Moreover, the Clause's wording is not limited to 'custom', but extends to the 'principles of humanity' and the 'dictates of public conscience', which can hardly be reduced to mean customary international law.

In a third interpretative approach, it has therefore been suggested that the Martens Clause affirms the existence of separate sources of international law that are to be distinguished from conventional and customary international law. Not only does the drafting history of the relevant treaties not support such a conclusion,[102] but it also remains unclear which rules would be deducible from the 'principles of humanity' and the 'dictates of public conscience' in the absence of conventional or customary international law. [103] It must thus be noted that in international and national

---

101 See eg the position of the UK in *Nuclear Weapons* (n 56) 'Statement of the Government of the United Kingdom' (16 June 1995) 48, para 3.58 <http://www.icj-cij.org/files/case-related/95/8802.pdf> accessed 30 October 2017: 'The terms of the Martens Clause themselves make it necessary to point to a rule of customary international law which might outlaw the use of nuclear weapons. Since the existence of such a rule is in question, reference to the Martens Clause adds little.'

102 Compare the ICRC draft preamble to the Additional Protocols to the Geneva Conventions of August 12, 1949 and their Commentary (Geneva, October 1973), 5 ('Recalling that, in cases not covered by conventional or customary international law, civilian population and the combatants remain under the protection of the principles of humanity and the dictates of the public conscience') with the final wording of Art. 1 (2) AP I. The Drafting Committee did not follow the ICRC's proposal and located the principles of humanity and dictates of the public conscience within the Martens Clause-formulation requiring the existence of 'principles of international law derived from … the principles of humanity and from the dictates of public conscience', see Michael Bothe et al, *New Rules for Victims of Armed Conflicts: Commentary on the Two 1977 Protocols Additional to the Geneva Conventions of 1977* (Martinus Nijhoff Publishers 1982) 44.

103 For a discussion about possible ways to identify the dictates of public conscience, see Dissenting Opinion of Judge Shahabuddeen in Nuclear Weapons (n 56) 410, who proposes to look to sources which speak 'with authority', like resolutions of the UN GA. See also the Treaty on the Prohibition

jurisprudence, in State practice or academic writings, it has never been found that a rule has emerged only as a result of these notions, but that conventional or customary international law was required for a positive rule to exist.[104]

Based on these considerations, a fourth approach to interpreting the Martens Clause seems preferable. It supposes that the Martens Clause prevents an *a contrario* argument based on the *Lotus* principle and that it provides that something which is not explicitly prohibited by a treaty is not *ipso facto* permitted in IHL.[105] The notions referred to in the Clause at least prevent a strict application of the *Lotus* principle: States are not entirely free to do what is not expressly prohibited by treaty or custom. More specifically, they must consider the principles of humanity and the dictates of public conscience, which may or may not provide guidance restricting or

---

of Nuclear Weapons (n 81) which in its preamble '[*reaffirms*] that any use of nuclear weapons would also be abhorrent to the principles of humanity and the dictates of public conscience' and hence takes a more affirmative stance than previous drafts which had reaffirmed 'that in cases not covered by this convention, civilians and combatants remain under the protection and authority of the principles of international law derived from established custom, from the principles of humanity and from the dictates of public conscience'.

104 See generally *The Prosecutor v Kupreskic et al* (Judgment) ICTY-95-16-T-14 (14 January 2000) 525 and Cassese, 'The Martens Clause' (n 98) 202-8 and Mary Ellen O'Connell, 'Historical Development and Legal Basis' in Dieter Fleck (ed), *The Handbook of Humanitarian Law in Armed Conflicts* (3rd ed, OUP 2013) 1, para 131. See also Jean-Philippe Lavoyer and Louis Maresca, 'The Role of the ICRC in the Development of International Humanitarian Law' (1999) 4 International Negotiation 501, 511-17, who (partially dissenting) note with respect to the Ottawa process to ban anti-personnel landmines: 'This process affirmed for many what the ICRC and others had always known to be true: that humanitarian law has its roots in the public perception about the acceptable limits of warfare. It has long been a maxim of humanitarian law that even in the absence of positive or customary rules, the conduct of armed conflict is limited by the "laws of humanity and the dictates of public conscience". Public conscience was a vital element in creating the necessary political will for action against anti-personnel mines in government, military and international circles. As a result, it became a stigmatised weapon, and the norm against its use was established before the adoption of the ban treaty. This element was an important factor in the decision of countries to continue developing a ban in a new context, closely linked with civil society.'

105 Louise Doswald-Beck, 'International Humanitarian Law and the Advisory Opinion of the International Court of Justice on the Legality of the Threat or Use of Nuclear Weapons' (1997) 79 IRRC 37, 49.

permitting certain conduct – such as detention – but which open up IHL to further development and other areas of international law.

D. Conclusion

The discussion about detention in NIAC illuminates the persistently diverse perceptions of international law and its treatment of situations which are not addressed by explicit legal rules. The issue whether and to what extent the *Lotus* principle applies to IHL is of fundamental importance in this context.[106] An analysis of the jurisprudence of the ICJ confirms a positivist approach which foresees the application of the *Lotus* principle within IHL. An examination of the norm structure of treaty and customary IHL also suggests that IHL is mainly restrictive in nature and compatible with a positivist vision of international law, meaning that belligerent conduct is permitted, if not prohibited by law. The principle of military necessity, if interpreted to constitute an independent legal rule of permissive nature and the Martens Clause, however, constrain the application of the *Lotus* principle within IHL. The Martens Clause especially serves to prevent *a contrario* arguments and to limit States' freedom in conducting armed conflict by introducing notions possibly inspired by natural law, such as the principles of humanity and dictates of public conscience. Forcedly vague, the notions require further legal interpretation to provide better guidance. However, it is foreseeable that a case-by-case approach to the application of a 'Martens Clause-restricted *Lotus* principle' (however well informed) does not produce pragmatic solutions to military and humanitarian needs which IHL seeks to balance with both resolve and caution. Thus, States are well advised to fill possible gaps in positive law and to work towards greater legal clarity.[107]

---

106 More generally, the operation of the *Lotus* principle within other branches of public international law seems worthy of more scholarly attention.

107 For scholarly contributions, see eg Brian Orend, 'The Next Geneva Convention: Filling a Law-of-War Gap with Human Rights Values' in Jens David Ohlin (ed), *Theoretical Boundaries of Armed Conflict and Human Rights* (CUP 2016) 363.

Comment: neither Sunken Vessel nor Blooming Flower! The Lotus Principle and International Humanitarian Law

Pia Hesse

A. Introduction

The *Lotus* case of the PCIJ is one of the most cited cases in international law. Formulating the voluntarist paradigm with international law as rules emanating from the free will of independent States, *Lotus* serves as an important point of reference for deliberations on legal positivism. From the appraisal that it is State consent that gives international law its binding force, the Court infers that

> … [t]he rules of law binding upon States therefore emanate from their own free will as expressed in conventions or by usages generally accepted as expressing principles of law and established in order to regulate the relations between these co-existing independent communities or with a view to the achievement of common aims. Restrictions upon the independence of States cannot therefore be presumed.[1]

This *Lotus* formula is often invoked as a meta-concept attesting international law a prohibitive nature and thereby reflecting a rigid positivist approach to international law. In their paper, *Katja Schöberl* and *Linus Mührel* essentially analyse the relevance of this concept to IHL.

In this comment, I argue that this frequently referenced passage of the PCIJ's case cannot be read in isolation, but must rather be understood in its context. In this way, the *Lotus* principle loses its significance as a doctrine to explain the nature of international law as a whole. To use *Katja Schöberl's* and *Linus Mührel's* words: The flower is not in full bloom, but it is much more than a sunken vessel. The *Lotus* formula is part of the PCIJ's more detailed elaborations on the broader question of jurisdiction in international law. Its relevance thus spans beyond the single case of the collision between a French and a Turkish steamer back in 1926. In fact, jurisdiction is the gist of the *Lotus* case. Understanding the *Lotus* formula

---

1 The Case of the S.S. "Lotus" (*France v Turkey*) [1927] PCIJ Series A No 10, para 44 (hereafter '*The Case of the SS Lotus*').

cited above as one statement of the Court's larger deliberations on jurisdiction, this comment claims that the *Lotus* formula is not readily applicable to IHL.

As a first step, I will turn to the international law on jurisdiction in more general terms. On this basis, I will then demonstrate how it relates to IHL and thereby underpin my assertion that *Lotus* is not apt to determine the nature of IHL.

B. The International Law on Jurisdiction

International law on jurisdiction is a vast field. It is basically a procedural mechanism to determine the application *ratione loci* of different substantive regulations.[2] In 1927, when the PCIJ was asked to resolve the dispute between the French and the Turkish government, substantive regulations were predominantly found in the domestic legal orders of States. In a decentralised international system of independent States, the key role of international law was to delimit spheres of competence between co-existing States. The substantive legal framework to then govern the given situation was the domestic law of the competent State. International law as a legal order performing a task of co-ordination between sovereign States: This was 'the spirit of the times'[3] and this is the image of international law adopted by the PCIJ in the *Lotus* case.

The question the PCIJ was confronted with was whether States actually need to 'point to some title *to* jurisdiction'[4] or whether States are free to exercise jurisdiction unless there is a rule of international law prohibiting it[5]. The exercise of jurisdiction can be performed by prescribing rules, or by enforcing these rules either through the executive branch or through courts. Here, and this is central to this comment, it is essential to make a differentiation. There is a distinction between the rules that are prescribed or enforced and the rules that provide the authorisation to prescribe or

2 Cedric Ryngaert, *Jurisdiction in International Law* (2nd edn, OUP 2015) 2 (hereafter 'Ryngaert, *Jurisdiction*').

3 Declaration of President Bedjaoui in Legality of the Threat or Use of Nuclear Weapons (Advisory Opinion) [1996] ICJ Rep 226, para 12 (hereafter 'Declaration Judge Bedjaoui').

4 This was the position of the French Government in the *Lotus* case, see *The Case of the SS Lotus* (n 1) para 41; emphasis added.

5 The position of the Turkish Government in the *Lotus* case, ibid.

enforce – the title 'to' jurisdiction. Whereas the former usually is found among domestic laws of States, the latter is one of international law. The *Lotus* formula, however, exclusively refers to the latter type of rules – those granting or not granting a title to jurisdiction.

International law on jurisdiction thus aims at demarcating the fields of competence between sovereign States and, thereby, at reducing conflicts between them.[6] As a consequence, the decision of the PCIJ that is put in a nutshell by the above cited *Lotus* formula can, originally, only apply to international rules concerning the 'if' of the exercise of jurisdiction by States in their international relations. The essential phrase supposedly explaining the nature of international law, '[r]estrictions upon the independence of States cannot therefore be presumed', is to be taken as meaning '[r]estrictions upon the exercise of jurisdiction by States cannot therefore be presumed'.

However, this statement, reflecting the consent theory underlying the positivist paradigm, is only half of the truth. The PCIJ made a distinction between different forms of exercising jurisdiction and established different relationships of rules and exceptions for them. Whereas States are generally free, if not restrained by a prohibitive rule of international law, to prescribe rules (prescriptive jurisdiction) even concerning situations and persons outside their territorial boundaries, the enforcement of its rules (enforcement jurisdiction) using coercive power in another State's territory is generally prohibited, unless a permissive rule to the contrary exists.[7] The international law of jurisdiction, however, has since developed and other principles have emerged, especially under customary international law.[8] But these need not be further elaborated here, as international law of jurisdiction is not the topic of this comment. This brief digression served only to demonstrate that the *Lotus* formula first and foremost is concerned with international jurisdiction and that the PCIJ in its decision adopted a view that regards international law as inter-State law, a system that operates in the horizontal dimension, regulating the relationship between independent entities.[9]

6 John E. Ferry, 'Towards Completing the Charm: The Woodpulp Judgment' (1989) 10 European Competition Law Review 58.

7 *The Case of the SS Lotus* (n 1) para 45.

8 See Ryngaert, *Jurisdiction* (n 2).

9 Roman Kwiecien, 'On Some Contemporary Challenges to Statehood in the International Legal Order: International Law Between Lotus and Global Administrative Law' (2013) 51 Archiv des Völkerrechts 281.

IHL, however, is the best illustration of the fact that international law is more than inter-State law, which, at the same time, disqualifies it from being subject to the *Lotus* doctrine.

C. The International Law on Jurisdiction and International Humanitarian Law

As has been shown, an allocation of competence by the law of international jurisdiction determines a State's scope of action and, as a corollary, the scope of application *ratione loci* of its laws. How does IHL relate to this differentiation between rules of international law that provide the ground of jurisdiction and a State's rules that are prescribed or enforced in exercising that jurisdiction?

As *Katja Schöberl* and *Linus Mührel* point out, IHL 'constitutes a distinct body of law with several specificities'. IHL's particularity within the international legal order also becomes evident when compared to international law on jurisdiction. IHL is an example of successful substantivism[10] and, as such, is quite the opposite of an instrument of co-ordination. IHL does not allocate competences in the sense of *Lotus,* but it presents a branch of international law that regulates a particular subject matter in substantive terms – the means and methods of warfare. This, of course, is due to the fact that, traditionally, the nature of the object of regulation of IHL – war – had a purely international character. As IHL is the applicable law to armed conflict in substantive terms, there is no need to (1) determine the competent State that then (2) applies its laws to the situation. The applicable substantive law can be found in international law itself, in IHL. Put bluntly, there is no room for *Lotus*. Whereas the law of jurisdiction is a procedural mechanism managing action of independent States within a decentralised system, IHL is a branch of international law providing for substantive regulation of a subject matter in a centralised manner. *Lotus* and international jurisdiction are concerned with territoriality and sovereignty. Non-State values, like the protection of those not participating in hostilities as is the case for IHL, are not addressed.

Katja Schöberl and *Linus Mührel* put forward the example of the alleged Taliban fighter *Serdar Mohammed* to accentuate the necessity of either

10 Cedric Ryngaert, 'The Limits of Substantive International Economic Law: In Support of Reasonable Extraterritorial Jurisdiction' in Bert Keirsbilck et al (eds), *Facing the Limits of the Law* (Springer 2009) 242.

'fill[ing] possible gaps in positive law' or alternatively determining the nature of IHL in order to be able to make sense of perceived gaps in positive law. This case provoked the debate about whether IHL provided for an authorisation to detain in NIACs and, as a consequence, evoked a debate about the nature of IHL itself.

Seen through the *Lotus* lens, the detention of *Serdar Mohammed* in Afghanistan carried out by the British armed forces in 2010 was an exercise of extraterritorial enforcement jurisdiction. Of course, this exercise of jurisdiction required an international principle of law to allow for this otherwise unlawful violation of Afghanistan's territorial integrity. The international principle of law, here, is the legal basis for the UK's overall military engagement in Afghanistan (initially the right of collective self-defence in support of the US, later the resolution of the UN SC mandating ISAF). However, the authorisation of foreign States was not required in order to identify the domestic law applicable to govern the situation, as international law itself provides for the substantive laws for situations of armed conflicts: IHL. As mentioned above, *Lotus* does not say anything about the actual exercise of jurisdiction by a State; rather, it concerns the permission/prohibition to exercise jurisdiction in the first place. Once the sovereignty hurdle has been overcome, here in the form of *jus ad bellum* norms, the *Lotus* principle is satisfied. The next step, namely the question of which law governs this exercise of jurisdiction, is based on other considerations, especially on those inherent to IHL, as offered by the humanitarian-law-specific approach of *Katja Schöberl* and *Linus Mührel*.

D. Conclusion

When claims are made that the *Lotus* principle is outdated as it is reflective of 'the spirit of an international society which as yet had few institutions and was governed by an international law of strict co-existence, itself a reflection of the vigour of the principle of State sovereignty',[11] I agree. I do not agree, though, that this is the reason why *Lotus* is unable to explain the nature of IHL. Whether Lotus is still the leading doctrine to regulate international jurisdiction or not is not of concern to this comment. The important finding is rather that this was its initial purpose. As shown above, the rule that '[r]estrictions ... cannot therefore be presumed' only applies to those international laws that qualify as rules allocating competences

11 Declaration Judge Bedjaoui (n 3) para 12.

between States. IHL does not qualify as such. It is true that the distinction between the two categories of rules established above is not always easily made. In fact, rules of international law may, at the same time, contain coordinating elements determining the State that is competent to exercise power, and are thus to be categorised as principles of international law within the meaning of *Lotus* on the one hand, and, on the other hand, may contain substantive elements that are applied by the State in the execution of its jurisdiction. IHL, however, clearly pertains to the second set of rules, which is also mirrored in the strict dichotomy of the *jus ad bellum* and the *jus in bello.*

When claims are made 'that international humanitarian law is mainly restrictive in nature, … meaning that belligerent conduct is permitted if not prohibited by law', I agree. I do not agree, though, that this is so because IHL, as a branch of international law, follows the logic of *Lotus.* As elaborated above, the *Lotus* formula provides the starting point in the law of international jurisdiction. As such, it has a meaning beyond the specific case before the PCIJ. It is more than the sunken vessel in the Mediterranean Sea. However, it does not serve to explain the nature of all international law. Especially developments discussed under the catchwords 'institutionalisation', 'integration', and 'globalisation', that advance the shift from an international society of co-existence to one of co-operation, prevent *Lotus* from coming to full bloom. The legal order increasingly emerges from one of allocating competences between independent States to one addressing global phenomena in substantive terms.

This, of course, is not to say that the question about the nature of IHL as either permissive or restrictive as *Katja Schöberl* and *Linus Mührel* raise it, is irrelevant. Exactly the opposite is true. But the answer to this question cannot be drawn from the *Lotus* doctrine. For this reason, *Katja Schöberl's* and *Linus Mührel's* analysis of the norm structure of IHL provides a very important contribution to the academic discourse on the topic.

Part II:
Detention in Non-International Armed Conflict

Detention for Security Reasons by the Armed Forces of a State in Situations of Non-International Armed Conflict: the Quest for a Legal Basis

Manuel Brunner

A. Introduction

During times of armed conflict, individuals are detained for security reasons by the armed forces of the State or States involved. In fact, this is a central feature of such situations. While such detention may last only for some hours or days in some cases, in others it may last for a much longer period. In any case, detentions in armed conflict give rise to a situation in which detainees are immensely vulnerable to the actions and omissions of their captors, and in which the detaining authorities are responsible for safeguarding the health and dignity of those in their custody.[1] However, the international law on detention in armed conflicts for security reasons is not entirely clear. A highly-disputed point in this respect is the legal basis for detentions in situations of NIACs. The different questions relating to this problem were discussed by Single Justice *Leggatt* of the High Court of Justice of England and Wales in the judgment in the case of *Serdar Mohammed v Ministry of Defence* of 2 May 2014.[2] The case involved the detention of a person during the conflict in Afghanistan by British Armed Forces. The work by Justice *Leggatt* in the case was so remarkable that one commentator called it 'a heroic effort, with the single judge grappling with a host of complex, intertwined issues of international law and acquitting himself admirably in the process'.[3] The decision was later upheld in almost

---

1 See ICRC, 'Strengthening international humanitarian law protecting persons deprived of their liberty: Concluding report' (October 2015) Conf. Doc 32IC/15/19.1, 8 <http://rcrcconference.org/wp-content/uploads/2015/04/32IC-Concluding-report-on-persons-deprived-of-their-liberty_EN.pdf> accessed 13 October 2017 (hereafter ICRC, 'Concluding Report').

2 *Serdar Mohammed v Ministry of Defence* [2014] EWHC 1369 (QB) (hereafter *Serdar Mohammed v Ministry of Defence* [2014]).

3 Marko Milanovic, 'High Court Rules that the UK Lacks IHL Detention Authority in Afghanistan' (*EJIL: Talk!*, 3 May 2014) <http://www.ejiltalk.org/high-

every aspect by the Civil Division of the Court of Appeal for England and Wales.[4] The last judgment in the case so far was delivered by the Supreme Court of the United Kingdom in early 2017.[5]

Along the lines of the judgments in the *Serdar Mohammed* case, this contribution explores the questions relating to the legal basis for detentions for security reasons in NIACs. The analysis begins with an inquiry into IHL (II.), where it will be shown that neither treaty-based law nor customary law applicable to NIACs provide a legal basis for detentions. In a second step (III.), the relevance and role of human rights law in respect to such detentions is explored. The third step (IV.) is dedicated to the potential legislation on which detentions in NIACs could be based. The analysis is rounded off by a summary and concluding remarks (V.).

B. *Does International Humanitarian Law Provide a Legal Basis for Detentions for Security Reasons?*

I. The Situation under International Humanitarian Law Applicable to International Armed Conflicts

The treaty law applicable in situations of IAC provides different grounds for detention or internment. Art. 21 (1) GC III permits that 'the Detaining Power may subject prisoners of war to internment'. Furthermore, according to Art. 27 (4) GC IV, 'the parties to the conflict may take such measures of control and security as may be necessary as a result of the war'. Such measures also include the power to detain protected persons. In relation to aliens in the territory of a party to an IAC, Art. 42 GC IV provides that 'the internment or assigned residence of protected persons may be ordered only if the security of the Detaining Power makes it absolutely necessary' and that 'if any person, acting through the representatives of the Protecting Power, voluntarily demands internment, and if his situation renders this step necessary, he shall be interned by the Power in whose hands he may be'. Moreover, Art. 43 GC IV grants several safeguards to an interned protected person. Lastly, according to Art. 78 GC IV, if, in an occupied territory, 'the

court-rules-that-the-uk-lacks-ihl-detention-authority-in-afghanistan> accessed 13 October 2017.

4 *Serdar Mohammed v Secretary of State for Defence* [2015] EWCA Civ 843 (hereafter *Serdar Mohammed v Secretary of State for Defence* [2015]).

5 *Serdar Mohammed v Ministry of Defence* [2017] UKSC 2 (hereafter *Serdar Mohammed v Ministry of Defence* [2017]).

Occupying Power considers it necessary, for imperative reasons of security, to take safety measures concerning protected persons, it may at the most, subject them to assigned residence or to internment'. In addition to this, the second and third paragraphs of Art. 78 GC IV provide several safeguards for the affected persons.

The legal logic behind incorporating those reasons for detention in the treaties concerning IACs is connected to the nature of such conflicts. In an IAC, a minimum of two sovereign States are pitted against each other.[6] Military operations by one or the other State take place on the territory of a foreign State and with respect to persons who are nationals of the foreign State in question. If rules to detain persons in IACs did not exist in international law, detention on foreign territory would be unlawful as States are prohibited to take such actions under general international law.[7] Therefore, only explicit provisions of international law can provide the State which is exerting military force on the territory of another State during an IAC with the legal authority to detain.[8]

II. The Situation under International Humanitarian Law Applicable to Non-International Armed Conflicts

1. Treaty-based International Humanitarian Law

In the treaty law applicable in situations of NIACs, no explicit provision can be found upon which the armed forces of a State could legally base the detention of individuals.[9] However, CA 3 as well as Art. 5 and 6 AP II contain several provisions both on the minimum treatment of individuals

6 Yoram Dinstein, *The Conduct of Hostilities under the Law of International Armed Conflict* (3rd edn, CUP 2016) 35.

7 Lawrence Hill-Cawthrone and Dapo Akande, 'Locating the Legal Basis for Detention on Non-International Armed Conflicts: A Rejoinder to Aurel Sari', (*EJIL: Talk!*, 2 June 2014) <http://www.ejiltalk.org/locating-the-legal-basis-for-detention-in-non-international-armed-conflicts-a-rejoinder-to-aurel-sari/> accessed 13 October 2017 (hereafter Hill-Cawthrone and Akande, 'Rejoinder to Sari').

8 Ibid.

9 Emily Crawford and Alison Pert, *International Humanitarian Law* (CUP 2015) 161.

who are subject to detention or internment and on criminal proceedings against such individuals in the context of a NIAC.[10]

Therefore, the British Ministry of Defence in the *Serdar Mohammed* case as well as some commentators in academic writing have argued that CA 3 and AP II provide inherent powers to detain.[11] Indeed, CA 3 explicitly refers to 'detention' and Art. 2, 4 (1), 5 (1) and (2) as well as 6 AP II refer to those 'deprived of their liberty or whose liberty has been restricted for reasons related to the conflict', 'detention' and 'internment'. The argument goes that

> ... the premise of those references and the existence of rules in Common Article 3 and AP II for the protection of those detained in non-international armed conflict [is] that there [is] an inherent power to detain provided that [it] is done in accordance with those rules.[12]

This interpretation of the law was met with opposition by Justice *Leggatt* in the *Serdar Mohammed* case for five convincing reasons:

(1) As a first reason, Justice *Leggatt* argued that, if CA 3 or AP II had been intended to provide a power to detain, the drafters of the provisions would have done so expressly, as is the case in GC III and GC IV. Justice *Leggatt* further correctly explained that it is not to be readily supposed that the parties to an international treaty have agreed to establish a power to deprive individuals of their liberty indirectly by implication and without saying so explicitly.[13] This is a reasonable argument as a power to detain is a coercive power; therefore, such powers should not too readily be read into applicable treaty rules without clear evidence of this being the collective intention of the State parties to the respective treaty.[14] Such evidence can neither be found in the *travaux préparatoires* of CA 3 nor of AP II.

---

10 *Serdar Mohammed v Ministry of Defence* [2017] (n 5) para 12.

11 *Serdar Mohammed v Ministry of Defence* [2014] (n 2) paras 232; Jelena Pejic, 'Procedural Principles and Safeguards for Internment / Administrative Detention in Armed Conflict and Other Situations of Violence' (2005) 87 IRRC 375, 377.

12 *Serdar Mohammed v Secretary of State for Defence* [2015] (n 4) para 200.

13 *Serdar Mohammed v Ministry of Defence* [2014] (n 2) para 242.

14 Lawrence Hill-Cawthorne and Dapo Akande, 'Does IHL Provide a Legal Basis for Detention in Non-International Armed Conflicts?' (*EJIL: Talk!*, 7 May 2014) <http://www.ejiltalk.org/does-ihl-provide-a-legal-basis-for-detention-in-non-international-armed-conflicts> accessed 13 October 2017 (hereafter Hill-Cawthorne and Akande, 'Legal Basis for Detention in NIAC').

This position is not inconsistent with the view taken, for instance, in an often-referred-to article of *Goodman*, who notes that the logical structure of IHL is such that what is permitted in IACs should, *a fortiori*, also be considered permitted in NIACs as States would never have intended to restrict them more in the latter than in the former.[15] It needs to be taken into account that IHL does not restrict States with regard to detention in NIACs any more than it restricts their ability to detain in IACs. Detention is nothing that is prohibited for States in NIACs, as States may detain individuals in such conflicts; however, IHL simply does not provide a legal basis for such detentions.[16]

(2) Justice *Leggatt's* second argument was that CA 3 and AP II recognise the fact that people are detained during NIACs, but, aside that, the law remains silent. Such detentions may be lawful under the law of the State on whose territory the armed conflict is taking place, or under another applicable law, otherwise the detention may be entirely unlawful. Nothing in the language in CA 3 and AP II suggests that those provisions are intended to authorise or confer legality on any such detention.[17] This argument is convincing, as it is largely recognised that the regulation of a specific conduct by international law does not imply authorisation or acceptance of the legality of that conduct.[18] Commentators *Hill-Cawthorne* and *Akande* underline this finding with a good example from the sphere of IHL itself: They put forward that the distinction between recognition and regulation of conduct, on the one hand, and authorisation or acceptance of the legality of that conduct on the other hand, constitute a key feature of IHL as a legal regime. This is due to the fact that IHL regulates the use of force by States in situations of armed conflict. However, IHL remains silent on the legality of the use of force under the *jus ad bellum*. The use of force that IHL recognises and regulates is not rendered lawful simply by virtue of

---

15 Ryan Goodman, 'The Detention of Civilians in Armed Conflict' (2009) 103 AJIL 48.

16 Hill-Cawthorne and Akande, 'Legal Basis for Detention in NIAC' (n 14); for an examination of the permissive/restrictive nature of IHL see Katja Schöberl and Linus Mührel, 'Sunken Vessel or Blooming Flower? Lotus, Permissions and Restrictions within International Humanitarian Law' in this volume 59 (hereafter Schöberl and Mührel, 'Sunken Vessel or Blooming Flower?').

17 *Serdar Mohammed v Ministry of Defence* [2014] (n 2) para 243.

18 Hill-Cawthorne and Akande, 'Legal Basis for Detention in NIAC' (n 14).

the fact that it is regulated by IHL. Rather, IHL simply accepts that armed conflicts exist and seeks to regulate various aspects of such conflicts.[19]

(3) In his third argument, Justice *Leggatt* explored the *telos* of CA 3 and Art. 5 AP II. He argued that the aim of the two provisions was to guarantee certain minimum standards of treatment to all individuals who are deprived of their liberty for reasons relating to the respective armed conflict. The need to observe those minimum standards is equally relevant to all people who are detained, and does not depend on whether or not their detention is legally justified. *Leggatt* therefore concluded that the clear purpose of CA 3 and Art. 5 AP II was inconsistent with the notion that these provisions provide a legal power to detain.[20]

(4) The fourth reason Justice *Leggatt* brought forward to support his argument follows from the fundamental principle that IHL applies without distinction to all parties to an armed conflict, both State and non-State actors alike. He argued that States subscribing to the four Geneva Conventions and the two Additional Protocols hereto would not have agreed by treaty to establish a power to detain in the circumstances of a NIAC. Given that CA 3 applies to 'each Party to the conflict' and AP II applies to organised armed groups who are able to implement it,[21] providing a power to detain would have meant authorising detention by dissident and rebel armed groups. That would be an anathema to most States dealing with a NIAC on their territory and who do not wish to confer any legitimacy to rebels and insurgents or accept that such groups have any right to exercise a function which is a core aspect of State sovereignty. This conclusion is backed by the *travaux préparatoires* of CA 3 and AP II as they contain plentiful references to this concern by the various delegates.[22]

(5) The fifth and last argument of Justice *Leggatt* related to the content of the power to detain.[23] He argued that he did not see how CA 3 or AP II could possibly have been intended to provide a power to detain, nor how they could reasonably be interpreted as doing so, unless it were possible to identify the scope of such a power. Justice *Leggatt* further correctly observed that neither CA 3 nor AP II specify who may be detained, on what grounds, in accordance with which procedures, or for how long. This

19 Ibid.
20 *Serdar Mohammed v Ministry of Defence* [2014] (n 2) para 244.
21 Ibid, para 245.
22 See Hill-Cawthorne and Akande, 'Legal Basis for Detention in NIAC' (n 14).
23 *Serdar Mohammed v Ministry of Defence* [2014] (n 2) para 246.

argument is also convincing. From a rule of law perspective, clarity, predictability, transparency and authority are important attributes when the State's interest interferes with the position of the individual.[24] An explicit legal basis for detentions in situations of NIACs would undoubtedly serve those attributes.

A further argument that was presented by the British Ministry of Defence in the *Serdar Mohammed* case was that the ability to detain insurgents whilst hostilities are ongoing would be an essential corollary of the authorisation to kill them. Those engaged in military operation must be able to both accept the surrender of somebody who poses a threat to them and their mission and must be able to engage an adversary without necessarily having to use lethal force. Furthermore, the Ministry of Defence pointed out that it would be a serious violation of IHL to deny quarter.[25] Justice *Leggatt* convincingly responded to this argument by stating that it would justify the capture of a person who may lawfully be killed; however, the argument would not go further than that. As soon as an individual had been detained, the use of lethal force against him would have no longer provided a basis for the detention of this individual.[26]

2. Customary International Humanitarian Law

If no legal basis for detention can be found in treaty-based IHL applicable to NIACs, such a legal basis may be found in the applicable customary IHL. Art. 38 (1) (b) ICJ-Statute describes customary law as 'a general practice accepted as law'. In this respect, the existence of a rule of customary international law requires the presence of two elements.[27] The first of these elements is the existence of a general State practice. There is no requirement regarding any particular duration; however, the practice must be extensive, representative and virtually uniform.[28] The second requirement is the *opinio*

24 ICRC, 'Concluding Report' (n 1) 29.

25 *Serdar Mohammed v Ministry of Defence* [2014] (n 2) para 252.

26 Ibid, para 253.

27 On the formation of customary international law in general, see James Crawford, *Brownlie's Principles of Public International Law* (8th edn, OUP 2012) 23.

28 North Sea Continental Shelf Cases (*Federal Republic of Germany v Denmark; Federal Republic of Germany v Netherlands*) (Judgment) [1969] ICJ Rep 43, para 74.

juris sive necessitatis, the belief that the practice is a matter of right or obligation.[29]

It seems that in the law of NIACs, no customary basis for detentions has been formed as yet in the way described above. In the *Serdar Mohammed* case, Justice *Leggatt* found that no evidence of any recognition by States involved in NIACs as providing a legal basis for detention was produced by the British Ministry of Defence.[30] Furthermore, the Justice correctly concluded that

> … to demonstrate general practice of detention in non-international armed conflict recognised as a matter of legal right, it would need to be possible to identify with reasonable certainty the scope of the alleged rule of law in terms of who may be detained, on what ground, subject to what procedure and for how long.[31]

Important work in the field of IHL on the international scene has so far been unhelpful in the demonstration of the existence of such a rule containing all the features described above. For instance, the ICRC's Customary International Humanitarian Law Study identifies 161 rules of customary nature in IHL.[32] Rule 99 is dedicated to the deprivation of liberty and reads very clearly: 'Arbitrary deprivation of liberty is prohibited'. While these rules are merely the result of an academic study and are therefore in no way binding, it is clear that, if a rule like Rule 99 exists, it cannot serve as a legal basis for detention as the rule is prohibitive and therefore requires States to abstain from the conduct regulated in the rule and in no way allow it. The Copenhagen Process on the Handling of Detainees in International Military Operations is another international forum which dealt with detention in the context of NIACs. It enjoys a certain degree of legitimacy as it was initiated by the government of Denmark and 24 States participated in it with the African Union, NATO, the European Union, the UN and the ICRC as observers. In October 2012, the Copenhagen Process was concluded with the publication of principles and guidelines which are intended to apply to international military operations in the context of NIACs and peace operations.[33] Principle 1 of the Copenhagen Process Principles applies to 'the detention of persons who are being deprived of their liberty for reasons related to an international military operation'. According to this principle,

---

29 Ibid, 44, para 77.

30 *Serdar Mohammed v Ministry of Defence* [2014] (n 2) para 257.

31 Ibid, para 258.

32 Jean-Marie Henckaerts and Louise Doswald-Beck, *Customary International Humanitarian Law*, vol. I: Rules (CUP 2005) 344.

33 The Copenhagen Process on the Handling of Detainees in International Military Operations (The Process): Principles and Guidelines (19 October 2012).

'detention of persons must be conducted in accordance with applicable international law'; furthermore, several conditions for detentions are laid down in the principle, but there are no conditions mentioned under which an individual can actually be detained. In fact, according to Principle 16:

> ... nothing in The Copenhagen Process Principles and Guidelines affects the applicability of international law to international military operations conducted by the states or international organisations; or the obligations of their personnel to respect such law; or the applicability of international or national law to non-state actors.

The official commentary to this principle clarifies it, as it reads:

> ... the saving clause ... recognise[s] that The Copenhagen Principles and Guidelines is not a text of legally binding nature and thus, does not create new obligations or commitments. Furthermore, The Copenhagen Process Principles and Guidelines cannot constitute a legal basis for detention. ... Since The Copenhagen Process Principles and Guidelines were not written as a restatement of customary international law, the mere inclusion of a practice in The Copenhagen Process Principles and Guidelines should not be taken as evidence that states regard the practice as required out of a sense of legal obligation.

Lastly, the problem of identifying a legal basis for detentions in NIACs was discussed at the 32nd International Conference of the Red Cross and Red Crescent, held in Geneva from 8 to 10 December 2015, which was dedicated to the strengthening of IHL protecting persons deprived of their liberty. The results of the conference confirmed that, currently, no customary IHL applicable to situations of NIACs exists upon which detentions for security reasons might be legally based. In the concluding report it was held that 'neither existing treaties nor customary law' applicable to NIACs 'expressly provide grounds or procedures for carrying out' detentions, and that

> ... although States had divergent views on the relevance of the principle of legality to IHL, the ICRC has understood them to believe that the specific grounds and procedures for internment should be set down in a source, or combination of sources, that is capable of safeguarding arbitrary internment.[34]

III. Conclusion

In consequence, the legal basis for the authority to detain individuals for security reasons in NIACs lies neither in treaty-based IHL nor in customary

34 ICRC, 'Concluding Report' (n 1) 15, 29.

IHL.[35] This, however, does not imply that detention is prohibited or not allowed in situations of NIACs; it simply means that a legal basis for detentions must be identified in another corpus of law.[36] State practice supports this result, as States often rely on domestic law to provide the legal basis for detention practices in situations of NIACs. Examples include the 'Terrorism and Disruptive Activities Act and Ordinance',[37] which was applied in the conflict between the Nepalese Government and communist insurgents, or the 'Prevention of Terrorism Act'[38], which was applied in the conflict between the Government of Sri Lanka and the Liberation Tigers of Tamil Eelam.[39]

The divergent approaches to the problem of detention (and other fields of application) in IHL applicable to IACs and to NIACs are rooted in the differences between the regulated types of conflict. While the former type of conflict, as explained above, involves military operations of two or more sovereign States, NIACs (mainly) take place in an environment of intra-State relations. Therefore, firstly, the rights of other States will, on a regular basis, not be engaged by NIACs and, secondly, the intra-State nature of NIACs entails that they take place within a pre-existing legal system, namely domestic law, which is applicable to the situation of the conflict.[40]

---

35 Hill-Cawthorne and Akande, 'Legal Basis for Detention in NIAC' (n 14).

36 For a different assessment, see Schöberl and Mührel, 'Sunken Vessel or Blooming Flower?' (n 16).

37 Nepalese Ministry of Law, Justice and Parliamentary Affairs, 'Ordinance No. 1 of the year 2058 (2001)' *Nepal Gazette* (Kathmandu, 26 November 2001) <http://nepalconflictreport.ohchr.org/files/docs/2001-11-26_legal_govt-of-nepal_eng.pdf> accessed 13 October 2017.

38 Parliament of the Democratic Socialist Republic of Sri Lanka, 'Prevention of Terrorism' (20 July 1979) Act No 48 of 1979 <http://www.satp.org/satporgtp/countries/shrilanka/document/actsandordinance/prevention_of_terrorism.htm> accessed 13 October 2017.

39 Hill-Cawthorne and Akande, 'Legal Basis for Detention in NIAC' (n 14).

40 Hill-Cawthrone and Akande, 'Rejoinder to Sari' (n 7).

C. Human Rights Law Applicable to Detention in Non-International Armed Conflicts

I. Rules on the Deprivation of Liberty in Human Rights Law

In the sphere of human rights law, detentions are in conflict with the right to liberty. The term liberty refers to the physical liberty of an individual as opposed to a mere restriction of the freedom of movement.[41] Confinement to a certain limited place for a not negligible length of time without valid consent constitutes a deprivation of the physical liberty of an individual.[42] Rules regulating the deprivation of liberty can be found in several universally and regionally applicable human rights treaties. According to Art. 9 (1) ICCPR, Art. 5 (1) ECHR, Art. 7 (2) ACHR, and Art. 6 ACHPR, a person may be deprived of his or her liberty only 'on such grounds and in accordance with such procedure as are established by law'[43].

The most detailed and restrictive of the aforementioned provisions is Art. 5 (1) ECHR, which allows the deprivation of liberty of an individual only in six cases. Three of those cases are of interest in situations of NIACs, namely:

> (a) the lawful detention of a person after conviction by a competent court;
>
> (b) the lawful arrest or detention of a person for non-compliance with the lawful order of a court or in order to secure the fulfilment of any obligation prescribed by law;
>
> (c) the lawful arrest or detention of a person affected by the purpose of bringing him before the competent legal authority on reasonable suspicion of having committed an offence or when it is reasonably considered necessary to prevent his committing an offence or fleeing after having done so.

Therefore, under human rights law, a legal basis for detention is required. If such a legal basis to deprive a person of his or her physical liberty is not in place, the detention is unlawful. Furthermore, human rights treaties provide for a number of legal safeguards for the affected individual whose liberty has been deprived. These safeguards include, for instance, the right

---

41 Ilias Bantekas and Lutz Oette, *International Human Rights Law and Practice* (2nd edn, CUP 2016) 369 (hereafter Bantekas and Oette, *Human Rights Law*).

42 Ibid.

43 This is the wording used in Art. 9 (1) ICCPR. The rules on the deprivation of liberty in regional human rights treaties display a slightly different wording; however, the content is identical.

to be informed about the reasons for the deprivation of liberty,[44] or the right to take proceedings before a court in order for the court to decide without delay on the lawfulness of the detention and order release if the detention is not lawful.[45]

II. The Applicability of Human Rights Law in Situations of Armed Conflict

Only if human rights law applies in situations of armed conflict, its rules on the deprivation of liberty may have an influence on the problem of detention in NIACs. While it is clear that IHL is the body of international law that regulates armed conflict, it was disputed whether human rights law also applies in the context of such situations. The main argument was that IHL is designed especially to regulate times of war, while human rights law protects the individual in times of peace.[46] However, international legal practice has not followed this line of argumentation. For example, in 1996, the ICJ stated in its advisory opinion on the Legality of the Threat or Use of Nuclear Weapons that

> In principle, the right not arbitrarily to be deprived of one's life applies also in hostilities. The test of what is an arbitrary deprivation of live, however, then falls to be determined by the applicable *lex specialis*, namely, the law applicable in armed conflict which is designed to regulate the conduct of hostilities.[47]

Later, in the advisory opinion of the Court concerning Legal Consequences of the Construction of a Wall in the Occupied Palestinian Territory (2004), it was stated:

> As regards the relationship between international humanitarian law and human rights law, there are thus three possible solutions: some rights may be exclusively matters of international humanitarian law; others may be exclusively matters of human rights law; yet others may be matters of both these branches of international law. In order to answer the question put to it, the Court will have to take into

---

44 Art. 9 (2) ICCPR, Art. 5 (2) ECHR, Art. 7 (4) ACHR.

45 Art. 9 (4) ICCPR, Art. 5 (4) ECHR, Art. 7 (5) ACHR.

46 For approaches to the relationship between IHL and human rights law, see Daniel Thürer, *International Humanitarian Law: Theory, Practice, Context* (AIL-Pocket 2011) 125.

47 Legality of the Threat or Use of Nuclear Weapons (Advisory Opinion) [1996] ICJ Rep 226, 240, para 25.

> consideration both these branches of international law, namely human rights law and, as *lex specialis*, international humanitarian law.[48]

Furthermore, the UN GA – already in its 25th session – stated in the resolution of 9 December 1970 on the 'Basic principles for the protection of civilian population in armed conflicts' that '[f]undamental human rights, as accepted in international law, and laid down in international instruments, continue to apply fully in situations of armed conflict.'[49] These quotes demonstrate that both bodies of law generally continue to apply in armed conflicts as such, while the exact details of the relationship between IHL and human rights law must be determined according to the specific rules governing a particular situation. Therefore, the rules on the deprivation of liberty, as laid down in human rights treaties, also continue to apply to situations of detention in NIACs. As the law of NIACs does not provide for a legal basis for detentions which are carried out for security reasons, the only applicable rules here are the ones of human rights law. Therefore, in the context of NIACs, a legal basis is required in order to make such a detention lawful under international law.[50]

III. The Extraterritorial Application of Human Rights Law

While it is clear that the guarantees enshrined in a specific human rights treaty apply to the persons on the territory of a State that is a party to the respective treaty,[51] the question arises whether this is also true for States which act on the territory of another State. In the context of a NIAC, this is of importance in cases of 'internationalised' internal armed conflicts when the government of a State is aided by foreign armed forces to suppress the activities of non-State armed groups. The extraterritorial applicability of human rights treaties has, in general, been affirmed by the ICJ,[52] regional

48 Legal Consequences of the Construction of a Wall in the Occupied Palestinian Territory (Advisory Opinion) [2004] ICJ Rep 2004, 178, para 106 (hereafter *Wall Advisory Opinion*).

49 UN GA Res 2675 (XXV) (9 December 1970) UN Doc A/RES/2675 (XXV), para 1 of the operative part of the resolution.

50 *Serdar Mohammed v Ministry of Defence* [2014] (n 2) para 293.

51 Bantekas and Oette, *Human Rights Law* (n 41) 82.

52 *Wall Advisory Opinion* (n 48) 178, paras 107.

human rights courts,[53] and UN institutions[54]. However, the details are debated extensively. The focal point of the problem is the interpretation of the term 'jurisdiction' as it can be found for instance in Art. 1 ECHR. Under this provision, the parties to the Convention guarantee the rights and freedoms enshrined in the treaty to all persons under their jurisdiction. Therefore, only if troops were to exercise 'jurisdiction' when detaining a person in a NIAC abroad, the relevant provisions of human rights law would become applicable.

One can understand the term 'jurisdiction' as relating primarily to the territory over which a State has sovereign authority.[55] This was the position taken for instance by the Grand Chamber of the ECtHR in the case of *Bankovic et al v Belgium et al* in 2001.[56] The Court took the position that Art. 1 ECHR reflects an essentially territorial notion of 'jurisdiction' and that an extraterritorial application is an exception.[57] However, the Court indicated that extraterritorial jurisdiction under the ECHR can be established if a State has established 'effective control' over an area of foreign territory and its inhabitants. In the words of the Court, this requires that a State, 'as a consequence of military occupation or through consent, invitation or acquiescence of the Government of that territory exercises all or some of the public powers normally to be exercised by that government'.[58] With this argumentation, the Court appeared to reject the notion that 'jurisdiction' can be based on effective control over an individual as this would render the scope of application of the ECHR limitless and jurisdiction would arise whenever an act imputable to a contracting State of the Convention had an adverse effect on anyone anywhere in the world.[59] Furthermore, the Court rejected the contention that a State's obligation under the ECHR could be 'divided and tailored in accordance with the particular circumstances of the extraterritorial act in question'.[60] The Court therefore took the position that the rights enshrined

53 *Loizidou v Turkey,* App no 15318/89, 18 December 1996, para 52.
54 UN HRC, *Sergio Ruben Lopez Burgos v Uruguay* in 'Communication no 52/1979' UN Doc CCPR/C/13/D/52/1979 (1981) para 12.
55 *Serdar Mohammed v Ministry of Defence* [2014] (n 2) para 120.
56 *Bankovic et al v Belgium et al,* App no 52207/99, 12 December 2001 (hereafter *Bankovic et al v Belgium et al*).
57 Ibid, para 57.
58 Ibid, para 69.
59 Ibid, para 71.
60 Ibid, para 73.

in the ECHR constitute 'a single, indivisible package'.[61] It further emphasised the regional nature of the Convention and indicated that its extraterritorial application is limited to acts executed on the territory of a State which is, or would, 'but for the specific circumstances' be covered by the Convention.[62] The Court also seemed to limit the scope for a more extensive and progressive interpretation of 'jurisdiction' in future cases by implying that Art. 1, unlike the provisions of the ECHR defining substantive rights, cannot be interpreted as a 'living instrument' in accordance with changing conditions.[63]

The narrow reading and interpretation of Art. 1 ECHR by the ECtHR in the *Bancovic* case was, however, not upheld in later cases before the Court. In its judgment in the case of *Al-Skeini and Others v the United Kingdom* in 2011, the Court set out a comprehensive restatement of the general principles, which determine when a State's jurisdiction under Art. 1 ECHR extends to actions outside its own territory.[64] While the Court in this judgment repeated its earlier position that jurisdiction under Art. 1 ECHR is primarily territorial in nature and that extraterritorial acts can give rise to jurisdiction only in exceptional cases,[65] it went on to explain that such an exceptional case is a situation where a contracting State of the Convention, 'as a consequence of lawful or unlawful military action exercises "effective control" of an area' outside of its own territory. Jurisdiction in such a case 'derives from the fact of such control, whether it be exercised directly, through the Contracting State's own armed force, or through a subordinate local administration'. Where the requisite degree of control exists

> … the controlling state has the responsibility under Art. 1 to secure, within the area under its control, the entire range of substantive rights set out in the Convention and those additional Protocols which it has ratified. It will be liable for any violations of those rights.[66]

However, in the *Al-Skeini* case, the Court recognised that, where a contracting State does not have effective control over an area of territory such that the State is required to secure to the inhabitants of that territory all

61 *Serdar Mohammed v Ministry of Defence* [2014] (n 2) para 122.
62 *Bankovic et al v Belgium et al* (n 56) para 80.
63 Ibid, paras 62.
64 *Al-Skeini and Others v the United Kingdom*, App no 55721/07, 7 July 2011 (hereafter *Al-Skeini v UK*); see *Mohammed v Ministry of Defence* [2014] (n 2) para 129.
65 Ibid, para 131.
66 *Al-Skeini v UK* (n 64) para 138.

the rights set out in the ECHR, extraterritorial jurisdiction may still arise on a principle of responsibility for acts of the State's agents operating outside of its territory.[67] Such a case can *inter alia* be given in situations where, through the 'consent, invitation or acquiescence' of the government of the territory, a State 'exercises all or some of the public powers normally exercised by that government'[68]; this case can also be given 'in certain circumstance[s]' in which 'the use of force by a state's agents operating outside its territory may bring the individual thereby brought under the control of the state's authorities into the state's art. 1 jurisdiction'. To underline the application of the principle, the Court cited four post-*Bankovic* cases of its case law 'where an individual is taken into the custody of state agents abroad'[69]. Firstly, in the case of *Öcalan v Turkey* (2005), jurisdiction of Turkey arose when its officials took custody of the applicant from Kenyan officials on the territory of Kenya.[70] Secondly, in *Issa and Others v Turkey* (2004), where it had been established – which in the facts of the case it was not – that Turkish soldiers had taken the applicants' relatives into custody in Northern Iraq, brought them to a nearby cave and killed them; the deceased would have therefore been within Turkish jurisdiction 'by virtue of the soldiers' authority and control over them'.[71] Thirdly, in *Al-Sadoon and Mufdhi v the United Kingdom* (2009), where two individuals detained in military prisons in Iraq which were under British control fell within the jurisdiction of the United Kingdom, since it 'exercised total and exclusive control over the prisons and the individuals detained in them'.[72] Lastly, in *Medvedyev v France* (2010), French naval forces exercised 'full and effective control' over a ship and its crew, which was intercepted in international waters.[73] The Court went on to explain in the *Al-Skeini* case that the decisive element which led to jurisdiction in the aforementioned cases 'is the exercise of physical power and control over the person in question'[74]. Furthermore, it explained that

---

67 Ibid, para 133.

68 Ibid, para 135.

69 Ibid, para 136.

70 *Öcalan v Turkey*, App no 46221/99, 12 May 2005.

71 *Issa and Others v Turkey*, App no 31821/96, 16 November 2004 (hereafter *Issa and Others v Turkey*).

72 *Al-Sadoon and Mufhdi v the United Kingdom,* App no 61498/08, Decision on admissibility of 3 July 2009.

73 *Medvedyev and Others v France*, App no 3394/03, 29 March 2010.

74 *Al-Skeini v UK* (n 64) para 136.

> … it is clear that, whenever the state through its agents exercises control or authority over an individual, and thus jurisdiction, the state is under an obligation under art. 1 to secure to that individual the rights and freedoms of that individual. In this sense, therefore, the Convention rights can be 'divided and tailored'.[75]

While the *Al-Skeini* case leaves several important questions relating to the application of the ECHR in extraterritorial settings unanswered,[76] it is now at least clear that jurisdiction can be established in cases in which 'an individual is taken into the custody of state agents abroad'.[77] This argumentation was later reaffirmed by the ECtHR for instance in the *Chagos Islanders v the United Kingdom* case (2013), in which the Court deemed that the circumstances in which 'state agents authority' gives rise to extraterritorial jurisdiction include 'using force to take a person into custody or exerting full physical control over a person through apprehension or detention'.[78]

The recent case law of the ECtHR shows that human rights law is applicable in extraterritorial situations in which a contracting party exercises control or authority over an individual abroad. The decisive element, according to the Court, is the 'exercise of physical power and control' over an individual; in general, detentions by the armed forces of States party to the ECHR in situations in which these forces are acting on the territory of another State to aid the government during a NIAC are covered by the Convention. Moreover, Art. 5 ECHR must be observed. The possibility to 'divide and tailor' the Convention rights does not alter this observation. When the conduct of a State gives rise to jurisdiction, in this case namely the exercise of physical control over an individual through arrest and detention, it is not possible to divide and tailor the basic obligation under Art. 5 (1) ECHR that any deprivation of liberty must be lawful and fall within one of the cases specified in Art. 5 (1).[79]

IV. Conclusion

All major human rights treaties in which civil and political rights are enshrined contain specific rules on the deprivation of liberty of an individual. All of these rules require a legal basis for such deprivations and,

---

75 Ibid, para 137.
76 *Serdar Mohammed v Ministry of Defence* [2014] (n 2) para 141.
77 *Al-Skeini v UK* (n 64), para 136.
78 *Chagos Islanders v the United Kingdom*, App no 35622/04, 11 December 2012.
79 *Serdar Mohammed v Ministry of Defence* [2014] (n 2) para 151.

therefore, for detentions; this also applies in situations of NIACs. While this is certainly true for 'traditional' NIACs, in which the government of a State is fighting against one or more non-State armed actors, States which are party to one of the human rights treaties mentioned above are equally bound by the rights laid down in those treaties when troops are acting abroad, as those instruments also apply extraterritorially.

D. Potential Legal Bases for Detentions for Security Reasons in Situations of Non-International Armed Conflict

While, on the one hand, IHL does not provide States with a legal basis for detention in NIACs, human rights law, on the other hand, requires one. This leads to the question of where such a legal basis might be found, how it can be implemented and if human rights rules may be displaced in specific circumstances. Depending on the context, domestic law and international law have a potential role to play in the prevention of arbitrary or unlawful detention.[80]

I. Domestic Law

The domestic law of the State on whose territory a NIAC is fought provides an important source of law for the detention of individuals. Legal grounds for such detentions may be found in domestic criminal and criminal procedure statutes, general statutes concerning the use of military forces, the police or other security forces or in special legislation concerning situations of large-scale violence. If no provision which suits the needs of the forces in respect to detentions in NIACs is in place in the domestic legal system or if the existing rules do not suffice, the national legislator is not hindered in introducing such rules or altering the existing rules. However, such legal reforms may be restricted by the constitutional law of the respective State. Restrictions might include time limits or the exclusion of specific grounds for detentions in the constitutional regulations providing the right to liberty. The requirements of the relevant provisions might also be altered on a constitutional basis if a state of emergency is declared in the respective State in case of large-scale internal violence amounting to a

80 ICRC, 'Concluding Report' (n 1) 29.

NIAC.[81] In these cases, the fundamental rights and freedoms laid down in the constitution of the respective State might be restricted much more easily than in times of non-emergency. Furthermore, the national legislation on detention in times of war must comply with the requirements of the human rights instruments which the respective State is a party to.[82]

In situations of 'internationalised' armed conflicts, a legal basis for detentions could also be established in the domestic legislation of the State who sends troops aborad. However, in order to fulfil the validity requirements established by the ECtHR, this legislation must meet several conditions: the text of the respective piece of legislation must expressly provide for its applicability to situations of NIAC as well as its extraterritorial applicability; furthermore, the procedural safeguards provided must be sufficiently comprehensive.[83]

II. Application of Rules on Derogation/Suspension in Human Rights Treaties

While domestic constitutional law might allow the derogation of fundamental rights and freedoms laid down in the constitution in the context of a national emergency, several human rights treaties also allow for derogation or suspension of several rights enshrined in those instruments. These are, for instance, Art. 4 (1) ICCPR: 'in time of public emergency which threatens the life of the nation'; Art. 15 (1) ECHR: 'in time of war or other public emergency threatening the life of the nation', or Art. 27 (1) ACHR: 'in time of war, public danger, or other emergency that threatens the independence or security of a State Party'.

As none of the lists of non-derogable rights in the second paragraphs of the quoted articles contain the right to liberty, it is clear that this right can be made subject to derogation/suspension.[84] Therefore, the possibility of derogating/suspending from the obligations concerning the right to liberty

81 See David Dyzenhaus, 'States of Emergency' in Michel Rosenfeld and András Sajó (eds), *The Oxford Handbook of Comparative Constitutional Law* (OUP 2012) 442.

82 Hill-Cawthorne and Akande, 'Legal Basis for Detention in NIAC' (n 14).

83 Claire Landais and Léa Bass, 'Reconciling the rules of international humanitarian law with the rules of European human rights law' (2015) 97 IRRC 1295, 1307 (hereafter Landais and Bass, 'Reconciling').

84 Bantekas and Oette, *Human Rights Law* (n 41) 81.

under the respective human rights treaties may both provide a solution to the problem of complying with the obligations under these human rights instruments and, at the same time, allow for the use of detention in situations of NIAC.[85]

However, such a solution encounters several obstacles. The first of these obstacles lies in the applicability of the derogation/suspension rules to situations of NIAC. It is not entirely clear whether the term 'war' used in Art. 15 (1) ECHR and Art. 27 (1) ACHR only applies to situations of IACs or also to NIACs; the latter may also be understood as public emergencies or public dangers. Yet, the situation must also 'threaten the life of the nation' or 'the independence or security of a State Party'. For instance, in 1961, the ECtHR already defined a situation which threatenes the life of a nation in the case of *Lawless v Ireland* as 'an exceptional situation of crisis or emergency which affects the whole population and constitutes a threat to the organised life of the community of which the State is composed.'[86] While this requirement may be met by a State in which a NIAC is actually taking place, the situation is different for a State which intervenes in an 'internationalised' NIAC abroad with its armed forces on behalf of a foreign government. It was rightly observed that, in this regard, 'it would appear that recent armed conflicts involving ECtHR countries in the territory of a third "host" State could not be deemed to have reached the requisite threat level to them'.[87] Indeed, it is, for instance, not easy to imagine that a NIAC in Central Asia, in which some forces from Western European States are fighting, might constitute a threat to organised life in the respective European States.

However, the ECtHR made reference to Art. 15 ECHR in the cases of *Al-Jedda v the United Kingdom* (2011) and *Hassan v the United Kingdom* (2014).[88] Both cases concerned human rights violations during the British military presence in Iraq. This could be read as an indication that the Court does not rule out the validity of a derogation in cases which concern a situation of an extraterritorial 'internationalised' NIAC. However, it is obvious that the Court must then move away from the case law it had

85 Landais and Bass, 'Reconciling' (n 83) 1302.

86 *Lawless v Ireland*, App no 332/57, 1 July 1961, para 28.

87 Jelena Pejic, 'The European Court of Human Rights' Al-Jedda judgment: the oversight of international humanitarian law' (2011) 93 IRRC 837, 850.

88 *Al-Jedda v the United Kingdom,* App no 27021/08, 7 July 2011, para 40 (hereafter *Al-Jedda v UK*); *Hassan v the United Kingdom*, App no 29750/09, 16 September 2014, para 101 (hereafter *Hassan v UK*).

previously established regarding the criteria relating to 'the whole population' being affected and the 'threat to the organised life of the community' as those criteria could not be met *a priori*.[89]

Another problem arises with regard to the issue discussed above concerning extraterritorial 'jurisdiction'. In the case of *Issa and Others v Turkey* (2004), the ECtHR stated that 'Article 1 of the Convention cannot be interpreted so as to allow a State party to perpetrate violations of the Convention on the territory of another State which it could not perpetrate on its own territory'.[90] Under this case law of the ECtHR, it does not seem possible for a State to derogate from its obligations under the ECHR only for an extraterritorial situation: If a State wants to derogate, it must also do so for its own territory.[91] However, it is politically unlikely that a State which sends a contingent of its armed forces into another country will derogate from certain human rights laid down in the ECHR for the people living on its own territory only for the benefit of human rights compliance in faraway places.

Furthermore, even if a State could derogate from its obligations under Art. 5 ECHR in a situation of extraterritorial NIACs, the application of Art. 15 ECHR would not release this State completely from various safeguards. The first of these safeguards is the duty to notify the Secretary-General of the Council of Europe of the measures which are taken and the reasons thereof.[92] The Grand Chamber of the ECtHR interpreted Art. 15 ECHR in the case of *A and Others v the United Kingdom* (1998) in the way that it allows States 'a wide margin of appreciation to decide on the nature and scope of the derogating measures necessary to avert the emergency.' At the same time, the Court stated that 'it is ultimately for the Court to rule whether the measures were "strictly required"'. It further declared that,

> where a derogating measure encroaches upon a fundamental Convention right, such as the right to liberty, the Court must be satisfied that it was a genuine response to

89 Landais and Bass, 'Reconciling' (n 83) 1303.
90 *Issa and Others v Turkey* (n 71).
91 Landais and Bass, 'Reconciling' (n 83) 1303.
92 A similar duty to notify of derogation measures is enshrined in Art. 4 (3) ICCPR with respect to the Secretary-General of the United Nations and in Art. 27 (3) ACHR with respect to the Secretary-General of the Organization of American States.

> the emergency situation, that it was fully justified by the special circumstances of the emergency and that adequate safeguards were provided against abuse.[93]

This leads to the situation that, assuming that Art. 15 ECHR allows States to derogate from the provisions of Art. 5 ECHR only in relation to detentions for security reasons which are carried out on the territory of a State that is not a party to the Convention, the ECtHR could nevertheless verify that the measures taken by that State are strictly required by the exigencies of the situation in question.[94]

Furthermore, the safeguards which are installed to the benefit of a person that is detained by the agents of a State party to the ECHR are decisive in a situation of derogation. The ECtHR has already treated such cases brought before it. For instance, in the cases of *Brannigan and McBride v the United Kingdom* (1993), which dealt with derogations at the domestic level providing measures which authorised the detention of individuals suspected of terrorist activities, the Court accepted a lack of judicial control for a maximum period of seven days. On the other hand, the Court did not accept a similar derogation in relation to a fourteen-day detention in the case of *Aksoy v Turkey* (1996). Other safeguards were discussed in those cases as well. For instance, in the cases of *Brannigan and McBride v the United Kingdom*, it was stated by the Court that 'the remedy of *habeas corpus* was available to test the lawfulness of the original arrest and detention' and that there is 'an absolute and enforceable right to consult a solicitor forty-eight hours after the time of the arrest and detainees were entitled to inform a relative or friend about their detention and to have access to a doctor'[95]. Furthermore, in the case of *Aksoy v Turkey*, the Court stated that

> … the denial of access to a lawyer, doctor, relative or friend and the absence of any realistic possibility of being brought before a court to test the legality of the detention meant that he was left completely at the mercy of those holding him.[96]

In sum, it seems that, under the ECHR with the relevant case law established by the ECtHR, Art. 15 does not provide a sufficient solution to entirely overcome the lack of a legal basis with regard to detentions for security reasons in NIACs, especially in extraterritorial ones.

---

93 *A and Others v the United Kingdom*, App no 3455/05, 23 September 1998, para 184.

94 Landais and Bass, 'Reconciling' (n 83) 1304.

95 *Brannigan and McBride v the United Kingdom*, Apps no 14553/89 and 14554/89, 26 May 1993, paras 62.

96 *Aksoy v Turkey*, App no 21987/93, 18 December 1996, para 83.

III. Resolutions of the United Nations Security Council

A legal basis for detention for security reasons in NIACs might also be found in a resolution by the UN SC. Under Art. 24 UN Charter, the UN SC has the 'primary responsibility for the maintenance of international peace and security'. Furthermore, under Art. 25 UN Charter, the Member States of the UN have a duty to carry out the decisions of the UN SC in accordance with the Charter. When the UN SC is acting under Chapter VII of the Charter (Art. 39 *et seq*), it possesses immense powers. The most prominent power is the authorisation of the use of force by Member States. Measures taken by the UN SC under Chapter VII are a cornerstone of the present international legal order.[97] While a resolution adopted by the UN SC is neither a treaty nor is it legislation, it is well established that such a resolution may constitute an authority binding in international law to do that which would otherwise be illegal in international law.[98]

A UN SC resolution which allows for the use of 'all necessary measures/means' is best suited to serve as a basis for detention in a NIAC; an example of this is Resolution 1386 of 20 December 2001,[99] which authorised the Member States of the UN participating in the International Security Assistance Force in Afghanistan in the post-9/11 conflict to take all necessary measures to fulfil its mandate. This is due to the fact that it authorises the use of the full range of measures available to the UN itself to maintain or restore international peace and security under Chapter VII of the UN Charter. Normally this involves the use of force under Art. 42 UN Charter. This is, however, subject to the requirement that such measures are necessary. The necessity of a measure depends primarily on the specific mandate as well as on the general context and any conditions or limitations laid down in the resolution.[100] While a resolution of the UN SC might not expressly allow for detention, the 'all necessary measures/means' formula can be interpreted in a way that it encompasses operational detention as one of such means, if necessary and might therefore constitute a legal basis for such detentions.[101] However, it is not clear what kind of detention is allowed under such a UN SC resolution. This point was disputed in the *Serdar*

97 *Serdar Mohammed v Ministry of Defence* [2017] (n 5) para 23.
98 Ibid, para 25.
99 UN SC Res 1386 UN Doc S/RES/1386 (2001) para 3 of the operative part of the resolution.
100 *Serdar Mohammed v Ministry of Defence* [2017] (n 5) para 26.
101 Ibid, para 27.

Mohammed case. On the one hand, Justice *Leggatt* argued in the first instance that a UN SC resolution which authorises the use for 'all necessary measures/means' only allows for detention for a very short period of time. He argued that once a prisoner was captured and disarmed, he no longer represented an imminent threat to security; he exemplified this through the role of the British Armed Forces and the civilian population in the case before him. Detention thereafter could not be justified under a UN SC resolution.[102] This argument was not followed by Lord *Sumption* of the UK Supreme Court on the other hand. He argued that if a person constituted a sufficient threat to the British Armed Forces and the civilian population to warrant detention in the first place, he would be likely to present a sufficient threat to warrant his continued detention after being disarmed. Unless the armed forces (of the UK) were in a position to transfer the detainee to the civil authorities for possible prosecution or further detention, the only alternative would be to release him and allow him to present the same threat to the armed forces or the civilian population as he did before, if one follows the argument of Justice *Leggatt*. Lord *Sumption* concluded his argument with the statement that this would undermine the missions, which constitute the whole purpose of the armed forces.[103] It cannot be denied that the argument of Lord *Sumption* seem to better reflect the realities of the fight against insurgencies and asymmetric warfare. However, which of the two views will prevail in future cases remains to be seen.

Furthermore, it needs to be considered that human rights law may also interact with UN SC resolutions. It may be a possibility that a resolution by the UN SC might have the effect of displacing provisions which protect human rights. This follows from Art. 25 and 103 UN Charter. Pursuant to these provisions, decisions by the UN SC are binding on Member States of the UN and override any other conflicting obligations the Member States might carry under other treaties; this also includes treaties protecting human rights.[104] However, in the recent decision of the Grand Chamber of the ECtHR in the case of *Al Dulimi and Montana Management Inc. v Switzerland* (2016) it was observed that

102 *Serdar Mohammed v Ministry of Defence* [2014] (n 2) paras 218.

103 *Serdar Mohammed v Ministry of Defence* [2017] (n 5) para 27.

104 However, this raises multiple problems from an international law perspective that cannot be discussed in the scope of this paper; for a detailed discussion, see Kjetil Mujrezionic Larsen, *The Human Rights Treaty Obligations of Peacekeepers* (CUP 2012) 314.

> … where a Security Council resolution does not contain any clear or explicit wording excluding or limiting respect for human rights …, the Court must always presume that those measures are compatible with the Convention. In other words, in such cases, in a spirit of systematic harmonization, it will in principle conclude that there is no conflict of obligations capable of engaging the primacy rule in Art. 103 of the UN Charter.[105]

This confirms the presumption the Court had previously established in the judgment in the case of *Al-Jedda v the United Kingdom* (2011).[106] It follows from this case law that the inclusion of a simple reference to detention in a resolution of the UN SC, without an explicit exclusion of Art. 5 ECHR, is not sufficient to displace this provision.[107] Furthermore, in the judgment in the case of *Hassan v the United Kingdom* (2014), the ECtHR established that a resolution of the UN SC would have to provide certain legal safeguards in order to be deemed constitutive as a legal basis for administrative detention; this could be 'accommodated' with the list of permitted grounds for deprivation of liberty laid down in Art. 5 (1) ECHR, which, however, does not include detentions that are solely carried out for security reasons.[108]

If these standards are applied to the resolutions of the UN SC, it is very unlikely that such a resolution might serve as a legal basis for detention. This is because the drafting of resolutions in the UN SC can be and regularly is subject to a highly delicate political negotiating process. As a result, precise language, as would be necessary to fulfil the standards laid down in the aforementioned case law of the ECtHR, is likely to be missing in the respective resolutions.[109] Furthermore, such a solution must be activated in every occurrence of a NIAC. This would bear two disadvantages: First, it is by no way guaranteed that the UN SC would adopt a resolution with the desired content for every conflict and, second, a resolution that needs to be activated prior to each operation is highly problematic from the perspective of the principle of legal certainty.[110]

---

105 *Al Dulimi and Montana Management v Switzerland*, App no 5809/08, 21 June 2016, para 140.
106 *Al-Jedda v UK* (n 88) paras 101.
107 Landais and Bass, 'Reconciling' (n 83) 1305.
108 *Hassan v UK* (n 88) para 104.
109 Landais and Bass, 'Reconciling' (n 83) 1305.
110 Ibid, 1306.

IV. International Agreements or Treaties

Other possibilities from the sphere of international law that might provide a legal basis for detention in situations of extraterritorial 'internationalised' NIACs are international agreements or treaties.[111] An example of this is a Status-of-Forces Agreement (SOFA), which is signed between the government of a State which is about to send its troops to the territory of another State and the government of the host State at the beginning of the military operations. In such an agreement, an explicit reference to the power of the sending State to use detention for security reasons whilst guaranteeing the required safeguards is possible. Only the sending State would need to undertake it to provide all the safeguards guaranteed to a detained individual, but not the host State. The host State would only undertake it to refrain from subjecting individuals transferred to it by the sending State to treatment that would violate basic human rights, for instance the right to life, enshrined in Art. 2 ECHR, and the prohibition of torture, enshrined in Art. 3 ECHR.[112] An example of a SOFA regulation in which such guarantees can be found in international practice is Art. 10 of the SOFA signed between France and Mali in 2013 relating to the military operation 'Serval', which was initiated to oust militants from the north of Mali:[113]

> La Partie française traite les personnes qu'elle pourrait retenir et dont elle assurerait la garde et la sécurité conformément aux règles applicables du droit international humanitaire et du droit international des droits de l'homme, notamment le Protocole additionnel aux Conventions de Genève du 12 août 1949 relatif à la protection des victimes des conflits armés non internationaux (Protocole II) adopté le 8 juin 1977, et la Convention contre la torture et autres peines ou traitements cruels, inhumains ou dégradants du 10 décembre 1984.
>
> La Partie malienne, en assurant la garde et la sécurité des personnes remises par la Partie française, se conforme aux règles applicables du droit international humanitaire et du droit international des droits de l'homme, notamment le Protocole

111 *Medvedyev and Others v France*, App no 3394/03, 29 March 2010, paras 82 (hereafter *Medvedyev v France*).

112 Landais and Bass, 'Reconciling' (n 83) 1306.

113 Décret n° 2013-364 du 29 avril 2013 portant publication de l'accord sous forme d'échange de lettres entre le Gouvernement de la République française et le Gouvernement du Mali déterminant le statut de la force 'Serval', signées à Bamako le 7 mars 2013 et à Koulouba le 8 mars 2013 (1), Journal officiel de la République Française no 0101 du 30 avril 2013 (1), 7426 <https://www.legifrance.gouv.fr/affichTexte.do?cidTexte=JORFTEXT000027376103> accessed 13 October 2017.

additionnel aux Conventions de Genève du 12 août 1949 relatif à la protection des victimes des conflits armés non internationaux (Protocole II) adopté le 8 juin 1977, et la Convention contre la torture et autres peines ou traitements cruels, inhumains ou dégradants du 10 décembre 1984.

Compte tenu des engagements conventionnels et constitutionnels de la France, la Partie malienne s'engage à ce que, dans le cas où la peine de mort ou une peine constitutive d'un traitement cruel, inhumain ou dégradant serait encourue, elle ne soit ni requise ni prononcée à l'égard d'une personne remise, et à ce que, dans l'hypothèse où de telles peines auraient été prononcées, elles ne soient pas exécutées.

Aucune personne remise aux autorités maliennes en application du présent article ne peut être transférée à une tierce partie sans accord préalable des autorités françaises. La Partie française, le Comité international de la Croix-Rouge (CICR), ou, après approbation de la Partie malienne, tout autre organisme compétent en matière de droits de l'homme, dispose d'un droit d'accès permanent aux personnes remises.

Les représentants de la Partie française, du Comité international de la Croix-Rouge et, le cas échéant, d'un autre organisme mentionné à l'alinéa précédent, sont autorisés à se rendre dans tous les lieux où se trouvent les personnes remises; ils auront accès à tous les locaux utilisés par les personnes remises. Ils seront également autorisés à se rendre dans les lieux de départ, de passage ou d'arrivée des personnes remises. Ils pourront s'entretenir sans témoin avec les personnes remises, par l'entremise d'un interprète si cela est nécessaire.

Toute liberté sera laissée aux représentants susmentionnés quant au choix des endroits qu'ils désirent visiter ; la durée et la fréquence de ces visites ne seront pas limitées. Elles ne sauraient être interdites qu'en raison d'impérieuses nécessités militaires et seulement à titre exceptionnel et temporaire.

La Partie malienne s'engage à tenir un registre sur lequel elle consigne les informations relatives à chaque personne remise (identité de la personne remise, date du transfert, lieu de détention, état de santé de la personne remise).

Ce registre peut être consulté à leur requête par les Parties au présent accord, par le CICR ou, le cas échéant, par tout autre organisme compétent en matière de droits de l'homme mentionné au cinquième alinéa du présent article.

Les dispositions précédentes sont sans préjudice de l'accès du Comité international de la Croix-Rouge aux personnes remises. Les visites du CICR aux personnes remises s'effectueront en conformité avec ses modalités de travail institutionnelles.

However, such a solution might face problems regarding the necessary foreseeability and accessibility requirements for constituting a legal basis for detention in conformity with human rights law.[114] The ECtHR considers legal certainty as particularly important in cases where deprivation of

114 Landais and Bass, 'Reconciling' (n 83) 1306.

liberty is concerned; therefore, the conditions for deprivation of liberty must be clearly defined under domestic law or under international law. Moreover, the law itself must be foreseeable in its application to meet the standard of 'lawfulness' set by the advice in order to foresee, to a degree that is reasonable in the circumstance of a given case, the consequences which a given action may entail.[115] The quoted provision from the Agreement between France and Mali for instance does not fulfil this standard, as it does not lay down the reasons under which a person may be detained. Therefore, it is not foreseeable for the affected person at which point he or she can be made subject to detention for security reasons by the external power.

IV. Conclusion

It is possible to base detentions in NIACs either on domestic legislation or international legislation; moreover, one can also set aside the relevant human rights provisions on grounds of derogation/suspension or a resolution by the UN SC. However, in cases of States bound by the ECHR in light of the text of the Convention and the presented relevant case law of the ECtHR, the manoeuvring space for such legislation is extremely limited, especially as Art. 5 (1) ECHR does not explicitly mention detention for security reasons as a reason for lawful detention.

E. Summary and Conclusions

IHL applicable to situations of NIACs does not, at the present stage of its development, provide a legal basis for the armed forces of a State to detain individuals for security reasons.[116] This, however, does not mean that detention is prohibited or illegal in NIACs; one must merely look for the legal basis either in international or domestic law. Furthermore, a legal basis for detention is required by the rules enshrined in universal und regional human rights instruments, as the right to liberty of the individual is affected. Nevertheless, the implementation of adequate legislation faces several obstacles in the light of human rights law. The situation is especially complex regarding States bound by the EHCR, as the wording of this human

115 *Medvedyev v France* (n 111) paras 80; see also Landais and Bass, 'Reconciling' (n 83) 1306.

116 See also *Serdar Mohammed v Ministry of Defence* [2014] (n 2) para 293.

rights instrument does not allow a detention for security reasons. Additionally, the case law of the ECtHR is very strict with regard to the legal requirements of domestic and international legislation in relation to detention. It remains to be seen how the future human rights jurisprudence will both handle and solve the various problems involved.

Comment: Detention in Non-International Armed Conflict by States – Just a Matter of Perspective on Areas of Limited Statehood?

Anton O. Petrov

Manuel Brunner's well-elaborated contribution illustrates how detention in NIACs by States is permeating practice as much as legal discourse. It also demonstrates how much of a pressing issue it has become for lawyers approaching the issue from various angles of international and domestic law. In fact, detention is one of IHL's predominant aspects that receives legal attention and adjudication nowadays. From an IHL perspective, however, the approach usually taken in these fora raises a number of concerns.

In this regard, there are three themes of *Manuel Brunner's* contribution that I would particularly like to comment on: the quest for legal authorisation (1.), the doctrinal pitfalls of addressing detention in NIACs through the lens of human rights treaties (2.), and finally, the implications of addressing the issue from a human rights perspective for areas of limited statehood on the meta-level (3.). It will be shown that the conceptual understanding of areas of limited statehood lays open the underlying structures of the doctrinal questions surrounding a legal basis for States to detain in NIACs.

A. Rule of Law and the Need for Legal Authorisation

Manuel Brunner's contribution addresses the question of whether there is a legal basis for detention in IHL itself. Notably, it is not asked whether detention is *permitted* in IHL, but whether IHL provides a legal *authorisation* for it. Framing the research question in this particular way is based on a premise which warrants some consideration.

In fact, requiring a legal authorisation does not correspond to the traditional concept of international law. Despite the doctrinal controversy surrounding the *Lotus* principle, discussed already in other contributions of this volume,[1] international law was not built on the notion that sovereign exercise of power would *ipso facto* require a legal basis to authorise it. Quite the contrary, international law, as a basic principle, was rather indifferent to State action *vis-à-vis* individual persons, as this was the inherent domain of the State rooted in its international sovereignty.[2] Hence, the traditional question an international lawyer asks is whether something is not prohibited, and thus permitted.[3]

The question of legal authorisation is rather known from the domestic legal context. In German administrative law, for instance, the legal basis of authorisation to act is called *Ermächtigungsgrundlage* – it provides the basis for empowering the State to act face to face with its citizens, particularly to intervene in their individual rights. These individual rights create the need for such authorisation by law, the principle of statutory reservation.[4] IHL, in contrast, is usually thought of in restrictive terms.[5]

Why *Manual Brunner* nonetheless chose to apply this mode of thinking to IHL with a view to detention becomes apparent further into his contribution; there, he offers the interim conclusion that, 'under human rights law, a legal basis for detention is required'. This is a crucial statement as it reveals that the question of the legality of detaining in NIACs is approached from a human rights perspective. The individual right to liberty of the person detained makes it necessary that an authorisation in law exists as a basis.[6]

---

1 See Katja Schöberl and Linus Mührel, 'Sunken Vessel or Blooming Flower? Lotus, Permissions and Restrictions within International Humanitarian Law' in this volume 59 (hereafter Schöberl and Mührel, 'Sunken Vessel or Blooming Flower?'); Pia Hesse, 'Comment: neither Sunken Vessel nor Blooming Flower! The Lotus Principle and International Humanitarian Law' in this volume 80 (hereafter Hesse, 'Comment').

2 Cf Samantha Besson, 'Sovereignty' in MPEPIL (online edn, OUP April 2011) para 70.

3 Cf Dissenting Opinion of Judge Van Den Wyngaert in Case concerning the Arrest Warrant of 11 April 2000 (*Democratic Republic of the Congo v Belgium*) (Judgment) [2002] ICJ Rep 3, para 51.

4 See Peter Lerche, 'Vorbehalt des Gesetzes und Wesentlichkeitstheorie', in Detlef Merten and Hans-Jürgen Papier (eds), *Handbuch der Grundrechte*, vol. III (C.F. Müller 2009) 301.

5 Hans-Peter Gasser, 'International Humanitarian Law' in MPEPIL (online edn, OUP December 2015) paras 1, 3.

6 Oliver Dörr, 'Arbitrary Detention' in MPEPIL (online edn, OUP March 2007) paras 12 et seq (hereafter Dörr, 'Arbitrary Detention').

It is, of course, in no way wrong to apply this requirement to detention in NIACs. However, one needs to be conscious of the fact that it is a deliberate move to search for authorisation, not simply permission, in international law.[7] At least, on the international plain there is no abstract rule of law that requires an authorising legal basis for State action. This requirement surfaces when human rights are concerned. With this in mind, some of the doctrinal questions appear in a different light.

B. Concerns Regarding the Human Rights Paradigm

The question of whether IHL provides an express authorisation for detention in NIACs is *a priori* alien to IHL as a legal system. Unsurprisingly, neither Justice *Leggatt* nor the judges at the ECtHR or any other court could find such a provision in international humanitarian treaty or customary law. Of course they were not able to, as IHL does not provide an express authorisation to kill non-civilians in NIAC either.[8] Yet, one can hardly claim that killing a non-civilian in a NIAC would be illegal under international law due to a lack of express authorisation.[9]

The simple reason for this, as *Manuel Brunner* delineates in the beginning, is that the original lawmakers of IHL considered NIACs a (largely) internal affair of the State. At that time, it would have been completely beside the point to consider that international law could bar a sovereign State from killing or detaining members of armed non-State groups in a NIAC. There was no need to provide for positive authorisation in international law. As *Manuel Brunner* points out, IHL addresses only some aspects of *how* detention in NIACs may be conducted. In fact, addressing the 'if' of such acts – even if this meant authorising them – would have been more intrusive to States' sovereignty than leaving it unaddressed. Excluding it upheld the original freedom of States. Hence, the contemporary quest for express authorisation by IHL in the context of NIACs runs fully counter to this legal regime's original conception and *raison d'être*.

---

7 The doctrinal twists of this difference are addressed with a view to the infamous Lotus principle by Schöberl and Mührel, 'Sunken Vessel or Blooming Flower?' (n 1) as well as by Hesse, 'Comment' (n 1).

8 See also Sean Aughey and Aurel Sari, 'Targeting and Detention in Non-International Armed Conflict' (2015) 91 ILS 60, 88-89.

9 Cf *Federal Prosecutor General (Germany), Targeted Killing in Pakistan Case*, Case No 3 BJs 7/12-4, 157 ILR 722, 748.

There is also a methodological concern in this regard. It pertains, on a first level, to the relationship between IHL and IHRL. The traditional bold *lex specialis* displacement of IHRL as the general regime by IHL as the special one is obsolete. The debate seems to have settled on a situation-specific case-by-case analysis: this means that it needs to be inquired in each instance whether there is a particular *lex specialis* of IHL that can partially displace human rights law or inform its interpretation.[10] Taken as such, these case-specific approaches can provide reasonable solutions.

However, the problem starts when the demanding requirements of contemporary IHRL are applied to the rather antique treaty rules of IHL without the necessary interpretive sensitivity. If the circumstances have changed from a *Lotus*-inspired world to a rule-of-law-based one, this change must be reflected in how IHL provisions are interpreted. Yet, this is often not sufficiently done. IHL is – foreseeably without result – frequently scanned in search for sufficiently clear, predictable and transparent rules. In effect, the lack of regulation by IHL in NIACs is used to incorporate the much more restrictive IHRL regime although this restraint of IHL was originally intended to guarantee States' freedom.

C. Areas of Limited Statehood as a Challenge to the Dichotomy of International Armed Conflicts and Non-International Armed Conflicts

An explanation for this push for international regulation of NIACs via IHRL can be found in the pluralistic setting of areas of limited statehood. It is, however, in this context that the benefits of applying the requirements posed by IHRL indiscriminately to NIACs become doubtful.

When a consolidated State is involved in a NIAC on a foreign State's territory, IHL's essential dichotomy of international and non-international armed conflicts dissolves. This dichotomy, however, had been the rationale behind the structurally different regimes of IHL applying to IACs and NIACs. IACs required comprehensive international legal rules because two sovereign States clashed; thus, authorisation by international law was needed to infringe upon another State's sovereignty. This was a completely

10 For an overview of the three main concepts, i.e. total displacement, partial displacement as the norm conflict resolution and an interpretive solution, see Marko Milanovic, 'The Lost Origins of Lex Specialis: Rethinking the Relationship between Human Rights and International Humanitarian Law', in Jens D. Ohlin (ed), *Theoretical Boundaries of Armed Conflict and Human Rights* (OUP 2016) 78, 103-14.

different case in an internal conflict: there, IHL only needed to prohibit certain acts out of humanitarian considerations. The law of NIAC thus gave States much more liberty in conducting warfare because other States were not directly affected. An extraterritorial NIAC involves an inter-State element which potentially calls for more international regulation, arguably also authorisation.

Yet, is the approach taken convincing with a view to detention? The mechanical application of the human rights regime to extraterritorial NIACs in areas of limited statehood leads, to some extent, to absurd results. I would also question that the formal insistence on an expressly authorising black-letter rule benefits those concerned.

My first concern regards derogations. Derogations have been proposed as a solution to the conflict of the various legal regimes; in particular, the UK is considering derogating from the ECHR.[11] However, a closer scrutiny of the requirements of derogation clauses in human rights treaties reveals that they do not fit the situation. Is it a threat to the life of the host State's nation, for instance Afghanistan's, which would allow the United Kingdom to derogate from its own human rights obligations as Justice *Leggatt* has suggested in *Serdar Mohammed,*[12] or is it only a threat to that of the sending State's, in that case the United Kingdom's, which would allow it not to comply with its human rights obligations when fighting a war on Afghan soil as *Lord Bingham* proposed in *Al-Jedda*[13]? Case law and scholarship diverge on these questions, which does not come as a surprise as every answer appears arbitrary.

Another concern relates to detention itself. It seems rather odd that British troops could act on the basis of Afghan law to comply with their obligations under the ECHR. Although such relationships are not unknown in the realm of legal and administrative cooperation, particularly in law enforcement, they must fulfill a specific purpose, namely to 'allow the persons concerned to foresee the consequences of their actions'[14]. Would any of the potential sources that *Manuel Brunner* discusses in this regard

11 See the website of the UK Joint Committee on Human Rights regarding the Government's proposed derogation from the ECHR inquiry, <https://www.parliament.uk/business/committees/committees-a-z/joint-select/human-rights-committee/inquiries/parliament-2015/government-proposed-echr-derogation-16-17> accessed 30 October 2017.

12 *Serdar Mohammed v Ministry of Defence* [2014] EWHC 1369 (QB) para 156.

13 *Al-Jedda v Secretary of State for Defence* [2008] 1 AC 332 para 38.

14 Dörr, 'Arbitrary Detention' (n 6) para 12.

substantively improve the protection of persons engaged in areas of limited statehood?

In the end, detention in NIAC is a paradigm example in which the underlying values and structures of the law of IAC, the law of NIAC and IHRL clash. Reconciling them is a worthwhile effort, but will not be achievable in all instances. Understanding the guiding values and structures involved can, at least, allow to make more prudent doctrinal choices.

Detention by Organised Armed Groups in Non-International Armed Conflicts: the Role of Non-State Actors in a State-Centred International Legal System

Vincent Widdig

A. Introduction

Following the swift change in nature of armed conflicts in recent history, the number and importance of NIACs and non-State actors especially has grown significantly.[1] Conflicts are also increasingly taking place in areas where State influence is limited or even absent. Especially the recent conflicts in Syria, Iraq, Yemen and the Democratic Republic of Congo have powerfully illustrated which devastating impact armed groups can have on the lives and livelihoods of the respective civilian populations.[2] Although it is well-established by now that non-State actors / OAGs are bound by IHL to a certain extent, the scope of applicable norms remains very much unclear when dealing with the conduct of hostilities in the context of NIACs.[3] When touching upon human rights obligations of OAGs, the 'fog of law', *in concreto* the question of applicable norms, becomes even more obscure.[4]

---

1 See Annyssa Bellal (ed), *The War Report – Armed Conflict in 2014* (OUP 2015) 23-25 (hereafter Bellal, *War Report*) for a comprehensive overview of currently existing conflicts.

2 Daragh Murray, *Human Rights obligations of Non-State Armed Groups* (Hart 2016) 1-6 (hereafter Murray, *Human Rights obligations*), with further examples.

3 Yoram Dinstein, *Non-International Armed Conflicts in International Law* (CUP 2014) para 200 et seq (hereafter Dinstein, *NIAC*); for an analysis of IHL and its early relationship with human rights, see Charles Lysaght, 'The Scope of Protocol II and Its Relation to Common Article 3 of the Geneva Conventions of 1949 and Other Human Rights Instruments' (1983) 33 American University Law Review 9 et seq; René Provost, *International Human Rights and Humanitarian Law* (CUP 2002); UN SC Res 1564 (8 September 2004) UN Doc S/RES/1564.

4 For a detailed discussion, see: Andrew Clapham, 'Focusing on Armed Non-State Actors' in Andrew Clapham and Paola Gaeta (eds), *The Oxford Handbook of International Law in Armed Conflict* (OUP 2014), 766 (hereafter Clapham, 'Focusing on Non-State Actors'); Andrew Clapham, *Human Rights Obligations*

Notwithstanding their individual character and other issues in NIACs, OAGs[5] possess one common denominator in all conflicts: They all capture or detain individuals in a variety of situations. After the experiences in countries such as Afghanistan and Iraq, the international community still struggles both practically and conceptually with the detention of belligerents in NIACs; moreover, it is still very much unclear which legal obligations those groups actually are subject to when dealing with detainees.[6] In other words, to which standards of treatment must these groups adhere after having captured or detained individuals in the context of an armed conflict? The legal question that follows this debate, is inevitably linked to the role of a distinct legal personality, which may or may not be awarded to OAGs in order to assert their possible legal obligations under international treaty and customary law.[7]

Bearing in mind that there is an urgent need to improve the protection of civilians and those detained or deprived of their liberty in armed conflicts,

---

of Non-State Actors (OUP 2006) (hereafter Clapham, *Human Rights Obligations*). However, this uncertainty largely stems from the fact that, although armed conflicts and the deprivation of liberty are inexorably linked, IHL itself does not offer a specific internment regime in NIACs for States; moreover, States seem to be in considerable disagreement over the applicability of human rights law in those situations. For arguments on the legal basis of detention by States in NIACs, see Manuel Brunner, 'Security Detention by the Armed Forces of a State in Situations of Non-International Armed Conflict: the Quest for a Legal Basis' in this volume 89 (hereafter Brunner, 'Security Detention'); Marco Sassòli and Laura M. Olson, 'The relationship between international humanitarian and human rights law where it matters: admissible killing and internment of fighters in non-international armed conflicts' (2008) 90 IRRC 871.

5 Although the terms 'armed non-State actor', 'insurgents', etc. are used in differing manners to describe those involved in armed conflicts acting outside of State control, this contribution will refer to the terminology of organised armed groups following the *Tadić*-jurisprudence of the ICTY, see *Prosecutor v Dusko Tadić* (Decision on the Defence Motion for Interlocutory Appeal on Jurisdiction) IT-94-1 (2 October 1995) (hereafter *Prosecutor v Tadić*).

6 Chris Jenks, 'Detention under the law of armed conflict' in Rain Liivija and Tim McCormack (eds), *The Routledge Handbook of the Law of Armed Conflict* (Routledge 2016) 301 (hereafter Jenks, 'Detention').

7 In order to apply any legal rights and duties under international law, OAGs must possess an international legal personality. Since the question of legal personality is almost inevitably linked with legitimisation, some have coined that dilemma a legal 'Gordian-Knot' as it seems almost impossible to solve without a pragmatic approach to detention; Jenks, 'Detention' (n 6) 301. This approach will also be taken throughout this contribution.

this contribution in its outset, will try to set a legal framework on how and to what extent OAGs might be bound *de lege lata* to IHL and human rights law within the context of 'detention' in order to gain some legal clarity on the matter. Before dealing with the issue of detention itself *in intenso*, it is important to note, what is actually *not* covered by this terminology. Although armed groups are engaged in hostage-taking to a large extent, not every deprivation of liberty by an OAG also automatically amounts to hostage-taking since the latter requires a specific intention for the deprivation of liberty.[8] The focus of the present contribution will therefore be placed on the effect of the conduct of OAGs on treaty and customary obligations under the 1949 Geneva Conventions and its Additional Protocols, the 1907 Hague Regulations (as far as they can be related to NIACs) and international human rights law outside of the 'regime of hostage-taking'.[9] Since States differ in their use of terminology, sometimes explicitly avoiding any attribute that may link a non-State conduct to a State-like action, the inevitably linked debate of the distinction between detention and deprivation of liberty directed at the perceived risk of the group's legitimisation will be touched upon as well. This may constitute a relevant factor to ascribing them legal obligations under the regime of humanitarian protection.[10] It is therefore worth investigating whether the existing regime of IHL is still capable of regulating modern conflicts

8 The deprivation of liberty must be conducted through a threat to the life, integrity or liberty of the captured person in order to pursue concessions by a third party, as stated in Art. 1 of the International Convention against the Taking of Hostages (opened for signature 17 December 1979, entered into force 03 June 1983) 1316 UNTS 205. The convention currently has 176 States Parties, not including *inter alia* the Republic of the Congo, Democratic Republic of the Congo, East Timor, Gambia, Indonesia, Israel, Somalia, South Sudan and Syria. See also ICRC, 'ICRC position in hostage taking' (2002) 84 IRRC 467.

9 See, for example, ECHR, ICCPR, ACHR. For the broader scope of 'equality' (before the law), 'freedom' (right to liberty and security), 'dignity' (as the core principle) and 'solidarity' (collective effort to secure the rights in question) as the underlying principles of the human rights regime, see Ilias Bantekas and Lutz Oette, *International Human Rights, Law and Practice* (2nd edn, CUP 2016) 71 et seq (hereafter Bantekas and Oette, *Human Rights Law*) in that respect.

10 This is an argument put forward within the context of human rights law. Some differentiate between deprivation of liberty and detention; the latter usually entails a formal prolonged internment of the individual under the activation of all accompanying procedural guarantees, whereas the former is, by definition, short-lived and not necessarily conducted by the State or a State agent. The consequence may be a different scope of applicability of human rights.

properly and whether a reasonable discussion outside of CA 3 can take place.

When talking about applicable international law, the role of domestic law within the debate over the conduct of OAGs in NIACs should not be forgotten. The application of existing domestic law in the respective State where the conflict occurs (and its possible primacy over international obligations) might already represent an adequate tool to bind OAGs to a certain legal standard. In other words, do we even need to create legal obligations for non-State actors at the international level or is the existing domestic law already sufficient to deal with the matter?

Without prejudice to the nature of the applicable law, the case of a possible accountability of non-State actors for violations of IHL and human rights needs to be investigated in order to complete the picture.

B. The Legal Personality of Organised Armed Groups and the Risk of their Legitimisation

To gain a certain degree of legal certainty, the answer to this highly debated and (at first glance) contradictory question can only be found in international law. Given the prohibitive character of IHL and its function as a minimum legal order,[11] once all efforts to a peaceful settlement of the conflict have failed, the question of legal personality of OAGs under international law is central to the complementary protection offered by IHL for victims of the conduct of hostilities in armed conflicts and the effective human rights protection in areas of limited statehood.

It may be argued that (a) a certain degree of legal personality and/or capacity should be the necessary prerequisite for OAGs to assert their possible legal obligations under international treaty and customary law in the context of detention, as only subjects of international law may be addressed by it, and (b) incorporating those actors into the existing

---

11 The prohibitive character of IHL remains the rule rather then the exception. Where there is an authorisation to act, the Geneva Conventions and their Protocols will mention it explicitly as in Art. 43 (2) AP I. It hereby deviates from its prohibitive nature. For a further interpretation of the prohibitive/permissive character of IHL, see Katja Schöberl and Linus Mührel, 'Sunken Vessel or Blooming Flower? Lotus, Permissions and Restrictions within International Humanitarian Law' in this volume 59 (hereafter Schöberl and Mührel, 'Sunken Vessel or Blooming Flower?').

protection regime might require a renunciation from the current State-centric public international law.[12] Before dealing with possible legal obligations of OAGs, it is important to define what can be perceived as an OAG in the first place. Its definition plays an important role within the debate, especially in terms of a distinct legal personality or even a legal capacity in international law, as, by their very nature, these groups are characterised by their diversity; the clarification of their definition will therefore add effectiveness and validity to the legal regime they might be involved in.[13] Thus, the variety of non-State actors involved in modern (non-international) armed conflicts requires different treatments depending on their specific legal character.[14]

I. Defining Organised Armed Groups in International Law

Although defining organised armed groups seems to be straightforward at the first glance, adequately defining the term in a legal sense is not without difficulties. The term OAG is used by political analysts and sociologists in international relations as well as in various other contexts.[15] For example, the UN Office for the Coordination of Humanitarian Affairs refers to OAGs as armed non-State groups and defines them as:

---

12 This is a change some expect to take place soon. For further details, see Janne E Nijman, 'Non-State Actors and the International Rule of Law: Revisiting the "Realist Theory" of International Legal Personality' (2009) Amsterdam Center for International Law Research Paper Series <http://dx.doi.org/10.2139/ssrn.1522520> accessed 16 November 2017.

13 David Tuck, 'Detention by armed groups: overcoming challenges to humanitarian action' (2011) 93 IRRC 759, 761, also elaborating on the (factual) humanitarian challenges regarding the internment by OAGs.

14 See, for example, Bantekas and Oette, *Human Rights Law* (n 9) 762, who negatively define non-State actors as 'entities that do not exercise governmental functions or whose conduct cannot be described as possessing a public nature'. This seems to exclude those entities from the vertical system of human rights obligations by definition.

15 For a detailed discussion on the interdisciplinary approach towards defining an OAG and the definition of an OAG, see Vincent Widdig, 'Perspektiven einer möglichen Einbindung bewaffneter organisierter Gruppen als nicht-staatliche Akteure in den Normsetzungsprozess des Völkerrechts' (2016) 29 J. Int'l L. of Peace & Armed Conflict 109, 110 et seqq (hereafter Widdig, 'Perspektiven einer möglichen Einbindung').

> ... hav[ing] the potential to employ arms in the use of force to achieve political, ideological or economic objectives; ... [being] not within the formal military structures of States, State-alliances or intergovernmental organizations; and [not being] under the control of the State(s) in which they operate.[16]

Other authors like *Philip Alston* have resorted to a negative approach to the definition for a long time already by defining non-State actors by what they are not, rather than by what they are.[17] When interpreting the term itself, three basic prerequisites can be identified. The actors in question ought to be (1) a group, (2) armed and (3) organised. Although there is no formal membership test and it is still disputed whether a 'certain function' or a 'continuous combat function' might be required for establishing the affiliation to the group,[18] it can be considered sufficient that gatherings take place on a more than just sporadic basis, bearing in mind that the affiliation criterion is ultimately met on a factual basis.[19] A certain degree of armament is rightly seen as a *conditio sine qua non* for such groups, since international law does not provide for specific technology standards. In general, possessing a political wing does not change the characterisation of the group as 'armed'.[20] The most interesting and relevant part of the definition is the organisation of the group in question. Since CA 3 and Art. 1 (1) AP II differ in their scope of requirements, this aspect must be dealt with carefully. In that respect, a certain command-and-control structure of the group is required.[21] This follows the line of the ICTY and its famous *Tadić*-Judgment, which was later specified in the *Boškoski*-jurisprudence in which the tribunal laid down five decisive criteria for the part of the definition referring to the organisation of a group.[22] Firstly, a chain of command, for

---

16 Gerard McHugh and Manuel Bessler, *Humanitarian Negotiations with Armed Groups, A Manual for Practitioners* (UN 2006) 6.

17 See Philip Alston, *Non-State Actors and Human Rights* (OUP 2005) (hereafter Alston, *Non-State Actors*), referring to the 'not-a-cat syndrome'.

18 See Dinstein, *NIAC* (n 3) para 128 et seqq.

19 Liesbeth Zegveld, 'Accountability of Organized Armed Groups' in International Institute of Humanitarian Law (ed), *Non-State Actors and International Humanitarian Law. Organized Armed Groups: A Challenge for the 21st Century* (FrancoAngeli 2000) 109, 112.

20 Dinstein, *NIAC* (n 3) para 129.

21 Bellal, *War Report* (n 1) 17; *Prosecutor v Ramush Haradinaj et al* (Judgment) IT-04-84-T (3 April 2008) para 60.

22 *Prosecutor v Tadić* (n 5); *Prosecutor v Jean Paul Akayesu* (Judgment) ICTR-96-4-T (2 September 1998), para 620 (hereafter *Prosecutor v Akayesu*) following the line of the ICTY; *Prosecutor v Boskoski et al* (Judgment) IT-04-82 (10 July 2008) paras 199-203.

instance the setting up of headquarters, the emergence of a military hierarchy or the issuance of directives to commanders in the field must be proved.[23] Secondly, organisational capacities to carry out military-style operations and coordinate efforts are required – a requirement that has to be established on a factual basis.[24] Thirdly, a logistical base for food, communications, training, etc. should be provided.[25] Fourthly, a certain discipline to obey IHL must exist. Fifthly, the group must speak with one voice, for instance in the form of common statements.[26] Although these criteria seem ample, they can only remain indicators as they merely touch upon some of the problems of defining an OAG[27]; thus, it might still prove difficult to factually establish the aforementioned facts when dealing with such a group. Nonetheless, the criteria remain a sufficient roadmap in order to better deal with this kind of actors. However, it should not be forgotten that these criteria will certainly not cover the majority of smaller groups involved in NIACs. Broadening the scope of definition too much would only hinder the effective application of the obligations in question. Thus, in sum, OAGs can be understood as actors who operate outside of State control, mainly pursue political goals which they enforce by resort to armed force, and who possess an effective organisational and commando structure which enables them to take part in hostilities.[28]

23 *Prosecutor v Limaj et al* (Judgment) IT-03-66 (30 November 2005), paras 46, 94-103 and 111.

24 Ibid, paras 108, 129, 158.

25 Ibid, paras 118-23.

26 Ibid, paras 113-17 and 125-29.

27 See Dinstein, *NIAC* (n 3) para 140, who also addresses the question of whether a group remains sufficiently organised when its members frequently violate IHL. Dinstein rightly argues that even if violating the laws of war may be a broader strategy or policy of an OAG, the group remains organised notwithstanding. It is only when members wantonly violate their obligations without any control of the group they belong to that they can be seen as 'unorganised'. See also Andrea Bianchi and Yasmin Naqvi, *International Humanitarian Law and Terrorism* (Hart 2011) 163.

28 Following a similar approach, see Orla Buckley, 'Unregulated Armed Conflict: Non-State Armed Groups, International Humanitarian Law and Violence in Western Sahara' (2012) 37 North Carolina Journal of International Law and Commercial Regulation 793, 797.

II. Arguments on International Legal Personality and/or Capacity of Organised Armed Groups

In order to assert the possible legal obligations of OAGs, the pretext of their legal personality and capacity has to be investigated and analysed, as only subjects of international law may be bound by the latter. That being said, it should be noted that the mere exercise of factual legal capacity is usually just the consequence of, but not the evidence for the existence of a legal personality.[29] Another issue that should be addressed in this context is whether the debate over the distinction between 'detention' and 'deprivation of liberty' directed at the perceived risk of the group's legitimisation and its connection to a State-like behaviour, might be a relevant factor to ascribing them legal obligations under the regime of humanitarian protection in the first place.

1. Arguing in favour of an international legal personality and/or capacity of Organised Armed Groups

International law and legal personality in particular have long been solely State-centric. However, since the ICJ's Advisory Opinion concerning reparations for injuries suffered in the service of the UN,[30] this perception has undergone some changes. Following the ICJ's Advisory Opinion, a subject of public international law may be every entity, that is (1) able to possess international rights and duties, (2) maintain those rights by bringing international claims[31] and (3) bear responsibility for the breaches of those obligations, for example by being subject to an international claim.[32] The core element that can be taken from this definition is the ability to take part

29 James Crawford (ed), *Brownlie's Principles of Public International Law* (8th edn, OUP 2012) 127 (hereafter Crawford, *Brownlie's Principles*).

30 Reparation for Injuries Suffered in the Service of the United Nations (Advisory Opinion) [1949] ICJ Rep 174, 179 (hereafter Reparation for Injuries Suffered).

31 Ibid.

32 Ibid; Crawford, *Brownlie's* (n 29) 115: 'an entity possessing international rights and obligations and having the capacity to maintain its rights by bringing international claims and to be responsible for its breaches of obligation by being subjected to such claims'; Antonio Cassese, *International Law* (2nd edn, OUP 2005) 71 et seq (hereafter Cassese, *International Law*).

in international legal relations independently and outside domestic law.[33] The inability to fulfil this last criterion will have important consequences for the quality of the legal personality in question; it will not lead to a negation of a legal personality as such, but rather results in limiting it to the application of rights and duties under existing customary international law.[34] A conclusion that was also reached by the ICJ in its Advisory Opinion. The mere acquisition of a (derived) international legal personality does not necessarily enable the entity to enjoy the same rights and duties as States. As States are the primary subjects of international law, they alone enjoy an unlimited legal personality.[35] This traditional approach, however, seems rather circular, as, in case of doubt, the decisive criterion of whether or not an entity possesses a distinct legal personality is the factual determination of its exercise of the capacity to enter into sovereign international relations with other subjects; more precisely, its capacity to bear rights and duties under international law.[36] Therefore, the ability to participate in international legal relations as well as the immunity from national jurisdiction is the result of a previously established legal personality, thereby empowering the entity as a bearer of rights and duties under international law as a consequence, and not as a prerequisite. Beyond that, the reality of international relations cannot always be reduced to a simple formula, which further complicates any attempts at determination.[37]

When arguing in favour of OAGs possessing a legal personality in the context of armed conflicts, it is well established by now that, once the non-State party has been recognised as a formal belligerent by the State party to the conflict (given that the insurgents exercise effective control over a certain part of the State's territory and their conduct reaches the threshold of an armed conflict), these actors enjoy partial legal personality in relation to the recognising belligerent State.[38] This partially enables them to act on

33 Crawford, *Brownlie's Principles* (n 29) 115.

34 Ibid.

35 Reparation for Injuries Suffered (n 30) 180; Volker Epping, 'Grundlagen' in Knut Ipsen (ed), *Völkerrecht* (7th edn, Beck 2018) para 7 et seq.

36 Crawford, *Brownlie's Principles* (n 29) 115; Clapham, *Human Rights Obligations* (n 4) 64.; Anna Meijknecht, *Towards International Personality: The Position of Minorities and Indigenous Peoples in International Law* (Intersentia 2001) 24.

37 Crawford, *Brownlie's Principles* (n 29) 116.

38 Cassese, *International Law* (n 32) 125; Andrew Clapham, 'Human Rights Obligations of Non-State Actors in Conflict Situations' (2006) 88 IRRC 491, 492 (hereafter Clapham, 'Human Rights Obligations in Conflict Situations').

the international legal plane and to enter into legal relations with other subjects of international law.[39] Some even argue that this includes the ability to conclude international agreements with third Parties.[40] However, this assertion seems highly doubtful, as third Parties would hereby regularly violate the principle of non-intervention. The conclusion of an international agreement with an OAG will always be accompanied with its recognition. Any legal relations in this case are limited to the belligerents and an interference with this constitutes a violation of matters within the sole domestic jurisdiction of the belligerent State. This formal recognition, however, rarely occurs in practice, as States are eager to avoid conferring any legal personality to insurgents in order to limit their own legal obligations and responsibilities when combatting insurgency to their own domestic sphere.[41]

Another approach in this context can be taken from the (limited) principle of reciprocity in armed conflict. The answer could lie in the form of a limited recognition of the OAG beneath the threshold of the recognition as a belligerent: the recognition as an insurgent. This theory relies on practical considerations. An insurgency is understood as 'a more substantial attack against the legitimate order of the State with the rebelling faction being sufficiently organized to mount a credible threat to the government'[42]. In this case, the limited recognition by the belligerent State is vested in the protection of its own interests – for instance a reciprocal standard of

---

Some argue that such a recognition of belligerency was set into effect by the conduct of the State of Israel within its conflict with the Palestinian Forces. Otherwise, the naval Blockade put in effect on the Gaza-shore would remain illegal.

39 Cassese, *International Law* (n 32) 118; Volker Epping, 'Sonstige Völkerrechtssubjekte' in Knut Ipsen (ed), *Völkerrecht* (7th edn, Beck 2018) para 11 et seq (hereafter Epping, 'Sonstige Völkerrechtssubjekte').

40 Gerald Fitzmaurice, 'The general principles of international law considered from the standpoint of the rule of law' (1957) 92 RdC 5, 10; UNYBILC 1958/II 24,32; UNYBILC 1962/II 161, the original Draft Articles on the Law of Treaties used the formulation 'States and other subjects of international law' thereby including insurgents.

41 Cedric Ryngaert, 'Non-State Actors and International Humanitarian Law' (2008) Institute for International Law K.U. Leuven Working Paper, <https://www.law.kuleuven.be/iir/nl/onderzoek/wp/WP146e.pdf> accessed 27 March 2018 (hereafter Ryngaert, 'Non-State Actors').

42 Lindsay Moir, *The Law of Internal Armed Conflict,* (CUP 2007) 4.

protection or a 'humane conduct of hostilities' – resulting in a *de facto*, but not *de jure* recognition as a belligerent.[43]

This mere factual recognition as insurgents for practical considerations can thereby only constitute a partial and particular legal personality of the OAG in relation to CA 3.[44] An argument that seems very convincing in the light of the object and purpose of CA 3, which predominately guarantees a minimum standard of protection for vulnerable persons in armed conflicts and which does not assert or regulate any international legal status between the parties to the conflict. Nevertheless, even in this case, there ultimately has to be some explicit recognition of the belligerent group by the State itself at some point in time.

Apart from the creation of a legal personality via recognition, an argument for its constitution is also made with the link to the threshold of applicability of IHL. The determination of the applicability of IHL transforms the previously national situation into an international one. This might be done by either the standard of CA 3 or Art. 1 (1) AP II, depending on the organisational structure of the group itself. As a consequence, a relative legal personality in international law is created for the non-State party to the conflict. The question of consent is often the centrepiece of the debate over the legal personality of OAGs, since, as a principle of international law, its subject may only be bound by consent; moreover, no third party shall be affected be an agreement which it has not consented to following the *pacta tertiis nec nocent nec prosunt* principle.[45] The rejection of the consent requirement would indeed overcome a major obstacle towards the direct applicability of international treaty law. Whether or not this principle only extends to States or represents a basic principle of public international law binding all of its subjects surpasses the scope of the

---

43 Ibid, 5; Hans-Peter Gasser, 'International Humanitarian Law and Human Rights Law in Non-International Armed Conflict' (2002) 45 GYIL 149 et seq.

44 Robert Frau, 'Entwicklungen bei der gewohnheitsrechtlichen Einbindung nicht-staatlicher Akteure' in Heike Krieger and Dieter Weingärtner (eds), *Streitkräfte und nicht-staatliche Akteure* (Nomos 2013) 28 et seq; Jean-Marie Henckaerts, 'Binding Armed Opposition Groups through Humanitarian Treaty Law and Customary Law' in Marc Vuijlsteke et al (eds), *Relevance of International Humanitarian law to non-state Actors* (College of Europe/ICRC 2003) 123, 129 et seq.

45 See Daragh Murray, 'How International Humanitarian Law Treaties Bind Non-State Armed Groups' (2015) 20 *JCSL* 101, who rejects the applicability of the *pacta tertiis nec nocent nec prosunt* principle on the basis of non-applicability to armed opposition groups.

present contribution. As OAGs – if at all – merely possess a limited legal personality that still is distinguished from that of States, it is convincing to solely limit this principle to the conduct of States at the level of international treaty relations, even under customary international law.[46]

2. Arguing against an international legal personality and/or capacity of Organised Armed Groups

Although recognition might be the easiest way to create some form of legal personality for the OAG, its actual implementation is highly unlikely as granting OAGs a relative or extensive legal personality always implies some form of legitimisation of the group's conduct – at least from a State-centric perspective. A position that was also taken by the ILC in its early drafts to Art. 10 ASR, which explicitly did not include any prerequisites for a legal personality of insurgents in order to avoid the emergence of a formal legal personality for the latter.[47] However, the stronger and bigger the group becomes, the harder it is for the international community to deny its existence on the international plane. Even if a legal personality of OAGs with the capacity to make treaties could be asserted in theory, there is almost no evidence in recent State practice that would prove their full legal capacity on the international plane, such as States claiming the group's international responsibility on the grounds of international law.[48] The rare exception to this rule is the American Alien-Tort Claims Act.[49] Under the Alien-Tort Claims Act, several cases were filed against the non-State actor as such, claiming his responsibility under international customary law.[50] Of course,

---

46 An Argument that can be supported by the interpretation of the principle itself. Since it derives from international treaty law, Art. 34 to 36 VCLT. The treaty itself only addresses States by its wording. An exception might has to be made of course, when conferring treaty-making capacities to a non-State actor.

47 UNYBILC 1975/I, 41-6.

48 James Crawford, *State Responsibility: The General Part* (OUP 2013) 81 (hereafter Crawford, *State Responsibility*).

49 28 U.S.C. § 1350 (1994). Applicable law in such cases is only customary international law. The acceptance thereof may be seen as evidence for an *opinio iuris*.

50 See eg *Mohamad et al v Palestinian Authority et al*, 556 US 494 (2012) (hereafter *Mohamad v Palestinian Authority*); *Tel-Oren et al v Libyan Arab Republic et al*, (1984) 726 F.2d 774, 233 U.S.App.D.C. 384 (hereafter *Tel-Oren v Libyan Arab Republic*).

the incidents as such cannot suffice to set a precedence for a new rule of international law or serve as evidence for sufficient State practice yet. On the contrary, in most cases, States implement their international obligations into their domestic law in order to avoid any legal interaction with the insurgents on the international plane.[51] Even in the case of recognition through the belligerent State, where a derived and limited subjectivity of international law is awarded to the OAG, a full legal capacity comparing to that of a primary subject of international law (which would enable the OAG to enter and participate in the creation of international treaties and therefore create an international common responsibility) must be negated. A capacity to make treaties therefore remains unrealistic and sometimes even undesirable for OAGs.[52] Some even deny any legal personality of an OAG as such and argue that this kind of groups ought to be seen as what they are: clusters of individuals, who jointly exercise their individual rights and duties under IHL; a collective legal personality is not created by this joint exercise.[53]

C. The Argument of Effectiveness

Although State practice seems to support this view until now, it might be worth asking whether the changing character of warfare and the ever-growing power of OAGs will inevitably alter the current discourse about their position in the international legal system, especially in areas of limited statehood. The central element of this discussion is the effective exercise of territorial control by OAGs.

It is often argued that international law must be obeyed in order for it to exert its full authority and to be effective. The specific reason for adherence to it is often deemed controversial: Sometimes law is obeyed due to the perceived (legal and political) threat of force and coercion by others. However, for more powerful actors, such as the permanent members of the UN SC or other strong nations, this might not be the motivation. Rather, it is the levelling of the playing field of the actors, the *do ut des* of traditional consensual public international law, which provides the true reason behind adherence to international law. The continued emergence of powerful non-

51 Crawford, *State Responsibility* (n 48) 81.
52 Clapham, 'Focusing on Non-State Actors' (n 4) 767.
53 See Dinstein, *NIAC* (n 3) para 210.

State actors seems to disrupt the playing field and shift it to a more three-dimensional sphere.[54]

Without prejudice to the very question of statehood, the argument and effect of the 'failed State' constellation may be invoked here to make a case for human rights protection in situations of limited statehood in order to level the playing field once more. The argument can be based on factual considerations for a determination of a possible legal personality in comparison to the prerequisites of statehood, as found in arguments within the 'failed State' debate. When adding the principle of effectiveness to the debate, it might be a valid point to ascribe some legal obligations to OAGs with regard to the protection of human rights in situations of deprived liberty within armed conflicts.

The main question to be asked is whether the exercise of effective control might be sufficient to confer legal obligations under the human rights regime to OAGs. In the context of prescribing a legal personality to OAGs *sui generis* on the basis of the common principle, it is often argued that international law cannot ignore actors with a certain presence on the international legal plane, despite their particular anomalous character.[55] This cannot be made dependent on their factual status.[56] Taken seriously and put in conjunction with the principle of effectiveness, a valid argument can be made. The effective exercise of permanent control over people and territory may very well be a factual criterion for international legal subjectivity. When a group is in fact effectively able to exercise control over a substantial area of a State's territory and enforce the rule of law, this threshold may be reached, as the group is organised in a State-like structure.[57]

From this point onwards, the OAG crosses the line towards a subject of international law that may even have the capacity to make and enter international treaties, as States can no longer ignore its existence.[58] Its legal

---

54 A sphere in which powerful non-State entities challenge the primacy of the States exercise of ultimate and sovereign power over everyone contained within their legal space, diluting the clear cut existing horizontal and vertical system.

55 Crawford, *Brownlie's Principles* (n 29) 124.

56 Ibid.

57 This will have be determined on a factual level. Although the gain and loss of captured territory is subject to change in the ebb and flow of a NIAC, the group must effectively control a substantial part of the territory permanently.

58 With regard to the principle of effectiveness, see Heike Krieger, *Das Effektivitätsprinzip im Völkerrecht* (Duncker & Humblot 2000) 35 et seq

personality is therefore created from its effective control: *ex facto jus oritur*.[59] A possible consequence might then be the ability to accede to international agreements; a convincing argument, considering that the effectiveness of an entity is a prominent criterion regarding the determination of statehood and governance, for instance in terms of effective jurisdiction to enforce and adjudicate.[60] Evidence for the effectiveness of an OAG can be deduced from its ability to be held responsible for its conduct at an international level. This, of course, depends to a certain extent on the definition of international responsibility. When taking the general approach, which defines international responsibility as 'legal relations which arise under international law by reason of an internationally wrongful act'[61], the ability of OAGs to fall under that system is not entirely farfetched. A conclusion that was already reached by special rapporteur *Ago* to the ILC when discussing the issue of State responsibility at the end of the 1960s; already then, he argued that 'an insurrectional movement which establishes its authority over a State's territory becomes a "separate subject of international law"'. This entailed the ability to have rights and obligations under international law and be held liable to claims.[62]

Even though his argument did not make it into the final draft, his point is still relevant today, especially in relation to the principle of effectiveness. Typical examples of an effective jurisdiction are the establishment of a 'domestic' court system or the setting up of a healthcare or taxation system.[63] Yet, this international legal subjectivity *sui generis* must be

(hereafter Krieger, *Effektivitätsprinzip*). For its basis in customary international law see 49 et seq.

59 See Robert Frau, 'Überlegungen zur Bindung nichtstaatlicher Gewaltakteure an internationale Menschenrechte' (2013) 26 J. Int'l L. of Peace & Armed Conflict 13.

60 Krieger, *Effektivitätsprinzip* (n 58) 82, relating to Art. 1 (d) 'capacity to enter into relations with other states' of the Montevideo Convention on Rights and Duties of States (opened for signature 26 December 1933, entered into force 26 December 1934) 165 LNTS 19.

61 Commentary on Art. 1 of the ILC Draft ASR, UNYBILC 2001/II 31.

62 UNYBILC 1972/II 129; see also earlier UNYBILC 1966/II 134.

63 A group that is worth noting here is the Liberation Tigers of Tamil Eelam (LTTE), which maintained an own 'judicial' system for the detention of persons captured under its authority and within the territory it controlled. This system reportedly amounted up to 17 courts with a hierarchical structure; see Kristian Stokke, 'Building the Tamil Eelam state: emerging institutions and forms of governance in LTTE-controlled Sri Lanka' (2006) 27 Third World Quarterly 1027 (hereafter Stokke, 'Building the Tamil Eelam state'). See also Sandesh

formally created in the first place, either by treaty or customary international law. The mere existence as an entity *sui generis* itself does not *per se* create an international legal personality in practice.[64]

However, if we compare an OAG which acts as a *de facto* authority by exercising effective control and jurisdiction to the concept of a 'failed State', the recognition of the existence of the former can only be declaratory in nature. As long as effective control in terms of government-like power is exercised, as in cases of the Tamil Tigers in Sri Lanka, the Fuerzas Armadas Revolucionarias de Colombia – Ejército del Pueblo (FARC) in Colombia or the Sudan People's Liberation Movement (SPLM) in Sudan, an international legal personality exceeding that created by CA 3 will be constituted as a consequence of the principle of effectiveness. Whether this extends to the applicability of human rights is highly debated.

Once an OAG, by its factual size and effective control over a relevant piece of territory, grows to be a State-like entity and therefore can be classified as a *de facto* authority,[65] it is not farfetched to attribute a distinct (partial) legal personality to it – at least with respect to IHL and basic human rights law.[66]

D. Provisional Summary

Concluding the arguments made above, OAGs can be seen as groups that exercise effective authority and have a certain standard of organisation and stability. Thus, they can be awarded a *de facto* limited legal personality in international law, which will bind them to existing international customary international law in NIACs. As a consequence, members of OAGs lose their status and protection as civilians following the wording and logic of both

---

Sivakumaran, 'Courts of armed opposition groups: fair trials or summary Justice?' (2009) 7 JICJ 489 (hereafter Sivakumaran, 'Courts of armed opposition groups').

64 Crawford, *Brownlie's Principles* (n 29) 124. To this day, the only traditionally recognised subjects of international law are the Order of Malta, the ICRC and the Holy See.

65 Epping, 'Sonstige Völkerrechtssubjekte' (n 39) paras 11 et seq. This will hold true especially once OAGs possess a military capacity equal to that of a State.

66 Ibid; Bantekas and Oette, *Human Rights Law* (n 9) 763 rightly arguing, that although some application of human rights can be conferred if the non-state entities do act state-like, it is not expected, that to provide the whole range of economic and social rights, since it would dilute the difference to the actual primary subject of international law, the state, too much.

CA 3 and AP II as well as the reasoning of the principle of distinction. The most effective argument in this case may be made when an OAG exercises substantial and effective control over a territory of a State Party to the GC, therefore becoming a *de facto* authority, or if its legal personality can be derived from the recognition by a belligerent State. However, State practice does not show any support for a creation of an international legal personality outside this narrow constellation. This may only cover a small group of entities, but everything else would be excessive and counter-productive to the validity of the legal argument, keeping in mind that States and their interactions on the international plane still build the normative foundation of modern international law. It is still unclear, however, to what extent such a legal commitment can actually be asserted. Since newly created subjects of international law are bound by a pre-existing foundation of (customary) rules of international law, this must be the vague minimum standard by which they have to live at the very least.

E. The International Normative Basis

When dealing with the framework of international legal personality and its effect on international obligations for OAGs, the international normative base, which may be applicable in situations of armed conflict, is the focal point of current debates as well as the legal authority for the act of detention under IHL itself. Since the deprivation of liberty by OAGs in NIACs is neither an irregular occurrence nor a small-scale issue, this debate should not be taken lightly.[67] Evidently, this should lead to the conclusion that, whenever there is an armed conflict, international law must also regulate the treatment and protection of those detained by OAGs. Although CA 3 and the AP II differ in their scope of application, the minimum requirement for an armed conflict would be, 'a resort to … protracted armed violence between governmental armed authorities and organized armed groups or between such groups within a State'[68].

Setting aside internal disturbances since they are solely governed by domestic law, it is important to factually distinguish between the two legal

67 Groups worth mentioning in this context are the Communist Party of Nepal-Maoist (CPN-M) in Nepal, the LTTE in Sri Lanka, the Forces Nouvelles de Côte d'Ivoire (FAFN) in Ivory Coast, the Taliban in Afghanistan, the SPLAM in Sudan, the FARC and the Ejército de Liberación Nacional (ELN) in Colombia, the Separatists in Eastern Ukraine and ISIS in Syria and Iraq, among others.

68 *Prosecutor v Tadić* (n 5) at para 70.

bodies of CA 3 and AP II for the determination of the specific conflict status of a NIAC. From the beginning, the two regimes displayed a very different approach. This becomes clear when looking at the drafting of AP II and the question of rules on the conduct of hostilities implemented in the protocol. In this context, the final draft of AP II contained almost the same set of rules and obligations for all parties to the conflict as AP I. Nevertheless, these provisions were ultimately deleted from the treaty before its final conclusion.[69] Notwithstanding the deletion of many of the provisions, AP II still contains a variety of precise regulations with respect to detention which may become applicable once its threshold of application is reached. CA 3 in its wording is vague and only determines very basic obligations; it therefore contains a very different set of rules for the respective parties to the conflict. This, however, does not change the overarching object and purpose of both frameworks, which is to create an 'equality of belligerents' in a sense. This entails a binding effect on all parties falling within its applicability, regulating their conduct and protecting those affected by the conduct of hostilities regardless of the characterisation as State or non-State entities.

As a consequence, members of OAGs will lose their status as civilians and become 'fighters' or so-called 'unprivileged combatants'; they are hence rendered lawful targets. Apart from their own specific status under IHL, members of OAGs are also often engaged in the detention of enemy 'combatants' outside the sphere of national law.[70] This implied lack of status and privilege, for example the lack of combatant-immunity, may be easily connected to obligations under IHL, resulting in a factual imbalance in rights and duties. This conclusion is, however, not quite convincing, as the Geneva Conventions and the AP II specifically address all entities involved in armed conflicts equally. The original distinction between OAGs and State entities is mainly rooted in the regulation of the conduct of

---

69 Nils Melzer, *International Humanitarian Law: A comprehensive Introduction* (ICRC 2016) 125 (hereafter Melzer, *IHL*). The reasoning behind this shift was ultimately seen in the desire of States to avoid any possible legitimisation or privilege of non-State parties to a conflict, be they insurgents or non-State belligerents. This hesitation is particularly interesting because CA 3 (2) itself states that '[t]he application of the preceding provisions shall not affect the legal status of the Parties to the conflict.' Ultimately, this legal containment of the non-State entity aside its political implications may be a finding that is reasonable in theory, but almost impossible to uphold in practice.

70 Ibid, 126.

hostilities itself, without prejudice to status and, therefore, rights and duties under internment.

I. Applicability of International Humanitarian Law with Respect to the Deprivation of Liberty

The major sources of applicable international law in the specific context of the deprivation of liberty and OAGs may be found first and foremost in treaty law and customary international law. Although OAGs never became parties to the Geneva Conventions and will not be able to do so in the future due to their limited legal personality, the direct applicability of the Geneva Conventions seems to be excluded for them at the first glance, thereby limiting the range of applicable law to customary international law. Customary international law seems to be the appropriate legal tool set at first, since it is able *qua* its legal nature to apply to OAGs with a limited legal personality.[71] A direct treaty-based application of at least CA 3 however, can be derived from interpreting CA 3 itself. Once the threshold of applicability of CA 3 is reached and the OAG in question is qualified as a party to the conflict, the convention, by its wording, addresses the OAG directly under international treaty law. Whether or not the obligation may stem directly from an international treaty or only from customary law is irrelevant at this point, as the binding nature of customary law to OAGs is undisputed.[72]

Although the Geneva Conventions offer some protection under CA 3 by demanding a 'humane treatment' of detainees and safeguarding the fundamental guarantees offered by Art. 4 and 5 of AP II, there is no specific detention regime in NIACs that regulates further procedural guarantees of the deprivation of liberty. Something that is usually found in human rights treaties.[73]

---

71 With respect to applicable international customary law, see Murray, *Human Rights obligations* (n 2) 82 et seq.

72 Ibid, 89 et seq.

73 To cope with this difference in regulation, a distinction between detention and the deprivation of liberty is often invoked. Whereas detention is perceived as a specific conduct by a state entity, the deprivation of liberty re is referred to the either procedural part regulated by human rights (for example the internment of a suspected pirate on board a ship at the High Seas (deprivation of liberty) until a port is reached to present him before a judge (detention)) or a vague term to

The protection by the conventions is not necessarily linked to the status of the detaining power. They follow a rather conduct-based approach by not prohibiting the internment by any party to the conflict *per se* without referencing to a victim and perpetrator narrative, but rather regulating the situation of internment once it occurred.[74] This reasoning hereby follows the same logic as for the authority for the participation to a conflict itself. The reference by the Geneva Conventions to civilians, combatants, fighters, etc. is solely made with respect to the level of protection and regulation of the conduct of hostilities and not with respect to any authority to participate.[75]

Indeed, a legal authority to detain cannot be found in the framework of IHL.[76] A conclusion, that was also reached by the High Court of England and Wales in its famous *Serdar Mohammed v Ministry of Defence* decision where it held that neither the relevant portions of the Geneva Conventions nor AP II contain:

> … any express statement that it is lawful to deprive persons of their liberty in an armed conflict to which these provisions apply. All they do is to set out certain minimum standards of treatment which must be afforded to persons who are detained during such an armed conflict.[77]

Hereby following this argument and applying the old *Lotus* principle, if international law does not prohibit a particular conduct, that conduct is permitted.[78] Even then, the consent-based reasoning of the *Lotus* case is still valid.[79] Critics argue that the *Lotus* principle may only be applied in inter-State relations, since it was developed in an inter-State dispute at a time where no debate over other possible subjects of international law existed. It then would only be applicable to State parties to AP II and the Geneva

---

differentiate from a state-conduct when talking about non-state actors. This however is mere semantics and driven by political reasoning and can have no effect on the legal regulation of the conduct itself.

74 Melzer, *IHL* (n 69) 208.

75 Ibid; although prohibited under national law, the direct participation in hostilities is not prohibited *per se* by international law. The only consequence is the loss of the protected status as a civilian.

76 See also Brunner, 'Security Detention' (n 4).

77 *Serdar Mohammed v Ministry of Defence* [2014] EWHC 1369 (QB) 239.

78 For a critical reading of the *Lotus*-case and its current interpretation, i.e. the *Lotus*-principle, see Pia Hesse, 'Comment: neither Sunken Vessel nor Blooming Flower! The Lotus-Principle and International Humanitarian Law' in this volume 80. For the role of the *Lotus*-principle concerning IHL, see Schöberl and Mührel, 'Sunken Vessel or Blooming Flower?' (n 11).

79 The Case of the S.S. "Lotus" [France v Turkey] [1927] PCIJ Series A No 1.

Conventions. Nevertheless, the reasoning behind the principle, i.e. that a subject of international law may only be bound by it through consent, is easily transferable to the current debate. A strict reliance on the *Lotus* principle itself is therefore not necessary. Moreover, the intent of the Geneva Conventions was clearly not to deal with any matters of authorisation in this respect, as they follow a conduct-based approach aimed to provide protection to those vulnerable, but not to legitimise a party to the conflict. However, the authority to detain and its penal regulation may still be found in domestic law.

1. Application of CA 3

Although the Geneva Conventions do not provide a definition of what a conflict *not of an international character* might be, they in essence require as a minimum, that the OAG is organised, has control over some territory and is able to obey the rules of war.[80]

Although humane treatment remains a vague concept, it does include, as a minimum, the prohibition of any violence to life or threats thereof, insults and public curiosity including the physical and mental well-being of the internees; moreover, it specifically prohibits murder, torture, corporal punishment, mutilation, outrages against human dignity, collective punishment and hostage-taking as well as the prohibition of any physical and psychological coercion.[81] Although CA 3 (1) (d) explicitly mentions the prohibition of passing out sentences or carrying out executions without *due process*, it does not authorise the establishment of specific courts for OAGs in which these cases could be dealt with, again following the

80 Emily Crawford and Alison Pert, *International Humanitarian Law* (CUP 2015) 63 (hereafter Crawford and Pert, *IHL*); Lindsay Moir 'The Concept of Non-International Armed Conflict' in Andrew Clapham et al (eds), *The 1949 Geneva Conventions: A Commentary* (OUP 2016) para 2 et seq.

81 Melzer, *IHL* (n 69) 195. The extent to which medical care and adequate food has to be provided to detainees found some clarification in the *Aleksovski* Judgment by the ICTY, where the tribunal defined certain minimum standards. Judging, that a standard that would fail to meet the requirement of peace times would still be sufficient in times of war; *Prosecutor v Aleksovski* (Judgment) IT-95-14/1-T (25 June 1999).

conduct-based approach of the Conventions.[82] Although CA 3 itself does not offer procedural guarantees, it does contain the prohibition of arbitrary detention as a minimum standard. Arbitrary deprivation of liberty, for instance detention without any due process of law, may already inherently constitute a violation of human dignity contained in the meaning of cruel treatment under CA 3.[83] Whether or not this constitutes a war crime, the prohibition of arbitrary deprivation of liberty constitutes a basic element of protection guaranteed by CA 3.

2. Application of Art. 4 and 5 Additional Protocol II

As mentioned before, AP II differs in its scope of application. According to Art. 1 (1), AP II applies to all conflicts not regulated by AP I and further requires the conflict to:

> … take place in the territory of a High Contracting Party between its armed forces, dissident armed forces or other organized armed groups which, under responsible command, exercise such control over a part of its territory as to enable them to carry out sustained and concerted military operations and to implement this Protocol.

A discussion on the binding effect of AP II is therefore only reasonable once the OAG reaches this specific threshold. In relation to the deprivation of liberty, the most comprehensive obligations are contained in Art. 4 AP II, including the obligation to respect the fundamental guarantees of persons who are not directly taking part, or who have ceased to take part in hostilities as well as the obligation to protect persons deprived of their liberty. Apart from their binding effect on all States parties, these obligations represent customary international law.[84]

This limitation of the scope of application of AP II actually serves the interests of the Protocol (and the Conventions) itself, as, only when OAGs can effectively exercise their duties under it, an effective protection of those interned by such groups can be guaranteed. Broadening the scope of application would merely serve to water the obligations down, ultimately leaving no satisfactory result.

---

82 See Melzer, *IHL* (n 69) 215; Lawrence Hill-Cawthorne, *Detention in Non-International Armed Conflict* (OUP 2016) 77 (hereafter Hill-Cawthorne, *Detention*).

83 *Prosecutor v Limaj et al* (Prosecution's final Brief [Confidential]) ICTY-03-66 (20 July 2005) para 391-2. This position was later overthrown by the trial chamber.

84 Crawford and Pert, *IHL* (n 80) 257.

3. The Hague Regulations

Another international norm which mentions the internment of parties to a conflict is Art. 3 Hague Regulations which provides that 'the armed forces of the belligerent parties may consist of combatants and non-combatants. In case of capture by the enemy, both have the right to be treated as prisoners of war'.

This regulation was later taken up by Art. 4 (4) and (5) GC III. However, it remains doubtful whether one can actually draw from the Hague Regulations here, as they (as well as Art. 4 GC III) are only applicable to IACs. The question is, therefore, whether or not OAGs can be qualified as combatants and whether the argument of Art. 3 Hague Regulations can be extended to NIACs in order to further root their legal obligations in international law. One could argue that Art. 3 not only contains legal obligations under the Hague Regulations, but is also a basic rule of IHL itself. A rule that ought to be applicable irrespective the character of the conflict, as this distinction may be one of the basic principles of IHL; there is no reason why it should not to be applied to modern asymmetric armed conflicts. After all, the drafters of the Hague Regulations certainly did not have NIACs in mind at the time.

Both CA 3 and AP II do not explicitly refer to the parties as combatants. The concepts of the mentioned 'armed forces' as well as 'dissident armed forces' and 'other organised armed groups' are unfortunately not further defined in the practice pertaining to such NIACs. However, those taking direct part in hostilities in NIACs are sometimes referred to as 'combatants'.[85] This wording is often only used as a generic term with the main purpose of distinguishing between the persons in question and protected civilians, without implying a formal combatant status or prisoner-of-war status, which would be the consequence in IACs.[86] Additionally, the

---

85 See UN GA Res 2676 (9 December 1970) UN Doc A/RES/2676 referring to 'combatants in all armed conflicts' in the context of human rights or the Cairo Declaration and Cairo Plan of Action, UN Doc TD /B/EX(24)/2 (5 May 2000) at 68–69 and 82 resp. of 3–4 April 2000 adopted at the Organization of African Unity and the European Union Africa-Europe Summit.

86 The term 'combatant' is often used synonymously when translated into different languages, which adds to the confusion. Although its original meaning would have been 'fighter' instead of a formal 'combatant'; a mere interpretation of the wording alone cannot be wholly satisfactory. See also Michael N. Schmitt et al (eds), 'The Manual of Law of Non-International Armed Conflict: with Commentary' (2006) 36 IYHR 71, Rule 1.1.2 - Fighters.

assertion that the term 'combatant' might be extended to NIACs would need some proof in form of *opinio iuris* and a uniform State practice. As evidence for this is scarce, its direct application must be negated. However, the basic principle contained in Art. 3 Hague Regulations can, of course, be considered when interpreting possible legal obligations for OAGs under customary international law, as modern-day norms are a further development of that principle – even in NIACs.

II. Application of Human Rights Law in Cases of Deprivation of Liberty

No field of international law is more controversial than the application of human rights to non-State actors and to OAGs in particular. Bearing in mind the exception of the effectiveness argument made above, the special nature of human rights *per se* seems to bar non-State entities from its direct application. In current State-centric international law, only States may be the bearers of human rights obligations. Any violation of human rights should be seen as a violation of the domestic transformations of those obligations and, therefore, as a domestic criminal offense which the State must prosecute.[87] The failure to do so is seen as a due diligence violation of the respective State.[88] Setting aside the domestic argument for a second, we shall firstly examine whether human rights obligations may be invoked by international law directly.

1. General considerations concerning how and when human rights may become directly applicable

Much has been written and said about the direct application of human rights in the context of non-State actors and armed conflicts.[89] Unlike IHL, which

87 One might hesitate to incorporate non-State entities into the human rights realm, as that may require a reconsideration of the basic human rights architecture and rationale, since it is founded on the premise that only States may hold absolute and ultimate power over its people; on this, see Bantekas and Oette, *Human Rights Law* (n 10) 716. It remains to be seen whether this can be upheld in areas of limited statehood, where no or only a limited State authority is present.

88 Louise Doswald-Beck, *Human Rights in Times of Conflict and Terrorism* (OUP 2011) 118 et seqq.

89 See Alston, *Non-State Actors* (n 17); Clapham, *Human Rights Obligations* (n 4).

addresses OAGs directly as a party to the conflict and hereby imposes direct obligations on them, human rights almost always address States.[90] That being said, both the UN SC and the UN GA address non-State actors with respect to their human rights obligations in NIACs.[91] Even if one would apply certain customary IHRL to non-State actors, a number of difficulties would arise when applying such rules to them.[92] Neither the UN SC nor other bodies have yet clearly referenced the legal source of the proclaimed human rights obligations for OAGs, leaving it unclear why these actors should be bound in the first place.[93] As far as human rights obligations are already contained within the basic protection offered by CA 3, they only serve as a complementary protection regime under IHL. This may be relevant in cases of torture or degrading treatment in situations of internment. The minimum requirement for the applicability of human rights law is that the violation occurs on the territory of a State Party to the respective convention and that the respective entity exercises effective control over the territory in question. This approach seems to be adopted by other UN bodies as well.[94] An argument that has been put forward here is that the OAG in question would thereby be bound by human rights obligations of the State whose territory it controls, thus implementing a rule of succession.[95] This, however, is not very convincing in light of Art. 10

---

90 See Clapham, 'Human Rights Obligations in Conflict Situations' (n 38). An accession to the relevant treaties for non-State actors is still impossible. If any binding law exists, it will have to be customary in nature.

91 UN GA Res 67/262 (4 June 2012) UN Doc A/Res/67/262 with respect to the conflict in Syria or UN SC Res 1834 (24 September 2008) UN Doc S/Res/1834 and UN SC Res 1814 (15 May 2008) UN Doc S/Res/1814 with respect to Chad and Somalia.

92 Hill-Cawthorne, *Detention* (n 82) 217; Elizabeth Wilmshurst (ed), *International Law and the Classification of Conflicts* (OUP 2012) 90-1.

93 Hill-Cawthorne, *Detention* (n 82), 218. Apart from the factual addressing by the UN SC, the legal nature of its resolutions in the context of non-State actors is very much unclear, since resolutions can neither be classified as a classic treaty nor as customary international law, however they may have gained a separate legal status in international law in that respect altogether. See *Serdar Mohammed v Ministry of Defence* [2017] UKSC 2, para 23; Brunner, 'Security Detention' (n 4).

94 For extensive examples, see Hill-Cawthorne, *Detention* (n 82) 218.

95 UN HRC, 'General Comment No. 26: Continuity of Obligations' (8 December 1997) UN Doc CCPR/C/21/Rev.1/Add.8/Rev.1; Anthony Cullen and Steven Wheatly, 'The Human Rights of Individuals in de facto Regimes under the

ASR, which only retroactively converts acts of an OAG into an act of the State once the insurrection is completely successful. A direct application of human rights obligations to OAGs is therefore not convincing.

2. Applying the 'minimum standard' to Organised Armed Groups

Although the consideration of the application of a minimum human rights standard is an argument which is often put forward, it is not quite clear what this standard actually entails. A hint to what this standard may comprise can be found in the 1990s Turku Declaration:[96] Art. 3 restates the existing obligations under CA 3. Art. 4 specifically relates to the situation of

European Convention on human Rights' (2013) 13 Human Rights Law Review 691, 717-23.

96 Turku Declaration of Minimum Humanitarian Standards, UN Doc E/CN.4/Sub.2/1991/55 (2 December 1990). The declaration was adopted by a meeting of experts and organised by the Human Rights Institute of Åbo Akademi in Turku/Åbo (Finland) in cooperation with *inter alia* the ICRC, which participated in the drafting. It was designed as a draft treaty, but its international legal reception was controversial. Despite its positive reception within the UN, the declaration was never included in a formal treaty due to the lack of States willing to take on these broad obligations in internal conflicts. Nevertheless, it remained an important document for the development of human rights protection in NIACs, see Knut Ipsen, 'Die Entwicklung von Kriegsrecht zum Recht des bewaffneten Konflifts' in Knut Ipsen (ed), Völkerrecht (6th edn, Beck 2014) 1195, and paved the way for the complementary protection approach to human rights in armed conflict, see Hans-Joachim Heintze, 'Theorien zum Verhältnis von Menschenrechten und humanitärem Völkerrecht' (2011) 24 J. Int'l L. of Peace & Armed Conflict 4. It was also recognised by the ICTY in its *Tadić*-jurisprudence, which referenced the declaration when debating the core principles of customary humanitarian law, *Prosecutor v Tadić* (n 5) para 119. The ICRC had initially criticised the declaration in the drafting process for its progressive stance on human rights and humanitarian law, but later revised its opinion and contributed to its spreading, see Louise Doswald-Beck and Sylvian Vité, 'International Humanitarian Law and Human Rights Law' (1993) 75 IRRC 99; Djamchid Momtaz, 'The minimum humanitarian rules applicable in periods of internal tension and strife' (1998) 80 IRRC 487. It is noteworthy in that context that even this progressive draft expressly addressed armed groups without conferring any legal status to them, see Art. 2 of the declaration: 'These standards shall be respected by, and applied to all persons, groups and authorities, irrespective of their legal status and without any adverse discrimination', herby echoing Art CA 3.

detention referring to the obligations under Art. 5 AP II but exceeding it in its scope, declaring that

> 1. All persons deprived of their liberty shall be held in recognized places of detention. Accurate in-formation on their detention and whereabouts, including transfers, shall be made promptly available to their family members and counsel or other persons having a legitimate interest in the information.
>
> 2. All persons deprived of their liberty shall be allowed to communicate with the outside world including counsel in accordance with reasonable regulations promulgated by the competent authority.
>
> 3. The right to an effective remedy, including habeas corpus, shall be guaranteed as a mean to deter-mine the whereabouts or the state of health of persons deprived of their liberty and for identifying the authority ordering or carrying out the deprivation of liberty. Everyone who is deprived of his or her liberty by arrest or detention shall be entitled to take proceedings by which the lawfulness of the detention shall be decided speedily by a court and his or her release ordered if the detention is not lawful.
>
> 4. All persons deprived of their liberty shall be treated humanely, provided with adequate food and drinking water, decent accommodation and clothing, and be afforded safeguards as regards health, hygiene, and working and social conditions.

When thinking about customary international human rights obligations, applicable to OAGs exercising effective control over a territory, it is often referred to the core of human rights that may not be derogated from. Although arguments concerning effective control and jurisdiction may be made for OAGs such as Al-Shabab or the Kurdish militias in northern Iraq, the question remains whether or not OAGs fall within the scope of the conventions in the first place. Whereas CA 3 refers to 'the case of armed conflict not of an international character occurring in the territory of one of the *High Contracting Parties, each Party to the conflict* shall be bound to apply',[97] thereby differentiating between the territorial applicability and the applicability *rationae personae*, the basic human rights covenants expressly refer to States only with respect to their applicability.[98]

From a human rights perspective, the legal definition of the perpetrator in cases of internment may be almost irrelevant. For the victim it does not make a difference whether a violation of his or her rights occurs through a State or an OAG. As long as there is a manifest exercise of effective control or authority over a certain territory or area, the application of human rights

97 Emphasis added.

98 Eg Art. 1 ECHR: 'High Contracting Parties'; Art. 2 ICCPR: 'Each State Party'.

obligations following the argument of the *Al-Skeini* jurisprudence of the ECtHR with its 'divided and tailored' approach seems to be favourable.[99] It may well be argued here that the division and tailoring may not only be done by the applicable obligations, but also by the obligated actor himself. However, this specific jurisprudence was solely designed for the application in an inter-State realm and may not be easily transferred out of the vertical level of human rights protection. Indeed, neither State practice nor any judgment by an original human rights body would support the claim that this system is on the verge of changing. Whether those actors are able to actually fulfil their possible obligations in the first place remains highly questionable. After all, the ability to enforce and provide human rights and their protection remains the essence of sovereignty and statehood. Humanitarian legal obligations for OAGs exceeding the minimum standards under IHL therefore remain highly doubtful.

F. The Domestic Argument

Picking up the debate opened above, the question to be dealt with now is the application of domestic law in the State where the conflict occurs. As mentioned, this might already constitute an adequate tool to legally bind organised armed groups to a certain legal standard regarding the deprivation of liberty. Within this debate, the question of the primacy of existing domestic law over possible international obligations will also be dealt with. In other words, do we even need to create international legal obligations for non-State actors or is the existing domestic law sufficient to deal with the matter? Problems arise especially when international and national obligations contradict each other. Is the applicable international law only a complementary protection alongside national law as the primary source of law in NIACs?

I. Domestic Relations of International Law

The case that is often put forward here is the argument of legislative jurisdiction. Not only in terms of applicable domestic, but also international

---

99 *Al-Skeini and Others v the United Kingdom*, App no 55721/07, 7 July 2011, 134; confirmed in *Al-Jedda v the United Kingdom,* App no 27021/08, 7 July 2011.

law. It is argued that, since the belligerent State in question has already ratified the international treaty and may even have implemented it into its domestic law, the obligation is therefore automatically binding for non-State actors operating on its territory and within its jurisdiction.[100] The advantage of this theory is that OAGs operating in the State's territory may be bound without their explicit consent, as the State exercises the will of the people it represents. However, this argument is not convincing on two grounds. Firstly, it ignores the sometimes divergent inner structure of States that either follow a dualistic or monistic system and, secondly, especially in areas of limited statehood, the further the insurgents progress, the less authority and factual existence of State there is. Thus, there would be no one liable to the violations of IHL and human rights law for the duration of the conflict. For example, notwithstanding the principle of continuity and the assumed continuous sovereignty over Somalia, it is highly doubtful that the Somali government may be held accountable for human rights violations perpetrated by Al-Shabab within the vast territory it effectively controls.

II. Primacy of Existing Domestic Law over International Obligations

Apart from the argument of legislative jurisdiction, the actual relation between national and international law with respect to non-State actors offers a further obstacle which would have to be overcome first. Existing national law often already deals with the deprivation of liberty on the penal und public law level. If an authority for OAGs to detain existed in international law, it would consequently entail an immunity from penalisation for the act of detention under national law and maybe even for taking part in the conduct of hostilities in the first place, analogous to the combatant immunity in IAC. This, however, might not be a concept the drafting States of AP II and especially the Geneva Conventions had in mind when regulating the treatment of OAGs in NIACs. National law must remain applicable alongside international law during conflicts. Furthermore, in most cases, the existing national law regulating the deprivation of liberty is the implementation of existing human rights obligations, for example the prohibition of arbitrary deprivation of liberty

100 Sandesh Sivakumaran, 'Binding Armed Opposition Groups' (2006) 55 ICLQ 369, 381; Antonio Cassese, 'The Status of Rebels under the 1977 Geneva Protocol on Non-International Armed Conflicts' (1981) 30 ICLQ 416, 429.

as well as regulations concerning the procedural requirements regarding the establishment of an independent judicial body and a fair trial. What it does not regulate is an authorisation of such acts – neither for State Parties nor for other actors involved. The authority to detain under international human rights law may only be found in national law itself or by particular acts of the UN SC.[101] Additionally, States will most likely avoid any authorisation for OAGs to detain under international law for reasons of enforcing their own domestic penal law.

In areas of limited statehood, the validity of this argument can be questioned. It may well be argued here that, in such cases, the effective protection of human rights should to be prioritised. If neither the State nor the OAG can be held accountable for their actions, at least for the prolonged duration of the conflict, a gap of protection arises.[102] This is especially the case when rights and duties in that respect are only provided by domestic law and the interests of the individual in the international sphere are assumed by the respective State through the voluntary system of diplomatic protection.[103] Additionally, from the perspective of a victim, the factual violation of an individual's right and the legal character of the perpetrator do not make a substantial difference anyway.

III. Conclusion

Ultimately, the answer of applicable domestic law to OAGs and their obligations for situations of internment will have to be found in the actual effectiveness of the OAG as an entity exercising territorial control and therefore in the effectiveness argument made earlier and or the absence of the State. A point that validity may be made comparing this case to the argument made in situations of failed States and their legal obligations under international law regarding the principle of effectiveness.

101 Cf Brunner, 'Security Detention' (n 4).

102 Although individual criminal responsibility deriving from international law directly will hold some individuals accountable, for instance in cases of war crimes, this might not suffice in all cases, for example regarding crimes against humanity, Bantekas and Oette, *Human Rights Law* (n 9) 764.

103 Ibid, 762.

G. Integrating Organised Armed Groups into the Process of 'Law-Making'

When accrediting OGAs with a distinct legal personality, thereby setting aside the primacy of domestic law and creating a legal framework for their involvement in the deprivation of liberty, the subsequent topic to be dealt with is the discussion of the relationship between OAGs and positive international norms, may they be treaty- or customary-law based. While certain groups do not seem to recognise any substantial standards of internment, some OAGs expressly recognise entitlements of their detainees under IHL and IHRL and regulate the conduct of its members according to those presumed obligations.[104] Therefore, the focus should be placed on the conduct of such groups and their conducts effect on treaty and customary obligations under the Geneva Conventions and international human rights. This also relates to the basic question of whether or not those actors remain 'law-takers' as opposed to 'law-makers' and how they affect the international (State) practice of those norms.[105] In the end, it must be asked to what extent OAGs should be incorporated into the process of the creation of rules of international law in the first place. Taking OAGs seriously in that respect might help to enhance compliance with international norms by these actors but might also just be a political argument.[106]

104 See the example of the FAFN in Ivory Coast, which secured and maintained territorial control over a substantial part of northern Ivory Coast between 2002 and 2007. The Group established routine detention operations utilising the captured facilities of the State and even segregated conflict-related detainees from regular persons detained under their control. The behaviour of the FAFN can largely be recognised as 'State-like', see David Tuck, 'Detention by armed groups: overcoming challenges to humanitarian action' (2011) 93 IRRC 759, 761. As mentioned above, the LTTE maintained an own 'judicial' system for the detention of persons captured under their authority and within their controlled territory, see Stokke, 'Building the Tamil Eelam state' (n 63), 1027. For the usage of detention to implement an OAG's own 'rule of law' within its controlled territory to ensure its continuous exercise of power over the area, see Sivakumaran, 'Courts of armed opposition groups' (n 63) 489.

105 For further details, see Widdig, 'Perspektiven einer möglichen Einbindung' (n 15) 109 et seqq.

106 For the compliance argument, see Annyssa Bellal and Stuart Casey-Maslen, 'Enhancing Compliance with International Law by Armed Non-State Actors' (2011) 3 GOJIL 175.

I. The Integration of Organised Armed Groups into the Creation of International Treaty and Customary Law

The question of the relationship between OAGs and international treaties remains highly controversial. The basic argument in this debate is, in fact, not a legal one, but rather one of compliance. If we accept that some conduct of OAGs (for instance detention), even though banned under national law, is not illegal or at least tolerated under international law, there should be an incentive for them to respect the laws of war. Taking the process of detention out of the illegality from the States perspective, might be an incentive for the respective group to detain those captured and respect their dignity and due process rights, rather than simply kill them.[107] This is something that might be achieved by the incorporation of OAGs into the 'law-making' process. However, the question remains of whether this is possible at all.

Art. 2 in accordance with Art. 1 VCLT defines international treaties as agreements between States. Today, most States accept and recognise this definition of an international treaty, thereby rendering it customary international law.[108] By this standard, the incorporation of OAGs into the process seems to be impossible. However, Art. 3 VCLT stipulates the fact that the Convention does not apply to international agreements concluded between States and other subjects of international law or between such other subjects of international law, shall not affect their legal force, nor the applicability of certain rules of the convention, as far as these rules constitute customary international law.

Consequently, agreements that qualify under Art. 3 VCLT can be seen as an international treaty, although not concluded between two primary subjects of international law.[109] The inclusion of OAGs in international agreements therefore seems not to be completely out of the question.[110] The formal requirements for such an inclusion would be the competence and

107 Andrew Clapham, 'Detention by Armed Groups under International Law' (2017) 93 ILS 1, 2-3.

108 For its basis in customary international law, see Duncan Hollis, 'Defining Treaties' in Duncan Hollis (ed), *The Oxford Guide to Treaties* (OUP 2012) 12 et seq.

109 Ibid, 13.

110 Ibid, 23; Yves Le Bouthillier and Jean-Francois Bonin, 'Article 3' in Olivier Corten and Pierre Klein (eds), *The Vienna Conventions on the Law of Treaties: A Commentary*, vol. I (OUP 2011) 72.

jurisdiction of the actor in question and the free will of the other party to enter the agreement.[111] This might apply to a stabilised *de facto* regime or an effective *de facto* authority. Ultimately, there is no positive obligation or rule neither within the VCLT nor in international law in general which prescribes what OAGs may or may not regulate with States through an international agreement. [112] Even if convincing in theory, this argument simply lacks sufficient State practice to be proven correct.

Therefore, it remains to be asked whether there are other ways for OAGs to be incorporated into the process of international 'law-making'. Art. 38 (1) (b) ICJ-Statute requires 'international custom as evidence of a general practice accepted as law' for the genesis of new customary international law. The influence of OAGs on that custom seems to be limited at first, but its indirect effect is quite substantial, as the conduct of States often is motivated by or is a reaction to the conduct of OAGs and their newly consolidated power in modern NIACs.[113] The OAG's influence or incorporation therefore is only an indirect one, which may come in the form of a (formal) recognition of its conduct and/or statements and declarations in the process of the creation of new rules.[114] This comprehensive approach can actually be beneficial to States, since it increases the probability of non-State actors complying with new rules of law as they were involved in the process to a certain extent.[115]

---

111 Duncan Hollis (ed), *The Oxford Guide to Treaties* (OUP 2012) 664 et seq.

112 Thomas Grant, 'Who Can Make Treaties? Other Subjects of International Law' in Duncan Hollis (ed), *The Oxford Guide to Treaties* (OUP 2012) 145.

113 Ryngaert, 'Non-State Actors' (n 41) 1, 6: referring to *Prosecutor v Tadić* (n 5) para 70, where the Appeals Chamber is said to also incorporate the practice non-State actors as proof for the formation of new customary international law at paras 107 et seq; Sandesh Sivakumaran, 'Lessons from the law of armed conflict from commitments of armed groups: identification of legitimate targets and prisoners of war' (2011) 93 IRRC 1 (hereafter Sivakumaran, 'Lessons').

114 An approach also recognised by the ICRC study on existing customary IHL, which concludes that conduct or practice by OAGs *per se* may not be qualified as State practice and classifies their conduct as 'other practice' or gives it an auxiliary character in the process. See Jean-Marie Henckaerts and Louise Doswald-Beck, *Customary International Humanitarian Law*, vol. I: Rules (CUP 2005) xlii.

115 See Anthea Roberts and Sandesh Sivakumaran, 'Lawmaking by Nonstate Actors: Engaging Armed Groups in the Creation of International Humanitarian Law' (2011) 37 Yale J. Int'l L. 108, 126 et seq (hereafter Roberts and Sivakumaran, 'Lawmaking by Nonstate Actors').

However, putting too much emphasis on the conduct and practice of non-State actors may hold the risk of a mere regression of customary international law.[116] Some OAGs explicitly do not want any attribution to human rights or other State-like obligations and duties and, by definition, oppose any legislative action that derives from the regime they fight against, even on the international plane. Yet, it is not entirely out of the question to take into consideration statements made by OAGs in relation to IHL. For example, the so-called Deeds of Commitments facilitated by the NGO Geneva Call allows OAGs to express their perception of binding humanitarian norms.[117] The relevance of such actions can be asserted following the argument of the ICJ; for proof of international custom as evidence of a general practice, emphasis has to be put on the subjects of international law that contribute to the practice and whose interests are touched by the relevant provision.[118] This might be a very progressive and dynamic interpretation of the decision as the court might have only had States in mind at the time of judgment, but the argument itself still holds some validity. Aside this indirect influence on customary international law, a further incorporation is not possible. Only if the rebellion of the OAG is successful, its conduct and practice will become that of a State and therefore gain relevance retroactively.[119]

II. The Integration of Organised Armed Groups into Law-Making through Unilateral Declarations

The nature of unilateral declarations made by OAGs is disputed; some see them as meaningless, and as a mere political tool for negotiation, whereas

---

116 Ryngaert, 'Non-State Actors' (n 41) 6.

117 Although they are intentionally not called 'treaties', the content of such agreements essentially resembles that of the respective treaty and *de facto* reflects the practice of existent international obligations. An approach that was most likely also taken by the ICTY in *Prosecutor v Tadić* (n 5) para 108 with reference to the abovementioned declarations by the FMLN in El Salvador (para 107 of the judgment).

118 North Sea Continental Shelf Cases (*Federal Republic of Germany v Denmark; Federal Republic of Germany v Netherlands*) (Judgment) [1969] ICJ Rep 3, para 73 et seqq; Wolff Heintschel von Heinegg, 'Völkergewohnheitsrecht' in Knut Ipsen (ed), *Völkerrecht* (6th edn, Beck 2014) para 11; Maarten Bos, *A Methodology of International Law* (Elsevier 1984) 231 et seq.

119 Art. 10 ASR.

others grant them a certain legal value. However, OAGs regularly make use of unilateral declarations to voice their perception of existing binding legal obligations. The scope of such declarations ranges from the mere restatement of the law to explicit violations of existing international standards.[120] Therefore, the nature and effect of such declarations on customary international law deserves some further investigation.

In its famous *Nuclear Test Cases*, the ICJ elaborated on the binding effect of unilateral declarations (by States), arguing that, by public unilateral declaration of the existence of a positive legal obligation, the declaration becomes binding for the declaring actor itself. However, further implications and legal effects on third parties may not be established with the exception of obligations having an *jus cogens* character.[121] It may be argued that now, although this reasoning was construed with only States in mind, there is no apparent obstacle in applying it to OAGs as well, particularly because States have a genuine interest in binding OAGs to their statements. For the respective group its binding character will come from its own consent to be bound and or held accountable.[122] This legally self-binding ability seems favourable, at least in cases in which *de lege lata* the group is bound by international law anyway.

Although it can be effectively argued that unilateral declarations have a binding effect on the group that issues them, the question of the legal nature of the agreement itself remains. Is it governed by international law or can its legal nature only be derived from the sovereign (domestic and political) decision of the responding State that engages the actor? Looking at State practice, evidence of States reacting to declarations by OAGs is fragmented,

---

120 Sivakumaran, 'Lessons' (n 113) 3-4. Groups such as the SLM-Unity in Darfur or the UNITA in Angola.

121 Nuclear Tests (*Australia v France*) (Judgment) [1974] ICJ Rep 253; Nuclear Tests (*New Zeland v France*) (Judgment) [1974] ICJ Rep 457; ILC, 'Guiding Principles applicable to unilateral declarations of States capable of creating legal obligations, with commentaries' (2006) UN Doc A/61/10, Guiding Principle 1.

122 In some cases, OAGs even go beyond the scope of existing international law. The Moro Islamic Liberation Front, for example, issued a declaration obliging itself to not conduct any operations that may cause collateral damage to civilians; see the Agreement on the Civilian Protection Component of the International Monitoring Team (20 October 2009) <http://www.opapp.gov.ph/sites/default/files/Terms_of_Reference_of_the_International_Monitoring_Team.pdf> accessed 27 March 2018. As far as a declaration exceeds existing international law, its involvement in the international legal process will remain at the political level only.

but existent. The accession to the 1997 Ottawa Convention[123] by the Sudanese government, for example, was said to be the result of a declaration issued by the SPLMA stating to be bound by it.[124] The recent peace agreement between the State of Colombia and the FARC or the ongoing negotiations between the Taliban and the Afghan government through an intermediary in Doha are further examples of States engaging in a legal agreement following declarations by OAGs to adhere to certain standards.

However, although these agreements did and will involve the implementation of obligations under international law, they remain within the sovereign decision and will of the negotiating State and, therefore, governed within its domestic sphere. Moreover, these agreements were deemed a national conciliation effort, but not a formal peace agreement which could be governed by international law. Nevertheless, international courts and tribunals tend to rely on those declarations as evidence for the international legal obligations of OAGs.[125] This, however, should only be interpreted as the exploration of the group's political intent to act and not as a direct influence on international legal practice. Its effect on international legal practice may only be an indirect one, as the conduct of the OAG in question certainly influences the State's conduct when dealing with it. Unilateral declarations by OAGs are therefore regulated by domestic law or, at most, have a *sui generis* character.

H. Accountability

Lastly, the question of a possible accountability of non-State actors for violations of IHL and human rights law should be briefly examined in order to complete the picture. International obligations may only come to their full effect, once they may also be enforced. The reparation for the damage caused may take the form of *restitutio in integrum*, monetary compensation or satisfaction, including a public apology with the acceptance of

---

123 Convention on the Prohibition of the Use, Stockpiling, Production and Transfer of Anti-Personnel Mines and their Destruction (opened for signature 18 September 1997, entered into force 1 March 1999) 2056 UNTS 211.

124 Roberts and Sivakumaran, 'Lawmaking by Nonstate Actors' (n 115)128-29.

125 See *Prosecutor v Akayesu* (n 22) para 627; Report of the UN Special Rapporteur on extrajudicial, summary or arbitrary Executions, 'Mission to Sri Lanka' (27 March 2006) UN Doc E/CN.4/2006/53/Add.5 para 30.

responsibility or guarantees of non-repetition.[126] Considering that the attribution of unlawful conduct and the hereby created obligation to compensate the damage caused is one of the core principles of international law, the inclusion of OAGs in this principle seems to be self-evident. However, existing compensation mechanisms mainly address States as the primary holders of international obligations for their unlawful conduct, most prominently the ASR. If the group succeeds in its insurrection, the question of responsibility is answered by Art. 10 ASR; thus, the group's conduct is retroactively treated as the conduct of a State. The question that remains is what happens in prolonged conflicts, where neither party can make decisive victories nor end the conflict. This especially holds true in the case of detention, where serious violations of international law occur.

Following the definition of OAGs set up above, requiring them to exercise effective control over a certain part of territory, and acting as de facto authorities, thereby conferring them a certain legal personality, it may not be farfetched though, to hold them accountable for their unlawful conduct.[127] As already argued above, ILC Special Rapporteur *Agos's* proposition that 'an insurrectional movement which establishes its authority over a State's territory becomes a '*separate subject of international law*' at the end of the 1960s is still valid in this context.[128] Even if we define international responsibility as 'legal relations which arise under international law by reason of an internationally wrongful act'[129], the decisive criterion for conferring those OAGs international legal responsibility is their actual capacity to fulfil those responsibilities and to

---

126 See UN SG, 'The Rule of Law and Transitional Justice in Conflict and Post-Conflict Societies' (23 August 2004) UN Doc S/2004/616 18-19.

127 Cf Ryngaert, 'Non-State Actors' (n 41) 4 et seq. For a further account in favour of the accountability of armed organised groups for violations under international law, see Jann Kleffner, 'The Collective accountability of organized armed groups for system crimes' in Harmen van der Wilt and Andre Nollkaemper (eds), *System Criminality in International Law* (CUP 2009) 238 (hereafter Kleffner, 'Collective accountability').

128 UNYBILC 1972/II 129; also earlier UNYBILC 1966/II 134.

129 Commentary on Art. 1 Draft ASR, UNYBILC 2001/II 31; See also UN GA, 'Basic Principles and Guidelines on the Right to a Remedy and Reparation for Victims of Violations of International Human Rights and Humanitarian Law' (21 March 2006) UN Doc A/Res/60/147, Basic Principle 15: '[i]n cases where a person, a legal person, or any other entity is found liable for reparation to a victim, such party should provide reparation to the victim or compensate the State, if the State has already provided reparation to the victim'.

enforce eventually existing claims against them, such as their 'jurisdiction to enforce'. Additionally, the mere establishment of an international responsibility *de jure* might not lead to a responsibility *de facto* for most OAGs, since the actual enforcement of those claims might prove difficult.

However, to this day, cases in which States hold OAGs responsible and accountable by international law and which could therefore be used as evidence for a broader existence of OAGs on the international plane, remain rare and selective incidents rather than precedents.[130] The only exception to this can be found in the US Alien Tort Claims Act[131]. Within the Alien-Tort-Claims-Act jurisprudence, cases can be found where the group as such is collectively held accountable for its actions.[132] Although legal proceedings are instigated at a national level, the applicable law within such cases remains international customary law; the cases are therefore used as supplementary evidence for the emergence or existence of a rule of law itself. However, this alone is not sufficient to serve as evidence for international custom, as it remains limited to the practice of the USA. The response by third parties on the international plane remains divided; States rather prefer to implement their international legal obligations into national law to avoid any interaction with those actors on the international legal plane.[133]

Setting aside the practical problems concerning the actual enforcement of claims, the international responsibility of OAGs for unlawful conduct therefore only remains a distant dream – if States deem it appropriate at all.[134] After all, the recognition of the existing mechanism of accountability

---

130 Crawford, *State Responsibility* (n 48) 81. For example, see the recommendation of the International Commission of Inquiry on Darfur to the UN SC, which noted that, apart from States, its agents or de facto organs, rebels and insurgents have a similar obligation to compensate for the crimes they committed, UN Commission of Inquiry on Darfur, 'Report of the International Commission of Inquiry on Darfur to the United Nations Secretary-General' (25 January 2000) para 600 <http://www.un.org/news/dh/sudan/com_inq_darfur.pdf> accessed 27 March 2018. Although Reports by International Commissions of Inquiry cannot be considered direct State practice, the recurrence on them may still be valid, as an auxiliary source of international law as in Art. 38 (1) (d) ICJ-Statute.

131 28 U.S.C. § 1350 (1994). Although the case may be tried before a national court, the applicable law in such cases will be customary international law.

132 Mohamad v Palestinian Authority (n 50); *Tel-Oren v Libyan Arab Republic* (n 50).

133 Crawford, *State Responsibility* (n 48) 81.

134 Kleffner, 'Collective accountability' (n 127) 250 also notes the practical issue of enforcement, but makes the argument for monitoring, compliance and sanctions with regard to their obligations.

of non-State actors outside the individual criminal responsibility will always be accompanied by some form of legitimisation. This, however, is something most, if not all, States certainly do not want to see happening.

I. Conclusion

For the time being, the deprivation of liberty by OAGs in areas of limited statehood remains an uneasy terrain. Although the legal obligations in CA 3 as well as, to a certain extent, Art. 4 and 5 of AP II (as far as they constitute customary international law) provide some protection to those captured in NIACs, the protection of human rights, especially those exceeding the scope of the 'minimum standards of humanity', which itself remains a rather murky concept, remains unsatisfactory *de lege lata* in most cases. The most common human rights treaties and the obligations set within their non-derogative provisions are not applicable to OAGs in general, as they exceed the protection provided by IHL. Although an argument can be made with respect to the principle of effectiveness in order to confer human rights obligations to these groups, future State practice will show whether international courts and State practice accept the idea of OAGs being involved in the delicate matter of detention to a more sophisticated level. Especially in cases when the principal organs of the State struggle to exercise control over the relative territory. Until then, it can only be restated that

> International Law is constantly evolving but still is State-centric in the way in which it is made and applied: treaties are made by States …, and customary law is formed primarily by State practice and State *opinio iuris*; international law still struggles to recognize entities other than States and IOs as legal persons.[135]

A resolution to this dilemma might be found at the policy level. Taking armed non-State actors seriously and engaging them as a legal actor in terms of policy on the international plane might be advantageous to all parties to the conflict, as reciprocal obligations offer the most effective contribution to the protection of civilians and other vulnerable persons in an armed conflict. This pragmatic conduct based on the engagement of OAGs without prejudice to status, ensuring their legality under national law and possible involvement into the international legal process might provide an effective tool to further one of the basic intentions of IHL: a humane conduct of hostilities.

---

135 Crawford and Pert, *IHL* (n 80) 261 et seq.

Comment: Detention by Armed Groups

Lars Müller

In his contribution, *Vincent Widdig* raised a number of questions concerning the role of armed groups in international law. To what extent are they bound by IHL or even IHRL? To what extent does this require them to possess a certain degree of legal personality and how could it be established? What are the further consequences of ascribing armed groups this kind of status? Would this legitimise their conduct and their goals on a political level? And would this also allow them to become law-makers, instead of mere law-takers, on a legal level? Finally, should armed groups be held accountable for their violations of international law?

All of the above are pertinent questions and inform us about the challenges international law, and especially IHL, faces in areas of limited statehood – where not only the exact meaning and scope of certain norms is contested, but the significance of international law itself is sometimes rejected.[1] We can approach these issues with the idea of ascribing armed

---

1 Concerning such a rejection by armed groups, see for example: Geneva Academy, 'Reactions to Norms: Armed Groups and the Protection of Civilians', Policy Briefing No. 1, (Geneva 2014) 13, 29 et seq; Olivier Bangerter, 'Reasons why armed groups choose to respect international humanitarian law or not' (2011) 882 IRRC 353, 380 et seq; Antonio Cassese, 'The Status of Rebels under the 1977 Geneva Protocol on Non-International Armed Conflicts' (1981) 30 ICLQ 416, 426; Andrew Clapham, 'The Rights and Responsibilities of Armed Non-State Actors: The Legal Landscape and Issues Surrounding Engagement' (Geneva Academy 2010) 23; Jann K. Kleffner, 'The applicability of international humanitarian law to organized armed groups' (2011) 93 IRRC 443, 446 (hereafter Kleffner, 'The applicability of international humanitarian law'); Michelle Mack, *Increasing Respect for International Humanitarian Law in Non-International Armed Conflicts* (ICRC 2008) 11; Anthea Roberts and Sandesh Sivakumaran, 'Lawmaking by Non-State Actors: Engaging Armed Groups in the Creation of International Humanitarian Law' (2012) 37 Yale J. Int'l L 107, 127.
However, also governments reject the applicability of international law in their conflict zones from time to time: Secretary-General, 'Minimum humanitarian standards: Analytical report of the Secretary-General submitted persuant to Commission on Human Rights resolution 1997/21' UN Doc E/CN.4/1998/87

groups a certain legal personality or capacity, thereby explaining that such groups are bound by international law obligations, but also prompting the conclusion that they could, or at least should, take part in the creation of international law.[2] This is one of the ideas international law is based on – sovereign equality, meaning that one should only be bound by rules one consented to. Hence, States either negotiate the law in State conferences or through their conduct on the battlefield, or at least they create their own obligations by adhering to a certain instrument or by not persistently objecting to a certain practice.

So, can we identify this kind of synchronicity of law-creation and corresponding obligations in the law of armed conflict or do we rather see non-State actors as being bound without having any influence? The fact that armed groups and their members are bound by and have obligations under international law – and can even be held accountable for their violations – seems to be settled.[3] The scope of these obligations is sometimes challenged, but that also holds true for States involved in NIACs, as for

(5 January 1998) 20; Michelle Mack, *Increasing Respect for International Humanitarian Law in Non-International Armed Conflicts* (ICRC 2008) 11; Theodor Meron, 'The Humanization of Humanitarian Law' (2000) 94 AJIL 239, 260 et seq; Lindsay Moir, *The Law of Internal Armed Conflict* (CUP 2002) 34, 67 et seq, 85 et seq (hereafter Moir, *The Law of Internal Armed Conflict*); Antonio Cassese, 'The Status of Rebels under the 1977 Geneva Protocol on Non-International Armed Conflicts' (1981) 30 ICLQ 416, 426; Dawn Steinhoff, 'Talking to the Enemy: State Legitimacy Concerns with Engaging Non-State Armed Groups' (2009) 45 Texas International Law Journal 297, 313.

2 On the concepts and consequences of international legal personality, see especially Janne E. Nijman, *The Concept of International Legal Personality: An Inquiry Into the History and Theory of International Law* (TMC Asser Press 2004) and Roland Portmann, *Legal Personality in International Law* (CUP 2010).

3 *Prosecutor v Akayesu* (Judgment) IT-96-4-T (2 September 1998) 617; *Prosecutor v Tadic* (Decision on the Defence Motion for Interlocutory Appeal on Jurisdiction) IT-94-1-AR72 (2 October 1995) 134; Kleffner, 'The applicability of international humanitarian law' (n 1) 445; Moir, *The Law of Internal Armed Conflict* (n 1) 53; Daragh Murray, 'How International Humanitarian Law Treaties Bind Non-State Armed Groups' (2015) 20 JCSL 101, 122; Marco Sassòli, Antoine Bouvier and Anne Quintin, *How Does Law Protect in War*, vol. I (ICRC 2011) chapter 12, 25 et seq.

example the debate on the power of the UK's armed forces to detain in the conflict in Afghanistan demonstrates.[4]

What hereby becomes apparent is the complete disregard of States and international organisations involved in the debate on the role of armed groups in international law, for the idea of international law being made by those who are bound by it. When we try to argue against that, we should analyse whether international law really accepts actors as being treated as mere objects or whether there is something in the law which might trigger a change of status from object to subject – at least in a limited area of the law.

Vincent Widdig correctly mentioned the principle of effectiveness in this regard. IHL is meant to effectively protect individuals from the consequences of war as far as possible. In contrast to most other fields of law, IHL refrains from taking into account the status of an actor and simply prescribes norms of behaviour to all those engaging in armed conduct. Therefore, the rules are formulated to either apply to each 'party to the conflict',[5] or do not mention the actor at all and simply prescribe that 'the wounded and sick shall be respected and protected in all circumstances'.[6]

In this sense, I would argue that IHL also effectively accepts attempts by any actor within an armed conflict to adjust the rules to the specific conflict or to expand the protection provided by its rules. Even if we understand international law to generally remain a State-centric system – and there are many reasons to do so – IHL already accepts other actors. Consider CA 3, which provides:

> The Parties to the conflict should further endeavor to bring into force, by means of special agreements, all or part of the other provisions of the present Convention.

Likewise, the UNESCO Convention on the protection of cultural property in armed conflicts[7] by itself includes only a limited protection regime in case of NIACs, but again provides in Art. 19 (2) that

---

4 Manuel Brunner, 'Detention for Security Reasons by the Armed Forces of a State in Situations of Non-International Armed Conflict: The Quest for a Legal Basis' in this volume 89.

5 For example, CA 3 (1).

6 For example, Art. 12 GC I; Art. 7 AP II.

7 Convention for the Protection of Cultural Property in the Event of Armed Conflict (opened for signature 14 May 1954, entered into force 7 August 1956) UNTS 249.

> The parties to the Conflict shall endeavor to bring into force, by means of special agreements, all or part of the other provisions of the present Convention.

Other treaties follow this example. In addition to this, all of them include a caveat,[8] stating:

> The application of the preceding provisions shall not affect the legal status of the parties to the conflict.

IHL, thus, already allows armed groups to change from mere objects of the law to real subjects, who are able to influence, at least in part, the law as it applies to their respective armed conflict. The trigger mechanism seems to be that the armed group must effectively be able to, first, engage in an armed conflict, and, second, to force their enemy into negotiating an agreement.

In other words: If an actor is in a position to effectively make the law applicable in a specific armed conflict, IHL will not ask for this actor to provide some further international status or legitimacy, but it will simply attempt to steer that actor's conduct on the battlefield and his law-making activities into certain directions, thus trying to maintain, or even to improve, the protection provided by IHL.

This also brings us back to the contribution by *Katja Schöberl* and *Linus Mührel* on the permissive and/or restrictive nature of IHL.[9] If this law is simply trying to steer the behaviour of those engaged in an armed conflict reaching a certain threshold, its goal is not to permit or otherwise legitimise this action as such. IHL, as the *jus in bello*, is concerned with how parties to a conflict behave, not about whether they should engage in an armed conflict at all. In the same way, it does not permit or forbid detention by armed groups, but rather provides certain standards to be observed during detention.

Looking at the applicable domestic law, we have to expect a totally different picture. States usually prohibit non-State actors from carrying out armed attacks as well as from detaining people, especially when this concerns the State's own armed forces. Here again, IHL does neither permit

---

8 For an early example, see Art. 152-55 of the Lieber Code (Instructions for the Government of Armies of the United States in the Field, prepared by Francis Lieber, promulgated as General Orders No. 100 by President Lincoln, 24. April 1863); see also African Union Convention for the Protection and Assistance of Internally Displaced Persons in Africa (Kampala Convention) (adopted 23 October 2009, entered into force 6 December 2012).

9 Katja Schöberl and Linus Mührel, 'Sunken Vessel or Blooming Flower? Lotus, Permissions and Restrictions within International Humanitarian Law' in this volume 59.

nor forbid States to prohibit non-State actors from doing so. This is articulated in Art. 6 (5) AP II, which states that

> … at the end of hostilities, the authorities in power shall endeavor to grant the broadest possible amnesty to persons who have participated in the armed conflict …

Thus, States are not obliged to accept activities by non-State armed groups, but are merely requested to contemplate amnesties at the end of hostilities. And not only States are asked to do so, but also 'the authorities in power'. As many post-conflict situations around the world have demonstrated, 'the authorities in power' are often not simply the government which has defeated a domestic armed group, or an armed group that has taken over State authority, but it is frequently both of them. Most internal armed conflicts are not terminated by the complete defeat of one party to the conflict, but by a negotiated settlement between the parties.[10] So, here again, IHL provides a way for armed groups to have an impact on the law, this time at the end of hostilities.

What all of this tells us is that, when trying to assess the law of detention in NIACs or any other aspect of this law, we should not limit ourselves by looking only into the universal treaties and customs of IHL, IHRL or even domestic law. Instead, we must consider agreements made between the parties to the specific conflict and what they provide, for example on detention. Looking ahead, the parties to armed conflicts should be encouraged to conclude such agreements, as they not only raise awareness for IHL in the first place, but also allow to translate the law into the specific context and, lastly, provide more legitimacy as both parties mutually agree to be bound by them.

10 Sidney D. Bailey, *How Wars End: The United Nations and the Termination of Armed Conflict 1946-1964*, vol. I (Clarendon Press 1982); David M. Morriss, 'From War to Peace: A Study of Cease-Fire Agreements and the Evolving Role of the United Nations' (1996) 36 VJIL 801.

Part III:
International Humanitarian Law and International Investment Law

Foreign Investments as Non-Human Targets

Ira Ryk-Lakhman Aharonovich

A. Introduction

On 23 July 1983, the LTTE, a separatist Sri Lankan militant group that was fighting for Tamil independence, ambushed and killed 13 Sri-Lankan soldiers. Over the next week, Sinhalese Sri Lankans, with the government's support, retaliated with Tamil blood shed across the country. These events ignited the 25-year civil war between the government and the LTTE. Shortly thereafter, the State created the Special Task Force (STF) to head counter-terrorism missions against the LTTE. By 1987, STF units were mainly deployed in the Batticaloa district, which quickly turned the area into a bloody battlefield.[1]

On 28 January 1987, an STF unit broke into a shrimp farm owned by Serendib Seafoods Ltd. in Batticaloa, which had been suspected of harbouring LTTE separatists.[2] Within hours, Serendib's manager and a dozen more employees were shot to death, yet not a single LTTE separatist was found on site. Before leaving, the STF destroyed the farm, causing it to go out of business. Accordingly, AAPL, a Hong Kong corporation which half-owned Serendib, filed an investment claim against Sri Lanka under the Sri Lanka – UK BIT,[3] claiming compensation for the losses. The *AAPL v Sri Lanka* Tribunal mostly accepted the claim and held that by failing to use less-deadly means and methods in its military operation, the State breached the BIT obligation to act in due diligence so as to protect the physical integrity of the investment. The Tribunal however, paid little attention to

1 Human Rights Watch, 'State Responsibility for "Disappearances" and Abductions in Sri Lanka', Section IV <https://www.hrw.org/reports/2008/srilanka0308/4.htm#_ftnref136> accessed 23 November 2017.

2 *Asian Agricultural Products Ltd v Sri Lanka* (Final Award) (1991) ICSID case No ARB/87/3 30 ILM 580 (hereafter *AAPL v Sri Lanka*).

3 UK-Sri Lanka BIT (1980). Unless explicitly stated otherwise, all investment treaties cited herein are available at UNCTAD – international investment agreement navigator http://investmentpolicyhub.unctad.org/IIA accessed 23 November 2017. For purposes of convenience these treaties are cited by their abbreviated version.

the existence of the protracted war in Sri Lanka, and made no reference to the laws that regulate the conduct of hostilities.

A similar occurrence concerned Kinshasa in the DRC, where Mr Mitchell had operated a boutique law firm, Mitchell & Associates. In March 1999, under a military court order that cited grounds of alleged illegal collaboration between the firm and the rebels, Congolese armed forces burst into the firm. They forcefully dragged the employees for detention, shuttered the business, sealed the premises, damaged the property, and seized several documents. Consequently, Mr Mitchell brought an investment claim against the State under the US-Zaire BIT arguing,[4] *inter alia*, that his investment was expropriated as a result of the State measures.

The State's primary defence was that the law firm did not qualify as an 'investment' and thus did not benefit from the standards of protection under the BIT. This objection was rejected by the *Mitchell v DRC* Tribunal. It held that the BIT's definition of 'investment', which covered 'service contracts', was wide enough to encompass the services of Mitchell & Associates. Since the Tribunal determined that the firm was a covered investment, which benefited from certain protection, it also held that the firm was expropriated as a result of the military operation.[5] Pertinently, at the time of the events subject-matter of the claim, Kinshasa was a conflict-ridden area, and the DRC was in the midst of the Great African War that had commenced in August 1998.[6] Nevertheless, neither the Tribunal nor the *ad hoc* annulment Committee, which annulled the award on grounds that the firm did not constitute an 'investment'[7] engaged in an IHL analysis in the assessment of the attack.

These examples illustrate that in practice investments may be the subject of military attacks. Yet in these cases, the lawfulness of the attacks was assessed in isolation from IHL; the tribunals focused rather on the classification of the object under the BIT's definition of 'investment' and on the standards of protection that were conferred upon this investment under the treaty. Nevertheless, these instances raise the question whether investments, in the forms of tangible economic objects, are in fact protected from direct and deliberate attacks or whether they can be lawfully targeted

4 US-DRC (formally Zaire) BIT (1989).

5 *Mitchell v Democratic Republic of the Congo* (Award) (2004) ICSID case No ARB/99/7.

6 Filip Reyntjens, The Great African War: Congo and Regional Geopolitics (CUP 2010), see generally 1-10 and chapter 7.

7 *Mitchell v Democratic Republic of the Congo* (Decision on the Application for Annulment) (2006) ICSID case No ARB/99/7, 25-33.

under certain circumstances. The answer to this question, it is argued, turns not only on the treatment that investment law prescribes for certain assets, but also on the treatment of these objects under IHL and the principles of distinction more specifically.

Distinction is a fundamental and 'intransgressible' principle of customary international law. It is anchored in Art. 48 of AP I, which mandates that attacks may be directed 'only against military objectives', while 'civilian objects shall not be the object of attack'.[8] The classification of investments under this principle may appear deceptively simple, since the term 'investment' is used in everyday language which forms the perception that it is necessarily a civilian economic asset that denotes a shared understanding. This classification however is far more complex in practice.

Accordingly, Section 2 establishes that the concept 'investment' encompasses a wide array of objects. An investment is potentially any economic asset in any sector that is owned or controlled by a foreign national. Such assets benefit from certain treaty standards of protection that remain operational during hostilities.[9] At the same time, Section 3 demonstrates that the scope of permitted targets under the definition of 'military objective' is as wide. Often objects are classified as targets for the economic sector in which they operate and for their ability to generate profits.

Building on the foregoing, Section 4 addresses the classification of investments into military objectives and civilian objects, and examines when, if at all, investments may be classified as lawful targets. Additionally, it is argued that the concrete rules that emanate from any such classification may result in a norm conflict, whereby what is permitted or required under IHL is prohibited under investment law. This norm conflict affects the treatment and protection of investments during hostilities and the invocation of international responsibility of the host State thereof.

---

8 Art. 48, 51 (2) and 52 AP I; Legality of the Threat or Use of Nuclear Weapons (Advisory Opinion) [1996] ICJ Rep 226, 257; Yoram Dinstein, 'Legitimate Military Objectives Under The Current Jus In Bello' (2002) 78 ILS 139, 139 (hereafter Dinstein, 'Legitimate military objectives').

9 Art. 3, 4, 7, and the Annex to Art. 7 ILC Draft Articles on the Effects of Armed Conflict on Treaties, Official Records of the General Assembly, Sixty-sixth Session, Supp 10, UN Doc A/66/10 <http://www.un.org/ga/search/view_doc.asp?symbol=a/res/66/99> accessed 9 December 2016.

B. The Classification of Assets under Investment Law

This section focuses on the classification of tangible economic objects under investment law and the international obligations that result thereof. Overall, this section establishes that 'investment' encompasses a very wide array of tangible objects in various economic sectors, that benefit from certain protections, in peacetime and hostilities.

International law of foreign investment is a field of public international law that is mostly regulated by investment treaties. This legal regime was described as the combination of substantive protections for foreign investors and investments, with remedial procedures that serve to enforce these protections.[10] Thus explained, the concepts of 'investment' and 'investor' are the foundations of investment law. The term 'investment' determines economic interests, to which States extend substantive protections in investment treaties, while the term 'investor' specifies the range of legal and natural persons who stand to benefit from any such treaty. The centrality of 'investment' notwithstanding, the concept has no universally accepted definition.

In economic parlance, a foreign direct investment, as opposed to a portfolio investment, entails, *inter alia*, regular income, long-term relationship, and business risk. The parlance of investment treaties however, goes beyond the meaning associated with economics. 'Investment' is defined in each instrument independently in a manner that arguably reflects the contractual bargain between the particular State parties to the treaty.[11] In this sense, the treaty definition serves to identify the types of investments that capital-importing States wish to attract and to ascertain the types of investments capital-exporting countries wish to protect overseas. Because treaties are forward-looking and since technology and provision of services is ever-evolving, there is some difficulty with defining 'investment' in exhaustive terms.

10 Julian D Mortenson, 'The Meaning of "Investment": ICSID's Travaux and the Domain of International Investment Law' (2010) 51(1) Harv. Int'l L. J. 257, 262.

11 Zachary Douglas, *The International Law of Investment Claims* (CUP 2009) 161-65.

To this end, two main approaches have developed in treaty practice.[12] The first approach uses an open-ended asset-based definition. In these cases, 'investment' is defined as 'every kind of asset' or 'any kind of asset', often accompanied by a non-exhaustive list of examples. For instance, the Albania-Cyprus BIT defines 'investment' as 'every kind of asset and in particular, although not exclusively, the following...'.[13] The second commonly found approach uses principle-based definitions, which elucidate the concept by reference to the economic features of an investment, frequently using an illustrative list. For example, the Morocco-Nigeria BIT defines 'investment' as:

> An enterprise within the territory of one State established, acquired, expanded or operated, in good faith, by an investor of the other State in accordance with law of the Party in whose territory the investment is made taken together with the asset of the enterprise which *contribute sustainable development of that Party and has the characteristics of an investment* involving a commitment of capital or other similar resources, pending profit, risk-taking and certain duration. An enterprise will possess the following assets ... For greater certainty, Investment does not include ...[14]

Recent investment instruments have attempted to develop a more nuanced definition by way of using a combination of both approaches and a list of inclusive and exclusive examples. Art. 8.1 of the EU-Canada Comprehensive Economic and Trade Agreement, for instance, reads:

> Investment means *every kind of asset* ... that has the *characteristics of an investment*, which includes certain duration and other characteristics such as the commitment of capital or other resources, the expectation of gain or profit, or the assumption of risk. Forms that an investment may take include ...[15]

The content and scope of these treaty definitions is asserted by way of treaty interpretation.[16] Thus, no particular debate arises over the classification of an object that is enumerated under the treaty.[17] Likewise, if the treaty provides for an asset-based definition, then 'the definition is open, general

---

12 Rudolf Dolzer and Christopher Schreuer, *Principles of International Investment Law* (2nd edn, OUP 2012) 62 et seq (hereafter Dolzer and Schreuer, *Principles of Investment Law*).

13 Art. 1 of the Albania-Cyprus BIT (2010).

14 Art. 1 of the Nigeria-Morocco BIT (2016) (emphasis added).

15 Emphasis added.

16 Art. 31 VCLT.

17 *Petrobart Limited v The Kyrgyz Republic* (Award) (2005) SCC case No 126/2003 24.

and not restricted'[18] and any economic asset could potentially qualify as an investment.

However, the growth of investment treaty disputes illustrated the implications of using broad treaty definitions of 'investment'. Arguably, States are often surprised at the type of asset that is considered as an investment under the relevant treaty, in that the meaning of 'investment' had been extended beyond what was envisaged by the host State. This results in frequent challenges of the jurisdiction of arbitral tribunals on the ground that the investor's assets do not constitute an investment. In response, arbitral tribunals that were constituted under the ICSID Convention, which limits the jurisdiction of the tribunal to legal disputes 'arising directly out of an investment',[19] but does not define the term, attempted to provide an 'objective' elucidation of 'investment'. Practically this means that the investor needs to demonstrate to the ICSID tribunal that the asset at bar meets the definition of 'investment' under both the applicable treaty 'and' Art. 25 of the ICSID Convention.

This 'objective' definition is commonly known as the '*Salini* criteria', whereby 'investment' entails: (a) duration, (b) regularity of profit and return, (c) assumption of risk, (d) substantive commitment, and (e) contribution to the host State's development.[20] To be sure, these criteria are far from widely accepted. For the purposes of the present discussion however several debates over the issue are put aside.[21] Namely, the relative weight of each of these features;[22] whether these are cumulative prerequisites, facultative characteristics, or an attempt to read into treaty

---

18 *RREEF v Spain* (Decision on Jurisdiction) (2016) ICSID case No ARB/13/30 156-60 (hereafter *RREEF v Spain*).

19 Art. 25 ICSID Convention.

20 *Fedax NV v Venezuela* (Award on Jurisdiction) (1997) ICSID case No ARB/96/03, 43; *Salini Costruttori SpA v Morocco* (Decision on Jurisdiction) (2001) ICSID Case No ARB/00/4 52; *Joy Mining v Egypt* (Award) (2004) ICSID case No ARB/03/11 53.

21 See *Beijing Urban Construction v Yemen* (Decision on Jurisdiction) (2017) ICSID case No ARB/14/30 124-38; David Williams and Simone Foote, 'Recent developments in the approach to identifying an "investment" pursuant to Article 25(1) of the ICSID Convention' in Chester Brown and Kate Miles (eds), *Evolution in Investment Treaty Law and Arbitration* (CUP 2011) 42.

22 *LESI SpA v Algeria* ICSID Case No ARB/05/3, Decision on Jurisdiction, 12 July 2006, para 72; *Bayindir v Pakistan* (Decision on Jurisdiction) (2005) ICSID case No ARB/03/29 131.

definitions what is simply not there;[23] and, whether these parameters apply only to disputes conducted under the ICSID Convention, to all investment claims, or not at all.[24] Nonetheless, at its lowest it may be said that the objective *Salini* criteria for 'investment' reflect the features that are mostly found in treaty definitions, economics, and investment practice.

Finally, the determination if a given asset is an 'investment' is detached from its area of economic activity. The protection of objects under investment law is independent from and non-contingent upon economic sectors. In practice, tribunals have exercised jurisdiction over a wide array of diverse economic activities and States indeed seek to promote and facilitate investment inflows in various sectors.[25]

The corollary of the classification of an asset as an 'investment' is that this object benefits from certain standards of protection. One such common standard, which was at the heart of the *AAPL* dispute, is 'full protection and security' (FPS). This provision requires states to take feasible precautions so as to protect investments from violence whether authored by the State or by a third party. It has been said to be designed to protect investments against violent actions, in particular during hostilities.[26] Another notable

23 *MCI v Ecuador* (Award) (2007) ICSID Case No ARB/03/6 165; *Malaysian Historical Salvors v Malaysia* (Award on Jurisdiction) (2007) ICSID Case No ARB/05/10; *Malaysian Historical Salvors v Malaysia* (Decision on the Application for Annulment) (2009) ICSID Case No ARB/05/10; *RREEF v Spain* (n 18) 156-60.

24 *Romak SA v Uzbekistan* (Award) (2009) UNCITRAL, PCA Case 173-243; *Alps Finance and Trade v Slovakia* (Award) (2011) UNCITRAL 240–241.

25 ICSID, 'Annual Report 2017' 33 et seq <https://icsid.worldbank.org/en/Documents/icsiddocs/ICSID%20AR%20EN.pdf> accessed 10 November 2017.

26 For arbitral jurisprudence, See *AAPL v Sri Lanka* (n 2) 77; *AMT v Zaire* (Award) (1997) ICSID case No ARB/93/1 6.05; *Tecmed v The Mexico*(Award) (2003) ICSID case No ARB (AF)/00/2 177; *Saluka v Czech Republic* (Partial Award) (2006) UNCITRAL 483 *PSEG v Turkey* (Award) (2007) ICSID case No ARB/02/5 258; *Pantechniki v Albania* (Award) (2007) ICSID case No ARB/07/2171-4; *Houben v Burundi* (Award) (2016) ICSID case No ARB/13/7 160-64. For scholarship see Giuditta Cordero-Moss, 'Full protection and security' in August Reinisch (ed), *Standards of Investment Protection* (OUP 2008) 134-39; Christopher Schreuer, 'Full Protection and Security' (2010) Journal of International Dispute Settlement 354; Helge Elisabeth Zeitler, 'Full protection and Security' in Stephan Schill (ed), *International Investment Law and Comparative Public Law* (OUP 2010) 183, 201; David Collins, 'Applying Full Protection and Security Standard of International Investment Law to Digital Assets' (2010) 12 Journal of World Investment & Trade 225; Cristopher

standard of protection, which was found to have been breached in the matter of *Mitchell v DRC*, concerns the dispossession of property. Almost all investment treaties recognise the right of States to expropriate investments as long as the taking is for a public purpose, in a non-discriminatory manner, under due process, and in return for compensation.[27] Finally, if a certain object constitutes an 'investment' that is owned or controlled by an investor, then the investor may also benefit from direct recourse to international adjudication.[28] There, he will be able to invoke the violation of, say, FPS, and claim reparations for losses owing to armed conflict.

In outline, the term investment potentially concerns a very wide scope of assets that are owned or controlled by foreign nationals. This definition, due to its width, confers certain standards of protection, in peacetime and hostilities, upon a varied range of tangible objects. Yet, the above referenced cases of *AAPL* and *Mitchell* demonstrate that in the reality of hostilities the determination that an asset is an 'investment' does not translate into its inviolability from attacks. In fact, it appears that the treatment of such investments during hostilities is predicated on a completely separate set of considerations. These considerations arguably stem from IHL and are therefore examined at the next step.

C. *The Classification of Commercial Objects under International Humanitarian Law*

This section focuses on the classification of tangible economic objects under IHL. The discussion below, first, analyses the wording of Art. 52 (2) AP I, which prescribes the binding definition of military objectives; and second, on two classes of targets that originate therefrom. This section demonstrates that the wide definition of 'military objectives' potentially allows for the deliberate destruction of objects, *inter alia*, for the economic sector in which the object operates and, for the financial contribution and profits that the object generates.

Schreuer, 'The protection of investments in armed conflicts' in Freya Baetens (ed), *Investment Law within International Law: Integrative Perspectives* (CUP 2013) 6.

27 Dolzer and Schreuer, *Principles of Investment Law* (n 12) chapter VI.

28 Subject to the provisions of the relevant treaty and issues of jurisdiction and admissibility.

Whereas 'investment' lies at the heart of investment law, the principle of distinction is the cornerstone of all IHL instruments. It mandates that attacks may be directed 'only against military objectives', while 'civilian objects shall not be the object of attack'.[29] Notwithstanding the centrality of this term, IHL defines 'civilian objects' *a contrario*, thus a civilian object is one which is not a 'military objective'.[30] This means that to learn what a protected object is, it is first necessary to identify what is a targetable objective. Art. 52 (2) AP I, which is widely recognized as customary law,[31] sets out the two-pronged definition of 'military objectives', whereby:

> [M]ilitary objectives are limited to those objects which by their nature, location, purpose or use make an effective contribution to military action and whose total or partial destruction, capture or neutralization, in the circumstances ruling at the time, offers a definite military advantage.[32]

Under the first prong of Art. 52 (2) AP I, the targetability of an object is determined by the examination of its use and function with the armed forces.[33] In this sense, an object can offer an 'effective contribution' to the military in four possible ways – nature, location, purpose, or use.[34] The

29 Art. 48, 51 (2), 52, AP I.

30 Art. 51 (1), AP I.

31 Jean-Marie Henckaerts and Louise Doswald-Beck, *Customary International Humanitarian Law*, vol. II: Practice (CUP 2009) practice on Rule 8. The most updated version of this authority is fully available online https://ihl-databases.icrc.org/customary-ihl/eng/docs/home accessed 23 November 2017 (hereafter ICRC Customary IHL Study). See also Horace B Robertson Jr., 'The Principle of the Military Objective in the Law of Armed Conflict' (1998) ILS 197, 201-4 (hereafter Robertson, 'The Principle of the Military Objective'); Julie Gaudreau, 'The reservations to the Protocols additional to the Geneva Conventions for the protection of war victims' (2003) 849 IRRC 143, 159-60; Yoram Dinstein, 'Legitimate Military Objectives' (n 8) 140; Ian Henderson, *The Contemporary Law of Targeting: Military Objectives, Proportionality and Precautions in Attach under AP I* (Martinus Nijhoff Publishers 2009) 51 (hereafter Henderson, *The Contemporary Law of Targeting*); Sandesh Sivakumaran *The Law of Non-International Armed Conflicts* (OUP 2012) 344 (hereafter Sivakumaran, *The Law of Non-International Armed Conflicts*); Stefan Oeter, 'Methods and Means of Combat' in Dieter Fleck (ed), *The Handbook of Humanitarian Law in Armed Conflicts* (3rd edn, OUP 2013) 170-71.

32 Art. 52 (2) AP I.

33 Henderson, *The Contemporary Law of Targeting* (n 31) 55.

34 Michael N. Schmitt, 'Fault Lines in the Law of Attack' in Susan Breau and Agnieszka Jachec-Neale (eds), *Testing the Boundaries of International*

criterion of 'location' concerns the geographical features of the object.[35] Civilian buildings, for instance, may become military objectives if they 'obstruct the field of fire for an attack on another valid military objective.'[36] An object that is 'owned or usually controlled' by the armed forces,[37] and possesses 'intrinsic military significance',[38] would qualify as a military objective by its 'nature'.[39] Such objects may include headquarters, military aircraft, and enemy warships.[40] 'Use' refers to the object's actual usage by the forces, i.e. whether it is presently used militarily either by the military itself or in a manner which benefits the forces.[41] Finally, 'military purpose' is construed from an established intention of the belligerent as regards 'future' use. Note, the purpose of an object refers to the adversary's known intentions, not to 'those figured out hypothetically in contingency plans'.[42]

At the next step, it is necessary to address the required level of 'effective contribution' that turns an object to a potential target. The original wording of the provision, as suggested by the ICRC, was concerned with objects that 'contribute effectively and *directly* to the military effort'. This qualifier however was deliberately omitted.[43] Beyond the drafting history of the provision, State practice indicates that 'effective contribution' comprises

---

Humanitarian Law (British Institute of International and Comparative Law 2006) 277, 278-80 (hereafter Schmitt, 'Fault Lines').

35 Ibid, 280.

36 Robertson, 'The Principle of the Military Objective' (n 31) 209.

37 Yaves Sandoz et al (eds), *Commentary on the Additional Protocols of 8 June 1977 to the Geneva Conventions of 12 August 1949* (Martinus Nijhoff 1987) 2020 (hereafter Sandoz et al, *AP I Commentary*)

38 Schmitt, 'Fault Lines' (n 34) 280.

39 Sandoz et al, *AP I Commentary* (n 37) 2020-2021; Dinstein, 'Legitimate military objectives' (n 8) 145-47; Henderson, *The Contemporary Law of Targeting* (n 31) 55-56.

40 Unless these objects were specifically exempt eg if aircrafts are used for medical transport.

41 Schmitt, 'Fault Lines' (n 34) 280; Henderson, *The Contemporary Law of Targeting* (n 31) 59.

42 Sandoz et al, *AP I Commentary* (n 37) 2022; Schmitt, 'Fault Lines in the Law of Attack' (n 34) 280; Dinstein, 'Legitimate military objectives' (n 8) 148; Henderson, *The Contemporary Law of Targeting* (n 31) 59-60; Sivakumaran, *The Law of Non-International Armed Conflicts* (n 31) 344.

43 Conference of Government Experts on the Reaffirmation and Development of International Humanitarian Law Applicable in Armed Conflicts (Second Session, Geneva, 3 May-3 June 1972), vol. I, 146-47, para 3.141 (emphasis added).

not only direct, but indirect contributions to the military action.[44] Thus, 'effective' does not denote a linear correlation or a direct causation, between the object and its military contribution.

Under the second-prong of Art. 52 (2), it is necessary to determine that given the circumstances 'ruling at the time', the 'total or partial destruction, capture or neutralization' of the objective 'offers a definite military advantage' to the military 'action'. The language 'circumstances ruling at the time' is inherent to IHL and to the notion that a conduct in warfare is to be assessed in consideration to all factors and existing possibilities as they appeared to the commander at the time.[45] A definite military advantage, in turn, is a term of limitation that requires a 'concrete' and perceptible military advantage rather than a 'hypothetical and speculative one'.[46] This means that there should be a reasonable connection between the destruction of property and the overcoming of the enemy forces.[47]

As regards the threshold 'definite', the drafting history of Art. 52 (2) AP I teaches that an 'extensive discussion took place' before agreement was

---

44 Human Rights Watch, 'Needless Deaths in the Gulf War: Civilian Casualties during the Air Campaign and Violations of the Laws of War', part 1, chapter 1 (1991) <https://www.hrw.org/reports/1991/gulfwar/CHAP1.htm> accessed 29 March 2017; Human Rights Watch, 'Off Target: The Conduct of the War and Civilian Casualties in Iraq II' (11 December 2003) <https://www.hrw.org/report/2003/12/11/target/conduct-war-and-civilian-casualties-iraq> accessed 30 July 2017.

45 *The United States of America v Wilhelm List, et al* (Judgment (Military Tribunal V)) (1948) case No 47 in Michael N. Schmitt (ed), *Yearbook of International Humanitarian Law – 2010* (Springer 2010) 234; Eric Jensen, 'Article 58 and Precautions against the Effects of Attacks in Urban Areas' (2016) 98 IRRC 147, 166.

46 Henderson, *The Contemporary Law of Targeting* (n 31) 63; Yoram Dinstein, *The Conduct of Hostilities under the Law of International Armed Conflict* (2nd edn, CUP 2010) 106 (hereafter Dinstein, *The Conduct of Hostilities*); Sivakumaran, *The Law of Non-International Armed Conflicts* (n 31) 346; Michael Bothe et al, *New rules for victims of armed conflicts: commentary on the two 1977 protocols additional to the Geneva Conventions of 1949* (2nd edn, Martinus Nijhoff 2013) 367 (hereafter Bothe et al, *New rules for victims of armed conflicts*).

47 Declaration Renouncing the Use, in Time of War, of Explosive Projectiles Under 400 Grammes Weight (adopted 11 December 1868, entered into force 29 November/11 December 1868) 138 Consol TS 297 (hereafter St. Petersburg Declaration) Preamble; Bothe et al, *New rules for victims of armed conflicts* (n 46) 367; Henderson, *The Contemporary Law of Targeting* (n 31) 62; Sivakumaran, *The Law of Non-International Armed Conflicts* (n 31) 346-47.

reached on the word 'definite'. Among the qualifiers that had been considered and rejected at the Diplomatic Conference were: 'distinct', 'direct', 'clear', 'immediate', 'obvious', 'specific', and 'substantial'.[48] The intentional rejection of these adjectives indicates that Art. 52 (2) AP I aims at a lower standard. As for its scope, a military advantage is not restricted to 'tactical gains'; the spectrum is necessarily wide, and it extends to the security of the attacking force.[49] Importantly, Art. 52 (2) AP I clarifies that any such 'definite advantage' ought to be of a 'military' category, character, or nature. This 'military' modifier excludes economic, civil, political, or national advantages from the scope of Art. 52 (2) AP I.[50] In sum, the definition of military objectives leaves a lot to be desired. In practice, this ambiguity resulted in several contentious classes of targets, namely dual-use and revenue-generating targets that are addressed below.

For the purpose of the present discussion, suffice it to explain that, in warfare particularly, the military also uses civilian infrastructure, telecommunications, and logistics. Objects which have both a civilian and a military application are commonly known as 'dual-use objects'. To illustrate, power-generating stations are used not only to grant civilians the access to clean water, but also to provide power to war industries.[51]

It is not plentifully clear that Art. 52 (2) AP I covers these targets. The provision focuses on the military contribution of the object, but pays no attention to the object's contribution to civilian life. This arguably indicates that the civilian benefits of an object are of little to no significance to its

---

48 Official Records of the Diplomatic Conference on the Reaffirmation and Development of International Humanitarian Law Applicable in Armed Conflicts, Geneva (1974–7) vol XV, CDDH/215/Rev. 1, 277, para 64.

49 James Burger, 'International humanitarian law and the Kosovo crisis: Lessons learned or to be learned' (2000) 82 IRRC 129, 132; Dinstein, 'Legitimate military objectives' (n 8) 144; US General Counsel of Department of State, *Department of Defence - Law War Manual* (June 2015, revised February 2016) section 5.7.7.3 (hereafter DoD LOAC Manual); ICRC Customary IHL Study (n 31) practice relating to Rule 8.

50 St. Petersburg Declaration (n 47) Preamble, prohibits any forms of economic activities; Sandoz et al, *AP I Commentary* (n 37) 2018 et seq; Henderson, *The Contemporary Law of Targeting* (n 31) 61; Dinstein, *The Conduct of Hostilities* (n 46) 108; Michael N. Schmitt, 'Targeting Narcoinsurgents in Afghanistan: The Limits of International Humanitarian Law' (2009) 12 YbIHL 30, 314.

51 Leslie C. Green, 'The Environment and the Law of Conventional Warfare' (1991) 29 Canadian Yearbook of International Law 222, 233; Michael N. Schmitt, 'Future War and the Principle of Discrimination' (1998) 28 IYHR 51, 68; Henderson, *The Contemporary Law of Targeting* (n 31) 129-42.

classification. Additionally, the term 'use' in the provision is not modified by any adjectives (e.g. 'primary'). Arguably, this suggests that any degree of military use may lead to the classification of an object as a military objective. In practice, bridges, factories, industrial plants, ports, mines, broadcasting stations, etc., are often treated as dual-use targets.[52]

As regards 'revenue-generating objects', these are any economic infrastructure that generate revenue for an enemy's armed forces,[53] such as production, transportation, storage, and distribution facilities of petroleum,[54] energy resources,[55] and generally any form of profit.[56] Note, the justification for targeting, say, oil assets does not arise from the military usage of the infrastructure as in the case of dual-use objects; the reasoning rather lies with the potential revenues from the object, which may (or may not) be transferred to the armed forces, who may (or may not) use the money to sustain their war-fighting.

Although revenues are not mentioned in Art. 52 (2) AP I, the ambiguity over the requirement that the object offers an 'effective' – but not 'direct' – contribution to the military action, arguably allows for this practice.[57] In the past, this doctrine justified the destruction of cotton storages and opium facilities. In today's warfare, revenue-generating targets mostly comprise petroleum infrastructure and bulk cash storage sites.[58] This is the most contentious, yet fast-growing, class of targets in modern warfare.

---

52 Dinstein, 'Legitimate military objectives' (n 8) 154-58; Marco Sassòli, 'Legitimate Targets of Attacks under International Humanitarian Law' (2004) HPRC 1, 6-8 <http://www.humanrightsvoices.org/assets/attachments/documents/Session1.pdf> accessed 20 October 2016.

53 Ryan Goodman 'The Obama Administration and Targeting "War-Sustaining" Objects in Non international Armed Conflict' (2016) 110 AJIL 663, 664 (hereafter Goodman, 'War-sustaining Objects').

54 DoD LOAC Manual (n 49) section 5.7.8.5 – 'Examples of Military Objectives – Economic Objects Associated with Military Operations'.

55 The White House, Office of the Press Secretary, 'Fact Sheet: Maintaining Momentum in The Fight against ISIL' (15 January 2016) <https://obamawhitehouse.archives.gov/the-press-office/2016/01/15/fact-sheet-maintaining-momentum-fight-against-isil> accessed 12 May 2017.

56 The speech of DoD General Counsel, Jennifer O'Connor at NYU Law School, published in Just Security, 'Applying the Law of Targeting to the Modern Battlefield' (*Just Security*, 28 November 2016) <https://www.justsecurity.org/34977/applying-law-targeting-modern-battlefield%E2%80%8E-full-speech-dod-general-counsel-jennifer-oconnor/> accessed 5 May 2017.

57 Goodman, 'War-sustaining Objects' (n 53) 663 et seq.

58 Ibid.

In sum, the definition of 'military objective' is broad and ambiguous enough to allow in practice for the classification of varied economic assets as military objectives, which may be subject to direct attack.

D. The Classification of Investments into Protected Civilian Objects and Permissible Military Targets

Building on the foregoing analyses, this section puts forth a twofold examination. First, the discussion outlines the instances when an object may constitute a covered and protected investment but at the same time be classified as a military objective susceptible of targeting. Alongside, the section outlines the implications of any such classification on the standards of treatment that the host State confers upon investments before and during hostilities, and the possible invocation of the international responsibility of the host State thereof.

I. Foreign Investments and the Language of Article 52 (2) AP I

Like any other civilian object, which may be targetable if it meets the two-prong test of Art. 52 (2) AP I, foreign investments may too be lawfully attacked. Thus, if a plant is used as headquarters or if it obstructs the line of fire, its military use or location may justify its targeting. The same is true if the plant is a foreign investment. Take the case of *AAPL v Sri Lanka*. Insofar and for so long as the shrimp farm at the heart of the dispute was in fact used militarily by the LTTE in a manner that offered an 'effective' contribution to their military action, the total or partial destruction of the investment may have been lawful under IHL,[59] regardless of the BIT's definition of 'investment'.

At the same time, the classification of this object as an 'investment' generates certain international obligations for the host State. In reality, the *AAPL v Sri Lanka* Tribunal held that by failing to use less-deadly means and methods in its military operation, the State failed to take the precautionary measures that a well-administered government would have taken in these circumstances.[60] Accordingly, the Tribunal found that the

59 Subject to additional conventional and customary constraints and limitations.

60 *AAPL v Sri Lanka* (n 2) 85(B).

State breached the FPS standard. To be sure, there is no IHL rule obliging States not to eliminate a military objective if it can be neutralized in other less-lethal means.[61] Arguably, here the rules on the treatment of the same object in the same situation may yield contradictory results.

II. Foreign Investments as Dual-Use Targets

In practice, foreign investments are often made in economic sectors which are prone to dual-use classification.[62] Investment in the form of, say, hydroelectric power plants,[63] airport security services,[64] telecommunications,[65] and certainly weapons production, are of primarily civilian nature, use, and purpose. But, these investments also possess secondary military qualities that may serve the armed forces in armed conflicts. Under certain circumstances such investments are legitimate targets. This classification generates international obligations for the host State. Under Art. 58 AP I, States are required, even before the outbreak of hostilities, to remove civilians and civilian objects from the vicinity of military objectives, to avoid locating military objectives within, or near, densely populated areas, and to take all other practicable precautions so as

61 This standard is rather taken from human rights law. See HCJ 769/02 *The Public Committee against Torture in Israel et al v Israel* (2006) 33, 40. Cf Marko Milanovic, 'Lessons for human rights and humanitarian law in the war on terror: comparing Hamdan and the Israeli Targeted Killings case' (2007) 89 IRRC 373, 389 et seq.

62 To illustrate, at least 153 disputes were focused on investments in electricity, gas, steam, and air conditioning supply; some 36 claims concerned investments in water supply, sewerage, waste management and remediation activities; 30 investment disputes concerned agriculture, forestry and fishing; 129 cases concerned mining and quarrying; (UNCTAD, Investment Dispute Settlement Navigator, Economic sector and subsector <http://investmentpolicyhub.unctad.org/ISDS/FilterByEconomicSector> accessed 14 May 2017).

63 Eg *Amlyn v Croatia* (pending) ICSID case No ARB/16/28. The dispute concerns investments in the construction of a biomass power plant.

64 Eg *Abed El Jaouni v Lebanon* (pending) ICSID case No ARB/15/3. The dispute concerns ownership of a company that operates a fleet of private jets for charter and lease throughout Europe and the Middle East.

65 Eg *Lauder v Czech Republic* (Final Award) (2001) IIC 205, UNCITRAL, and *CME v Czech Republic* (Final Award and Separate Opinion) (2006) 9 ICSID Rep 264. These disputes concerned an investment in the field of information and communication, and programming and broadcasting activities.

to protect the civilian population under its control from the effects of attacks.[66]

To illustrate, since the Second Lebanon War of 2006, Hezbollah leader *Hassan Nasrallah* repeatedly insisted that in any future armed conflict with Israel Hezbollah will target Haifa's ammonia storage tank, which mainly serves the agriculture sector; such an attack is alleged to have an effect tantamount to an atomic bomb.[67] True, a deliberate attack against a civilian industry plant is in breach of the principle of distinction and a war crime.[68] However, aside from its civilian usage, ammonia is also used militarily as an alternate fuel, namely for combat jets. Hence, the tank is prone to dual-use classification. Considering that the tank is located in the Haifa metropolitan area, the probability of an attack against it as evidenced in repeated threats by Hezbollah, and the magnitude of anticipated civilian damage thereof, the closure of the investment is not only permitted, but mandated, by Art. 58 AP I.

The same is true if the object is a foreign investment. In fact, this 12,000-ton storage container of ammonia is part a longstanding US investment in Israel.[69] If this foreign investment is a military objective, then Israel is obliged under Art. 58 AP I, 'already during peacetime',[70] to remove and avoid locating it within, or near, densely populated areas.[71] Indeed, on 28 May 2017 the Israeli Supreme Court instructed the government to discontinue the permit for the operation of the tank and ordered its closure, citing grounds of *inter alia* security concerns.[72] At the same time, this regulatory interference in the form of a revocation of a license unfavourably changed the regulatory environment in which the investment has operated for decades. This also caused the investor to lose control of the investment and enjoyment of the benefits thereof. In this instance, Israel's compliance

---

66 Art. 58 AP I. This provision is widely recognised as a rule of customary law and as such applies to IACs and NIACs. See ICRC Customary IHL Study (n 31) rule 22; Sivakumaran, *The Law of Non-International Armed Conflicts* (n 31) 351 et seq.

67 Noa Shpigel, 'Tens of Thousands of Israelis Could Die if Key Security Weak Spot Exploited, Experts Warn' Haaretz (Israel, 30 January 2017).

68 Art. 8 (2) (B) (I) ICC-Statute.

69 Haifa Chemicals is owned by the American holding company Trance-Resource Inc., which is controlled by the Trump Group, where Jules Trump, a US national, serves as chairman of the board.

70 Sandoz et al, AP I Commentary (n 36) 2244, 2247, and 2251.

71 Art. 58 (a) and (b) AP I.

72 PCA 2841/17 Haifa Chemicals v The City of Haifa et al (2017).

with what is required under IHL may give rise to an investment treaty claim.[73]

III. Foreign Investments as Revenue-Generating Targets

This category may prove the most challenging for investments. In fact, a closer examination reveals that the very first use of this doctrine concerned the destruction of British foreign investments by Union forces during the American Civil War.[74] In that case, the UK brought a claim against the US, arguing that the destruction of cotton was in breach of the FPS provision in the applicable treaties of amity.[75] The primary defence of the US was that, 'cotton in the insurrectionary States was peculiarly and eminently a legitimate subject for such destruction' because the revenues from cotton sustained the war-fighting of the Confederacy against the Union.[76] From its birth, the notion that the destruction of objects 'due' to their revenue-generating abilities is permissible, conflicted with the concurrent obligation to protect these objects 'for' their revenue-generating abilities.

Today, the doctrine of revenue-generation continues to challenge investment protection. Recently, this class of targets justified counter-narcotics operations in poppy-growing areas of Afghanistan. These operations aimed at collapsing the Taliban's financial base, which relied on

73 Namely, expropriation and fair and equitable treatment.

74 The 1980 US Air Force Commander's Handbook on the Law of Armed Conflict, 25 July 1980 (AFP 110-34); US Department of the Navy – JAG, 'Annotated Supplement to the Commanders Handbook on Naval Operations', NWP 1-14M (1989) 8.1.1; Ralph Thomas and James Duncan (eds), *Annotated Supplement to the Commander's Handbook on the Law of Naval Operations*, (1999) 73 ILS 403; Bothe et al, *New rules for victims of armed conflicts* (n 46) 2.4.3.

75 Art. 14 of the Treaty of Amity, Commerce, and Navigation, between His Britannick Majesty; and the United States of America, by Their President, with the advice and consent of Their Senate, 19 November 1794 (entered into force 29 February 1796); Article 1, Convention to Regulate the Commerce between the Territories of The United States and of His Britannick Majesty (3 July 1815). Both provisions contain a FPS obligation whereby, 'which stipulated that the 'merchants and traders of each Nation respectively shall enjoy the most complete protection and security for their Commerce'.

76 US Department of State, *Papers Relating to the Treaty of Washington: Report of the US Agent* (Washington 1874) vol. 6, 52–58.

the taxation of the production and sale of opium.[77] The success of the anti-drug campaign however forced the Taliban to look elsewhere for revenues. Today, foreign investments fill in the gap.

Illustratively, in November 2016, the Taliban publicly pledged to 'back all national projects' and to 'direct its Mujahideen to help in the security of projects that are in the higher interest of [Afghanistan]'.[78] This pledge also enumerated several national and foreign projects, including the investment of China Metallurgical Group Corporation's (MCC) in a copper mine 40 kilometers south-east of Kabul. To be sure, the Taliban does not volunteer its protection; it levies taxes on infrastructure which it 'guards' so as to sustain itself. Therefore, investors who pay protection-taxes effectively support the belligerent's financial base and risk turning their investment into a revenue-generating target.

As for MCC, its investment was the subject of repeated deadly attacks by the Taliban, until in 2014 it withdrew from the project.[79] After the Afghan President pleaded the insurgents to 'stop pursuing objectives of outsiders',[80] the Taliban propounded the protection of its Mujahideen. Put differently, the Taliban's support of foreign investments reflects an offer of taxation in

77 Judy Dempsey and John Burns, 'NATO Agrees to Take Aim at Afghan Drug Trade', *NY Times* (New York, 10 October 2008) <http://www.nytimes.com/2008/10/11/world/asia/11nato.html> accessed 12 July 2016; Dapo Akande, 'US/NATO Targeting of Afghan Drug Traffickers: An Illegal and Dangerous Precedent?' (*EJIL: Talk!,* 13 September 2009) <http://www.ejiltalk.org/usnato-targeting-of-afghan-drug-traffickers-an-illegal-and-dangerous-precedent/> accessed 10 May 2016; Schmitt, 'Narcoinsurgents in Afghanistan' (n 50) 301-5; Emily Crawford, *Identifying the Enemy: Civilian Participation in Armed Conflict* (OUP 2015) 198-201; Goodman, 'War-sustaining Objects' (n 53) 672.

78 Islamic Emirate of Afghanistan, 'Statement of Islamic Emirate regarding backing national projects in the country' (*Islamic Emirate of Afghanistan*, 29 November 2016) <https://alemarah-english.com/?p=7766> accessed 13 December 2016.

79 Global Witness, 'Copper Bottomed? Bolstering the Aynak contract: Afghanistan's first major mining deal' (*Global Witness,* 20 November 2012) <https://www.globalwitness.org/en/campaigns/afghanistan/copper-bottomed/?> accessed 13 December 2016.

80 Afghanistan, Office of the President, Press Release, 26 October 2012 <http://www.bakhtarnews.com.af/eng/politics/item/4659-president-karzai-calls-on-taliban-to-stop-pursuing-objectives-of-outsiders-but-rather-begin-a-life-of-dignity-and-honor-under-afghanistan-constitution.html> accessed 25 July 2017.

lieu of violence, leaving foreign investments and the State between a rock and a hard place.[81]

Modern operations against revenue-generating targets pose a particular challenge for the law and policy of foreign investment. In recent years the US launched a 'wave of strikes against oil infrastructure, tanker trucks, wells and refineries' in Iraq so as to undermine Daesh's financial base.[82] President Obama explained that 'thanks' to the American campaign, 'money is literally going up in smoke' and oil prices are reduced.[83]

The justification for these economically-motivated operations is very weak under IHL, but it is even harder to square this conduct with the law and policy of foreign investments. While the US Department of Defense cites revenue-generation as a justification for targeting oil assets in Iraq, the US State Department, simultaneously, encourages oil companies to invest in Iraq, stating that investments in petroleum represent a rewarding business opportunity for American corporations, as Iraq's economy depends mainly on the revenues from this sector.[84] Iraq on its part, with the encouragement of the international community,[85] goes to great length to promote and

81 Anders Corr, 'Sanction China for Its Support of Taliban Terrorists' *Forbes* (New York, 21 February 2017) <https://www.forbes.com/sites/anderscorr/2017/02/21/sanction-china-for-its-support-of-taliban-terrorists/2/#1e6ae1b14b31> accessed 10 October 2017.

82 Remarks by President Barack Obama on Progress Against ISIL, 25 February 2016 <https://www.whitehouse.gov/the-press-office/2016/02/25/remarks-president-progress-against-isil> accessed 24 November 2017; Statement by the President on Progress in the Fight Against ISIL, 13 April 2016 <https://obamawhitehouse.archives.gov/the-press-office/2016/04/13/statement-president-progress-fight-against-isil> accessed 7 May 2017.

83 Ibid. The current Trump Administration fully adopts this practice, see US DoD, 'US, Coalition Continue Strikes against ISIL in Syria, Iraq' <https://www.defense.gov/News/Article/Article/1056079/us-coalition-continue-strikes-against-isil-in-syria-iraq/source/GovDelivery/> accessed 16 May 2017.

84 US State Department, '2010 Investment Climate Statement – Iraq' <https://www.state.gov/e/eb/rls/othr/ics/2010/138084.htm> accessed 13 May 2017; US State Department, '2011 Investment Climate Statement – Iraq' <https://www.state.gov/e/eb/rls/othr/ics/2011/> accessed 13 May 2017; US State Department, '2013 Investment Climate Statement – Iraq' <https://www.state.gov/e/eb/rls/othr/ics/2013/204661.htm> accessed 12 May 2017; International Trade Centre, 'Iraq – Country Brief' <http://www.intracen.org/country/iraq/> accessed 12 May 2017.

85 OECD, 'Bringing Investments to Iraq' (OECD Insights, 21 September 2015) <http://oecdinsights.org/2015/09/21/bringing-investment-to-iraq/> accessed 20 October 2017.

facilitate revenue-generating investments in the energy and petroleum sectors. To that end, the State offers concession contracts, bids, and more relaxed licensing for foreign investors.[86] Indeed, investments in oil account for some 90% of Iraq's revenues; most of these are foreign investments, many of which are US-owned. Taken at face-value, this class of targets means that the assets of ExxonMobil in the West Qurna I oil field are permissible targets that may be lawfully attacked by Daesh under certain circumstances.

Put simply, the implication of conditioning the legality of attacks on revenue-generation is that revenue-generating foreign investments may too be targeted by the adversary. This class of targets seems to directly conflict with the law and policy on the promotion, facilitation, and protection of foreign investments.

IV. Foreign Investments as Civilian Objects

Finally, the classification of investments as civilian objects and the implications thereof should be considered. If the investment is not classified as a military objective under Art. 52 (2) AP I, and whenever there is any doubt as to its classification,[87] the investment is presumed to be is a civilian object. As such, an investment cannot be the subject of direct and deliberate attacks.[88] More so, this civilian classification imposes certain obligations on war-torn host States. These obligations require States to take precautionary measures to protect investments from attacks (Art. 58 AP I), however they do not guarantee inviolability.

The case of MCC's above referenced investment in Afghanistan is illustrative. Under Art. 58 AP I, Afghanistan, as the 'attacked' party, is required to take the practicable and practical precautionary measures, given the prevailing circumstances, to protect the civilian objects under its control (including foreign investments) from the attacks of the Taliban.[89] This obligation of due diligence is assessed against the particular means and

86 This fact has been consistently emphasised in the publications of the State Department (n 84).

87 Art. 52 (3) AP I.

88 Art. 48, 51 and 52 AP I.

89 Art. 58, AP I; Sandoz et al, *AP I Commentary* (n 37) 2239; Jean-Francois Queguiner, 'Precautions under the Law Governing the Conduct of Hostilities' (2006) 88 IRRC 796, 818-19; Jensen (n 45) 162.

circumstances of each State.[90] In this case, it may be that Afghanistan complied with Art. 58 AP I notwithstanding the damage to the investment.[91]

At the same time, it may be that the FPS obligation under investment law holds Afghanistan to a higher threshold of diligence, whereby it should have taken more or other measures than what is required under IHL.[92] In such a case, both norms prescribe different standards of vigilance with respect to the same situation.

Furthermore, IHL accepts that in the harsh reality of hostilities civilian objects, foreign investments inclusive, may be incidentally hurt during attacks against legitimate military targets. This is recognised under the customary principle of proportionality, which prohibits launching an attack against a lawful target which is 'expected' to cause incidental civilian damage that would be excessive in relation to the military advantage 'anticipated'.[93] Therefore, not all losses to investments owing to military operations invoke the international responsibility of the attacking party.

Take the situation of *Mitchell v DRC* where the investment sustained damage as a result of the State's attack. If the damaged investment was not a military objective but, say, a victim of mistaken target identification (in good faith), its destruction may have been lawful under IHL. The same is true for the damage that was caused to the investment in *AAPL v Sri Lanka*, if it was not excessive relative to the anticipated military advantage from the destruction of, assume, a permissible LTTE target. At the same time, it may be that these State measures (attacks) breach the standards of investment protection under the applicable investment treaty, as indeed the *Mitchell* and *AAPL* Tribunals found.

---

90 Kimberley Trapp, 'Great Resources Mean Great Responsibility: A Framework of Analysis for Assessing Compliance with AP I Obligations in the Information Age' in Dan Saxon (ed), *International Humanitarian Law and the Changing Technology of War* (Brill Nijhoff 2013)163-64; Michael N. Schmitt, 'War, Technology, and the Law of Armed Conflict' (2006) 82 ILS 137, 163-65.

91 Afghanistan deployed armed forces to guard the investment, provided the workers with armed vehicles, built bunkers and shelters on site, and spread checkpoints around the area. Farhad Yavazi, 'Mes Aynak Archeological Project', Project Management Unit PMU (January 2014) 43 <http://mom.gov.af/Content/files/Mes-Aynak-Complete_January_2014.pdf> accessed 21 December 2017.

92 *Ampal-American Israel Corporation v Egypt* (Decision on Liability) (2017) ICSID case No ARB/12/11 283-91.

93 Art. 51 and 57 AP I; ICRC customary IHL (n 30) practice on Rule 14.

In sum, investments may be, and are, classified as military objectives. The concrete obligations that flow from this classification may result in a conflict with applicable investment treaty standards. In each of the above discussed situations, IHL arguably permits, and even mandates, what investment law prohibits or restricts. Since in these situations both IIL and IHL norms are valid and applicable and point to incompatible decisions, a choice must be made between them.[94] For each of the above described situations, it is necessary to ascertain which of the two norms, IHL or IIL, prevails under the priority rules of international law namely, the *lex specialis* rule.[95] Any such determination must be made on a case-by-case basis, and therefore exceed this discussion. Nonetheless, for its implications of State responsibility, the recognition that a norm conflict may arise in the assessment of losses to investments owing to armed conflict has an intrinsic significance. In practical terms of State responsibility, under a conflict in the applicable law only the special rule that must be applied can be breached and, in turn, result in responsibility.

E. Concluding Remarks

This chapter was concerned with the status of investments, as tangible economic objects, in armed conflicts. In this sense, the discussion examined when, if at all, investments may be the subject of a lawful attack, and the implications for the treatment of investments and State responsibility thereof.

To that end, a twofold argument was proposed. First, the chapter demonstrated that the concept of 'investment' is broad enough to confer protection upon a very wide scope of economic assets. Further, it was established that an array of objects may be classified as permissible targets, often for the economic sector in which they operate (dual-use objects) or for their ability to generate revenues for the war-torn host State (revenue-

94 Joost Pauwelyn *Conflict of Norms in Public International Law* (CUP 2003) 278-98 (hereafter Pauwelyn, *Conflict of Norms in Public International Law*); ILC, 'Fragmentation of International Law: Difficulties Arising from the Diversification and Expansion International Law. Report of the Study Group of the International Law Commission' UN Doc A/CN.4/L.682 (13 April 2006) 1.

95 Pauwelyn, *Conflict of Norms in Public International Law* (n 94) 387-89; Marko Milanovic, 'Norm Conflicts, International Humanitarian Law, and Human Rights Law' in Orna Ben-Naftali (ed) *International Humanitarian Law and International Human Rights Law* (OUP 2011) 103-15.

generating targets). In some instances, this means that an object may be attacked as a 'military objective' precisely for the reasons for which it is protected as an 'investment'.

Second, the chapter addressed the rules that emanate from the classification of an object as a covered investment on the one hand, and as a military objective 'or' a civilian object, on the other. It was suggested that investment treaty standards often conflict with the treatment that IHL permits or mandates with respect to the same economic object. The protection of investments in armed conflict therefore may entail a conflict in the applicable law. In practical terms, only the rule that prevails in a norm conflict may be breached and invoke international responsibility.

Overall, it is suggested that in practice the protection and regulation of investments during armed conflicts is mainly a function of the principle of distinction.

The Protection of (Foreign) Investment during Belligerent Occupation – Considerations on International Humanitarian Law and International Investment Law

Charlotte Lülf

A. Introduction

An outbreak of hostilities disrupts day-to-day life in the affected State or region, posing a considerable challenge to both legal and contractual relations of the involved States. While complex situations of conflict generally endanger the rule of law and hamper the allocation of rights and duties as well as their practical implementation, it is the disruption and takeover of control by another sovereign State that poses an even more serious legal obstacle to the maintenance of regular State functions, including the protection of investment. The state of occupation requires a thorough analysis of the continuity or renunciation of legal relations between the occupied State, the occupying State and (foreign) private investors.

During conflict, investments are often the target of hostile action or collateral damage, resulting in the destruction, seizure or, broadly phrased, loss of value of the investment in question.[1] IHL aims at regulating the conduct of hostilities and restricts or reduces damages to civilians and civilian objects by prohibiting direct attack or destruction. Its regulation of the protection of investment in general and the protection of investment during occupation, however, is far from undisputed; moreover, situations of occupation in recent years have illustrated the need for legal certainty on the interpretation and application of IHL. In particular, the powers of the occupying State to control or change the economic landscape in the

1 Ofilio Mayorga, 'Occupants, Beware of BITs: Applicability of Investment Treaties to Occupied Territories' (2017) 19 Palestine Yearbook of International Law 1, 2 (hereafter Mayorga, 'Occupants, Beware of BITs').

occupied territory must be further examined, as, so far, no coherent practice on the economic legislative powers of an occupying State has emerged.[2]

IHL governs conduct during occupation; yet, it is investment law, most commonly in the form of BITs, which contains more specialised regulations for the matter at hand. International investment law has quickly evolved over the last decades and provides mechanisms aimed at the protection of investment and means of remedy both in times of conflict and violence. Therefore, with the help of factual examples, this contribution firstly analyses the protection of (foreign) investment in situations of occupation under IHL; secondly, it takes a closer look at the specific regime of BITs, their applicability during conflict and their interaction with the laws of occupation.

B. The Laws of Belligerent Occupation and the Protection of (Foreign) Investment

The laws of belligerent occupation cover a wide array of specific aspects occurring during occupation, of which the protection of (foreign) investment is only a minor, yet heavily debated one. Recent occurrences of situations of occupation, (un)lawful interventions and potential annexations highlight the need for providing legal clarity on both the means of protection and means of remedy. Occupation itself is not considered a permanent transfer of sovereignty in a territory; however, the recognition of a state of occupation is often a highly politicised matter. Therefore, as a first step, this paper highlights how the legal regime is applied in situations of occupation.

I. The Recognition of a State of Occupation and the Application of its Specialised Regime

When examining a state of occupation, one must be aware that, prior to the codification of modern IHL, a diametrical understanding of occupation was promoted. This entailed that, when the occupant took over powers as a

---

2 Robert Tadlock, 'Occupation Law and Foreign Investment in Iraq: How an Outdated Doctrine Has become an Obstacle to Occupied Populations' (2004) 39 The University of San Francisco Law Review 227, 245 (hereafter Tadlock, 'Occupation Law and Foreign Investment in Iraq').

conqueror, he emerged as the new rightful owner of the territory and, therewith, as the new sovereign. Yet, the prominent codification processes which took place at the turn of the century changed this perception: 'As the nineteenth century drew to a close, the distinction between conquest and military occupation had been firmly established,'[3] the latter being regarded merely as a phase of temporary change of *de facto*, but not *de jure* powers within a State territory. In this understanding, State sovereignty basically remained untouched despite the occurring transfer of control. Thus, occupation is not to be understood as the acquisition of a legal title over an occupied territory, but as the military ruling and exercise of administration in and over a, or parts of a, foreign State without consent of its sovereign. This conflict between two or more sovereign entities – one holding *de facto* powers, one holding *de jure* powers and none holding both – elucidates its integration into the laws of international armed conflict. Art. 1 (4) AP I reflects this understanding as it encompasses:

> situations ... includ[ing] armed conflicts in which people are fighting against colonial domination and *alien occupation* and against racist regimes in the exercise of their right of self-determination ...

In temporal terms, the point of time in which an occupation began is decisive in identifying the application of the corresponding legal regime. The main treaties of reference in this matter are the Convention Respecting the Laws and Customs of War on Land of 17 October 1907, the Geneva Convention relating to the Protection of Civilian Persons in Times of War of 12 August 1949 and AP I.[4] In Art. 3, AP I explicitly holds that the protocol is applicable:

---

3 Romulus A. Picciotti, 'Legal Problems of Occupied Nations after the Termination of Occupation' (1966) 33 Military Law Review 25, 29.

4 Beyond the application of treaty law, customary IHL must also be referenced and analysed in order to establish differences between the two. The corpus of the GC IV has been transformed into customary IHL as broadly, and among others, acknowledged in the prominent ICTY's *Tadic* Judgment: 'The extensive codification of humanitarian law and the extent of the accession to the resultant treaties ... have provided the international community with a corpus of treaty rules the great majority of which had already become customary ...', *Prosecutor v Tadic* (Judgment) [1997] IT-94-1-T, para 577. See also Advisory Opinion on the Legality of the Threat or Use of Nuclear Weapons (Advisory Opinion) [1996] ICJ Rep 226, para 79. 'Under customary international law, this duty begins once a stable regime of occupation has been established, but under the Geneva Conventions, the duty attaches as soon as the occupying force has any relation with the civilians of that territory, that is, at the soonest possible

> … (a) from the beginning of any situation referred to in the aforementioned Article 1 and (b) shall cease, in the territory of parties to the conflict, on the general close of military operation and, in the case of occupied territories, on the termination of the occupation except, in either circumstances, for those persons whose final release, repatriation or re-establishment takes place thereafter …

The change of control over the respective territory is the key question by virtue of Art. 42 Hague Regulations, which states that the 'territory is considered occupied when it is actually placed under the authority of the hostile army. The occupation extends only to the territory where such authority has been established and can be exercised'.

It is this takeover of factual control, irrespective of the lawfulness of the original deployment of armed forces or motives behind the engagement in hostilities, which triggers the application of the laws of belligerent occupation.[5]

The ICRC asserts that

> [t]here is no intermediate period between what might be termed the invasion phase and the inauguration of a stable regime of occupation. Even a patrol which penetrates into enemy territory without any intention of staying there must respect the Conventions in its dealings with the civilians it meets.[6]

While the focus on the factual change of control over territory aims at ensuring the application of the pertinent laws irrespective of the official position of actors involved, the fluid and highly politicised nature of situations of occupation *per se* nonetheless hampers the smooth transition to the occupation regime. For this reason, it is essential that IHL underlines the general and broad renunciation of official declarations in favour of the factual situation.[7] Positions brought forward by the State Parties, including any denial of a situation of occupation, are irrelevant for the legal finding

moment, a principle that finds reflection in U.S. military policy.'; Human Rights Watch, 'International Humanitarian Law Issues In A Potential War In Iraq' (*Human Rights Watch Briefing Paper*, 20 February 2003) <http://www.hrw.org/backgrounder/arms/iraq0202003.htm> accessed 08 October 2017.

5 Frederic Kirgis 'Security Council Resolution 1483 on the Rebuilding of Iraq' (*ASIL Insight*, 2003) <https://www.asil.org/insights/volume/8/issue/13/security-council-resolution-1483-rebuilding-iraq> accessed 11 March 2004.

6 Jean S. Pictet (ed), *The Geneva Conventions of 12 August 1949: Commentary*, vol. IV (Geneva 1958) 60 (hereafter Pictet, *Commentary*).

7 Art. 2 AP I: '... the present Convention shall apply to all cases of declared war or of any other armed conflict which may arise between two or more of the High Contracting Parties, even if the state of war is not recognized by one of them.'

and, thus, do not relinquish any arising obligations – at least in theory. The dispute over Ukraine in recent years and, more specifically, the status of Crimea between annexation, occupation and secession has illustrated the difficulties in both, ascertaining a certain legal status and demanding a subsequent application of law.[8]

Art. 1 (4) AP I furthermore emphasises that the occupation itself need not be armed; however, it is triggered when resistance against the occupation arises which could lead to active hostilities. Moreover, Art. 2 (2) GC IV applies 'to all cases of partial or total occupation of the territory of a High Contracting Party, even if the said occupation meets with no armed resistance'. This clarification allows it to encompass various situations, whether the control over territory stems from foreign military superiority or from foreign control through a puppet regime.[9] This broad scope of application is required to trigger the resulting obligations for the occupant while exerting its *de facto* control over the foreign territory.

II. The Protection of Private Property during Occupation

The international law of belligerent occupation contains general obligations concerning the security and basic necessities – such as food, medical supplies, or the provision of electricity – of the civilian population in the occupied territory. As such, it also aims at reconciling the disputed interests of the occupant, the occupied State and the population residing in the territory in question.[10] Art. 47 GC IV lays down the general obligation that

> Protected persons who are in occupied territory shall not be deprived, in any case or in any manner whatsoever, of the benefits of the present Convention by any change introduced, as the result of the occupation of a territory, into the institutions or government of the said territory, nor by any agreement concluded between the authorities of the occupied territories and the Occupying Power, nor by any annexation by the latter of the whole or part of the occupied territory.

8 Hans-Joachim Heintze, 'Völkerrecht und Sezession – Ist die Annexion der Krim eine zulässige Wiedergutmachung sowjetischen Unrechts?' (2014) 27 J. Int'l L. of Peace & Armed Conflict 129.

9 Eyal Benvenisti, *The International Law of Occupation* (2nd edn, OUP 2012) 4 (hereafter Benvenisti, *Law of Occupation*).

10 Christopher Greenwood, 'Book Review and Note: The International Law of Occupation by Eyal Benvenisti' (1996) 90 AJIL 712.

The 1907 Hague Regulations, while not directly referring to investment, codifies the general respect for private property and the prohibition of confiscation in Art. 46: 'Family honour and rights, the lives of persons, and private property, as well as religious convictions and practice, must be respected. Private property cannot be confiscated'. Furthermore, Art. 47 Hague Regulations generally prohibits pillage, and Art. 33 (2) GC IV[11] states that, 'Pillage is prohibited. (3) Reprisals against protected persons and their property are prohibited'.

Examples of the protection of private property during occupation can already be found in early investment disputes, such as the *Lighthouse Concession* Arbitration of 1956. The case concerned a lighthouse operated by a French company for which it held concessions granted by the Ottoman Empire in 1860. The lighthouse was located on territory that was later occupied by Greece. The tribunal set up decided that the occupying power, Greece, had to respect existing commercial rights in light of Art. 46 Hague Regulations, which were established by the concession contract of the occupied State prior to the occupation. Therewith, Greece was obliged to pay dues for its ships to the French company.[12]

The fundamental prohibition of IHL to directly attack civilians and civilian objects, in conjunction with the prohibition of disproportionality in targeting operations, offers a general protection mechanism for investments, both national and foreign, covering factories, offices, vehicles and any other form of assets.[13] One can generally presume that staff is

---

11 Generally, the GC IV in this regard operates with a limited scope of application to individuals, linking its provisions to protected persons as defined by Art. 4: 'those, who, at a given moment and in any manner whatsoever, find themselves, in case of a conflict or occupation, in the hands of a Party to the conflict or Occupying Power of which they are not nationals.' The commentary elaborates on this provision as referring to the whole population of the territory, which also includes foreign investors. See, Mayorga, 'Occupants, Beware of BITs' (n 1) 44 et seq. Arai argues that, if the home State of the investor maintains regular relations with the occupying power, then these cannot be considered 'protected persons', Yutaka Arai-Takahashi, *The Law of Occupation: Continuity and Change of International Humanitarian Law, and its Interaction with International Human Rights Law* (Martinus Nijhoff Publishers 2009) 306 (hereafter Arai-Takahashi, *The Law of Occupation*).

12 Administration of Lighthouses Arbitration (*France v Greece*) (Award) [1956] RIAA 155, para 201 et seq.

13 Art. 48 AP I, Art. 13 AP II, Art. 51 (4) and (5) AP I, Art. 51 (5) (b) and Art. 57 (2) (a) (iii) AP I.

considered civilian and is therefore protected; moreover, factories, offices and equipment such as vehicles are classified as civilian objectives unless they change their nature during hostilities.[14] This change in classification has more than often resulted in arbitration and compensation claims following an attack.[15] The GC IV in Art. 53 ascertains that

> Any destruction by the Occupying Power of real or personal property belonging individually or collectively to private persons, or to the State, or to other public authorities, or to social or cooperative organizations, is prohibited, except where such destruction is rendered absolutely necessary by military operations.

Moreover, Art. 52 Hague Regulations equally holds that no interference should be made unless it is of use for military purposes of the occupying military, as stated in the following:

> Requisitions in kind and services shall not be demanded from municipalities or inhabitants except for the needs of the army of occupation. They shall be in proportion to the resources of the country, and of such a nature as not to involve the inhabitants in the obligation of taking part in military operations against their own country.

The limitation of the protection granted is the test of military necessity.[16] This rationale stems from the attempt to separate the sphere of hostilities between the conflict Parties from the daily life and its procedures in the affected territory.[17] In the 1921 *Cessation of Vessels and Tugs for Navigation on the Danube* case, Arbitrator Hines proclaimed that '[t]he purpose of the immunity of private property from confiscation is to avoid throwing the burdens of war upon private individuals, and is, instead, to place those burdens upon the States which are the belligerents.'[18]

The protection of single or individual property, both national and foreign, is only one aspect of the broader issue of the protection of investment during occupation; there have been numerous incidents and disputes over economic intervention during occupation in past years. These illustrate not

---

14 Horace Robertson, The Principle of Military Objective in the Law of Armed Conflict (1997) 8 Journal of Legal Studies 35.

15 Ofilio Mayorga, *Arbitrating War: Military necessity as a defense to the breach of investment treaty obligations* (Program on Humanitarian Policy and Conflict Research, Harvard University 2013).

16 For the debate on the interpretation of military necessity, see Katja Schöberl and Linus Mührel, 'Sunken Vessel or Blooming Flower? Lotus, Permissions and Restrictions within International Humanitarian Law' in this volume 59, 73 et seqq (hereafter Schöberl and Mührel, 'Sunken Vessel or Blooming Flower?').

17 Arai-Takahashi, *The Law of Occupation* (n 11) 238.

18 *Cessation of Vessels and Tugs for Navigation on the Danube River* (Award) [1921] 1 RIAA 97, para 107 et seq.

only the importance of the protection of property as such, but rather the importance of more generally clarifying the status of law during occupation and the status of existing contractual relations.

III. Occupation, Law and Foreign Investment

The focus of this contribution does not solely lie on the protection of investment, but is concerned more specifically with foreign investments in occupied territory. Therefore, the status of existing laws in occupied territory as well as the power of the occupant to engage in substantive legislative changes is addressed in the following.

1. The status of law and the legislative powers of the occupant

Early during the negotiation and drafting processes at the Hague Peace Conference, the newly envisaged role of the occupant for modern IHL was debated. The later codified position of the *de facto* powers in occupied territories originated from a small group of States that strongly elaborated on their interests at the 1899 Conference – a group of States fearing potential future occupation.[19] Their goal was to introduce obligatory language to the developing occupation regime rather than to acknowledge or even strengthen any rights of occupying States.[20] The *travaux préparatoires* emphasised that

> … it has been formally said that none of the articles of the draft can be considered as entailing on the part of the adhering States the recognition of any right whatever in derogation of the sovereign tights of each of them, and that adhesion to the regulations will simply imply for each State the acceptance of a set of legal rules restricting the exercise of power that it may through the fortune of war wield over foreign territory or subjects.[21]

---

19 See the delegates debating at the Sixth, Seventh and Eighth Meeting, James Brown Scott, *The Proceedings of the Hague Peace Conferences: Translations of the Official Texts: The Conference of 1899* (OUP 1920) 503 (hereafter Scott, *The Proceedings of the Hague Peace Conferences*).

20 See also Schöberl and Mührel, 'Sunken Vessel or Blooming Flower? (n 16) 71 et seq.

21 Report annexed to the minutes of the Fourth Meeting, 5 July 1899 in Scott, *The Proceedings of the Hague Peace Conferences* (n 19) 418.

Art. 43 Hague Regulations is the main result of this successful attempt and contains the regulation on the distribution of power and entailing rights during occupation:

> The authority of the legitimate power having in fact passed into the hands of the occupant, the latter shall take all the measures in his power to restore, and ensure, as far as possible, public order and safety, while respecting, unless absolutely prevented, the laws in force in the country.[22]

Generally, the obligation is considered as one of means rather than of result due to the special situation of occupation as well as the limited resources and powers of the occupying State.[23] The Article reflects the basic understanding that the state of occupation should disrupt the regular life in the occupied territory as little as possible. It represents a call for continuity – one that was already recognised as customary in nature at the International Military Tribunal in Nuremburg.[24]

While the more prominent way to ensure public order and safety is through criminal prosecution[25] and law enforcement operations, for the matter at hand, the occupying power's rights and obligations concerning 'the law in force' in the economic context is of greater relevance. As such, Art. 43 Hague Regulations acts as a means to restrain the occupying power.[26] The term 'laws in force in the country' is commonly perceived as a broad term, which does not solely cover legislation but, with minor exceptions, also the whole legal system.[27] This understanding is reflected in the longstanding (academic) debate over the scope of the Articles in question.

---

22 See Benvenisti, *Law of Occupation* (n 9) 8.

23 Marco Sassòli, *Article 43 of the Hague Regulations and Peace Operations in the Twenty-First Century* (Background Paper prepared for the Informal High-Level Expert Meeting on Current Challenges to International Humanitarian Law, Cambridge, 25-27 June 2004) 4 (hereafter Sassòli, *Article 43 of the Hague Regulations*).

24 'Trial of the Major War Criminals, International Military Tribunal in Nuremberg' reprinted in (1947) 41 AJIL 172, 248 et seq.

25 The limiting factors for the power of the occupying party were subsequently codified in GC IV, most prominently in Articles 66-74 on Penal Legislation and Procedure.

26 Sassòli, *Article 43 of the Hague Regulations* (n 23) 4 et seq.

27 Ibid, 6, with reference to Benvenisti, *Law of Occupation* (n 9) 16. See further Ernst Feilchenfeld, *The International Economic Law of Belligerent Occupation* (Carnegie Endowment for International Peace 1942) (hereafter Feilchenfeld, *International Economic Law*).

The GC IV addresses this approach in Art. 64:

> The penal laws of the occupied territory shall remain in force, with the exception that they may be repealed or suspended by the Occupying Power in cases where they constitute a threat to its security or an obstacle to the application of the present Convention …

In contrast to the Hague Regulations, the GC, however, explicitly refers to 'penal laws' rather than relating to the laws generally in force in the territory. For this reason, a dispute over its legal scope has arisen. In contrast to the above proclaimed rationale to restrict the (legislative) powers of the occupant, the terminology of Art. 64 GC IV can be interpreted as less restrictive, even as 'extensive and complex'[28]. While some stick to the exact wording and therewith support the strict reference to 'penal law', others opt for a broader and more encompassing interpretation, one that includes administrative and civil laws in force in the occupied territory. Art. 64 (2) GC IV backs up this argument as it solely refers to 'provisions' rather than to repeat the penal law wording of the previous paragraph.[29] *Benvenisti* promotes this idea of a conscious omission of reference and emphasises the broad reading of both paragraphs as referring to all types of laws.[30] Similarly, *Dinstein* argues that 'logic dictates that Art. 64 should be construed as applicable, if only by analogy, to every type of law (including civil or administrative legislation)'[31]. Moreover, the Pictet Commentary on Art. 64 underlines that

> [t]he idea of the continuity of the legal system applies to the whole of the law (civil and penal law) in the occupied territory. The reason for the Diplomatic Conference making express reference only to respect for penal law was that it had not been sufficiently observed during past conflicts; there is no reason to infer a contrario that the occupation authorities are not also bound to respect the civil law of the country, or even its constitution.[32]

---

28 Pictet, *Commentary* (n 6) 335.

29 Sassòli, *Article 43 of the Hague Regulations* (n 23) 6.

30 Benvenisti, *Law of Occupation* (n 9) 102 et seq, with reference to the Final Record of the Diplomatic Conference of Geneva of 1949 (1950), iii, at 139 et seq. For a very strong counter argumentation based on the *travaux préparatoires*, the Commentaries to the Convention and subsequent ICJ Advisory Opinions, see Jose Alejandro Carballo Leyda, 'The Laws of Occupation and Commercial Law Reform in Occupied Territories: Clarifying A Widespread Misunderstanding' (2012) 23 EJIL 179 (hereafter Leyda, 'Laws of Occupation').

31 Yoram Dinstein, *The International Law of Belligerent Occupation* (CUP 2009) 111.

32 Pictet, *Commentary* (n 6) 335.

The Article generally enshrines the obligation to respect and uphold existing legislation and contractual obligations of the occupied State. This not only acts in favour of the affected population, but it could equally provide security for foreign investors and their contractual relations in the territory. The major downside to the debate over the laws is the following: while the above referenced attempts to expand the scope of 'the laws in force' are an endeavour to expand protection from the occupant and limit his powers, they can also act as a door-opener to empower the occupant, not only to change the 'penal laws' but also to make changes to 'every type of law'.

The Article entitles the occupant to make alterations to the law. However, this power is limited, as it allows the occupant to introduce legislation in order to maintain or even enhance civil welfare. The maintenance of an orderly government is the explicit goal incorporated in paragraph two; the longer a situation of occupation exists, the more pressing additional legal changes might become in order to avoid a failing and disruption of governance in the territory.[33]

While it is generally considered that small interventions in the inherent nature of an economy can be initiated by the occupant, the definition and identification of the 'absolutely necessary' remains highly disputed and gives leeway for arbitrariness.[34]

2. The occupant's powers and the welfare of the population in the occupied territory

The abrogation of existing laws as well as the introduction of new laws can be instruments of drastic economic and political transformation in occupied territories – changes that depend on the occupant's general understanding of economic development, or specific positions towards protectionism, market liberalisation or global economic interaction.

The occupant is 'allowed to evaluate the modality and extent of investments in occupied territories, while bearing in mind the duty to ensure the welfare of inhabitants in that territory'.[35] The regulations both in the Geneva Conventions and the Hague Regulations encompass a balancing act

---

33 Sassòli, *Article 43 of the Hague Regulations* (n 23) 15. For example, see tax regulations as addressed under Art. 48 Hague Regulation.

34 Leyda, 'Laws of Occupation' (n 30) 188.

35 Arai-Takahashi, *The Law of Occupation* (n 11).

between the powers of the occupant as a permissive element and the welfare of the affected population as a restrictive element. Establishing when a balanced situation is achieved and defining what constitutes the welfare of the population, however, leaves a wide margin of discretion as well as options for unilateral change and intrusion.

In principle, Art. 55 Hague Regulations seems to contradict a too permissive reading by depicting the occupant 'only as administrator and usufructuary of public buildings, real estate, forests, and agricultural estates belonging to the hostile State, and situated in the occupied country'[36]. Nonetheless, Art. 43 Hague Regulations may provide an exception to such a 'conservationist premise'[37] as it entitles the occupying power to introduce changes for a specific purpose, for instance the improved welfare of the population. In particular, introducing new laws that affect the territory's economy – for instance through the negotiation of new foreign investments – may follow such a purpose. The pertinent regulations remain silent on the explicit issuing of new investments. Already in 1957, *von Glahn* considered that granting investments is not *per se* a breach of the law of occupation as long as it does not exceed the time of the occupation.[38]

Examples of this balancing act and the role of the occupying power in investment matters can already be found in early case law. For instance, arbitrary tribunals in Belgium decided on the economic and legislative powers of the occupant, Germany, after the First World War. In 1920, the Brussels Court of Appeal upheld a decree on the regulation of excessive pricing of produce introduced by Germany, stating that the latter had 'acted in the place of the legitimate authority which for the time being had been ousted, and in conformity with the provisions of Art. 43'[39]. In 1925, it argued that 'the circumstances of war-times, and particularly the increase of cost in raw materials and the necessity for providing the needs of the population, in fact justified the measures taken by the occupying authority'[40]. Rulings from the post-Second-World-War era addressed

36 For a detailed discussion on the scope of Art. 55, see Separate Opinion of M. Séfériadès in *Lighthouses Case between France and Greece* (*France v Greece*) [1934] PCIJ (ser. A/B) No. 62, para 205 et seq.

37 Arai-Takahashi, *The Law of Occupation* (n 11) 169.

38 Gerhard Von Glahn, *The Occupation of Enemy Territory – A Commentary on the Law of Belligerent Occupation* (University of Minnesota Press 1957) 209.

39 *Bochart v Committee of Supplies of Corneux* (1920) No. 327, AD 1919-1922, quoted by Feilchenfeld, *International Economic Law* (n 27) 148.

40 *City of Malines v Societe Centrale pour L'Exploitation du Gaz* (1925) No. 362, AD 1925-26, quoted by Feilchenfeld, *International Economic Law* (n 27) 148.

similar issues. For example, the *Singapore Oil Stocks* case concerned oil concessions in Sumatra granted to Dutch companies by the Netherlands East Indies Government. Following the invasion by Japanese troops in February 1942, oil was exported to Singapore to further strengthen the Japanese war effort. The UK later seized parts of the oil in question when taking control over Singapore in 1945. Based on the Defence Compensation Regulation of 1940, owners were entitled to claim compensation by the UK. The legal dispute arose over the question of who held this entitlement: the Dutch companies, or the occupying power, Japan. In a first decision, the claim of the Dutch companies was rejected. Then, however, the Court of Appeal of Singapore reversed the decision.[41] The leading argumentation was related to Art. 53 Hague Regulations, which did not cover the exploitation of the oil by the Japanese troops as it was conducted without consideration of the local economy.[42]

Thus, the considerations on the rights of the occupant do not solely affect the abrogation or introduction of a single new piece of legislation, but are even more sensitive when affecting the economy of the occupied territory or the State as such.

3. Balancing in practice: the example of occupied Iraq

The situation of occupied Iraq following the conflict in 2003 is a major example when discussing the legality of alterations made by the occupant or, in the pertinent case, the occupying coalition.[43] The questionable aspect at stake in this context was the introduction of rather neoliberal ideas by the Coalition Provisional Authority (CPA) in Iraq, which aimed at opening the State to foreign investment.[44] The scope and necessity of changes to the Iraqi economic system and the resulting evaluation of the laws of occupation and potential changes to the domestic legal regime have

---

41 Martins Paparinskis, 'Singapore Oil Stocks Case' in MPEPIL (online edn, OUP April 2010).

42 *N.V. de Bataafsche Petroleum Maatschappij and Others v The War Damage Commission* (1956) 23 ILR 810 para 833 (Singapore Court of Appeal).

43 See Arai-Takahashi, *The Law of Occupation* (n 11) 171.

44 See the preamble of CPA Order 39: '*Noting* that facilitating foreign investment will help to develop infrastructure, foster the growth of Iraqi business, create jobs, raise capital, result in the introduction of new technology into Iraq and promote the transfer of knowledge and skills to Iraqis'.

triggered debates on the role of an occupying power.[45] In contrast to prior situations of factual occupation such as in the Palestinian territories, in Northern Cyprus, or the Falkland Islands, the belligerent occupying armed forces acknowledged their own status as an occupying power and the Security Council also determined the occupation as such. In May 2003, the UN SC under Art. 41 UN-Charter explicitly recognised 'the specific authorities, responsibilities, and obligations under applicable international law of these States as occupying powers' and their obligation to fully comply with 'the Geneva Convention of 1949 and the Hague Regulations of 1907' in particular.[46] The SC's Resolution 1483 reaffirmed that no transfer of sovereignty would take place and emphasised the 'right of the Iraqi people freely to determine their own political future and control their own natural resources.' The application of the legal regime of occupation was consequently undisputed, but the scope of the occupant's rights and obligations became a matter of discussion.

Were the changes introduced necessary or did they go beyond Art. 43 Hague Regulations, therefore violating it? Prior to the occupation, the Iraqi economy was characterised by limitations on foreign investment, for instance with respect to immovable property for non-Arabic foreign corporations, the investments of such more generally as well as their ownership of Iraqi companies specifically.[47] The CPA, however, introduced laws that led to inherent changes in the nature of the Iraqi economy. CPA Order 39 of 2003 is the primary example of such a transformed new legislation.[48] By replacing 'all existing foreign investment', the CPA attempted to comprehensively dismantle all barriers to foreign investment.[49] Foreign investors were provided with protection 'no less favourable than those applicable to an Iraqi investor'[50] and no longer experienced

45 For a very critical view of occupation practices that are limiting the occupied territories' development for instance in the case of Iraq, see Tadlock, 'Occupation Law and Foreign Investment in Iraq' (n 2).

46 UN SC Res 1483 (22 May 2003) UN Doc S/RES/1483.

47 US Department of Commerce, Overview of Commercial Law in Pre-War Iraq (12 September 2003) 1, 6 et seq <http://www.aschq.army.mil/supporting-docs/Iraqi_Comm_Law.pdf> accessed 08 October 2017.

48 In particular, the Companies Law 21 of 1997, available under International Labour Organization, Iraq, General provision <http://www.ilo.org/dyn/natlex/natlex4.detail?p_lang=en&p_isn=83220&p_classification=01> accessed 14 October 2017.

49 CPA Order 39 (3) (1).

50 CPA Order 39 (4) (1).

restrictions regarding the percentage rate of full or partial ownership of Iraqi companies.[51]

With a transformation of this scope, the changes made are none that were restricted to the time of occupation, but rather shaped the economic system of the country far beyond the time of occupation. As such, they were criticised for 'completely overhaul(ing) Iraqi commercial law, in particular, its foreign investment law'[52]. Interestingly, the changes to the economic structure of Iraq constituted only one aspect of the attempt to induce an overall change in regime.[53] This undertaking, however, is exactly what IHL prohibits within its laws of occupation.[54]

C. The Role of Investment Law during Belligerent Occupation

IHL is not the only field of law that governs in times of conflict. While the law of occupation codifies regulations concerning the powers of the occupying State to enact or change existing (economic) laws, the field of investment law provides another angle on the status of foreign investment and its protection in occupied territories. The traditional instruments governing the protection of investment are BITs, the use of which has increased since the 1990s. BITs are agreements between two States regulating the terms and conditions of private investment of the respective State's nationals or companies in the other State's territory. Typically, these agreements contain treatment guarantees, protection regulations as well as recourse to an investor-State dispute settlement mechanism. During times

---

51 CPA Order 39 (4) (2). Only minor limitations remained or were put in place, among other restrictions on foreign investments into the sectors of natural resources, banking and insurances, CPA Order 39 (6) (1).

52 Tadlock, 'Occupation Law and Foreign Investment in Iraq' (n 2) 242.

53 For a more detailed analysis, see Sir Adam Roberts, 'The End of Occupation in Iraq' (*IHLRI*, 2004) Section D on the transformative purpose of the occupation of Iraq <http://www.ihlresearch.org/iraq/feature.php?a=51> accessed 02 March 2017

54 Knut Dörmann and Laurent Colassis, 'International Humanitarian Law in the Iraq Conflict' (2004) 47 GYIL 293, 306 (hereafter Dörmann, 'International Humanitarian Law'). For a partially different argumentation concerning regime change and human rights violations, see Rüdiger Wolfrum, 'The Attack of September 11, 2001, the War Against the Taliban and Iraq: Is There a Need to Reconsider International Law on the Recourse to Force and the Rules in Armed Conflict?' (2003) 7 Max Planck Yearbook of United Nations Law 1, 56.

of occupation, one can question whether and to what extent BITs are and remain applicable.

I. Bilateral Investment Treaties and their Application during Times of Conflict and Occupation

The general rule of public international law, *res inter alios acta,* emphasises that States are only bound by treaties that they have consented to.[55] This rule is codified in Art. 34 VCLT: '[a] Treaty does not create either obligations or rights for a third State without its consent'. In a situation of occupation, the occupying power itself is not a State Party to pre-existing BITs between the occupied State and third States. From the *res inter alios acto* rule, one could infer that the occupying power, since it had never consented to the treaty, is not bound by it. Does that mean that no obligations arise out of the BIT as such and is it only the occupied State, the original BIT host State – a party without effective control over the territory in which the investment is located – that must adhere to its obligations? Or does the law of occupation that renders the occupant the new administrator of the territory transfer these obligations to the occupant – without his direct consent?

The classical international law presumption concerning treaties during times of occupation stems from the traditional and clear-cut separation of the regime of law of peace and the regime of law of armed conflict.[56] Generally, one assumed a discontinuity of all existing treaties and State relations as IHL replaced all laws belonging to the law of peace.[57] This understanding of the relation of law of peace to the law of armed conflict has since changed. The Draft Articles on the Effects of Armed Conflict on

55 See Schöberl and Mührel, 'Sunken Vessel or Blooming Flower?' (n 16).

56 Arnold Pronto, 'The Effect of War on Law – What happens to their treaties when states go to war?' (2003) 2 Cambridge Journal of International and Comparative Law 227, 230.

57 Hans-Joachim Heintze, 'On the Relationship between Human Rights Law Protection and International Humanitarian Law' (2004) 86 IRRC 789, 790. The 1958 commentary of the Geneva Convention mirrors such an understanding by stating that the occupant 'is not bound by the treaties concerning the legal status of aliens which may exist', see Pictet, *Commentary* (n 6) 49.

Treaties[58] are illustrative of this development as they do not support the *ipso facto* termination support in Art. 3 treaty continuity. The general assumption of the continuity of treaties explicitly includes a situation of occupation, which they subsume under situations of armed conflict through Art. 2.[59]

In addition to this general assumption of continuity, the Draft Articles furthermore directly address treaties on finance as one type of treaty that continues to apply in the absence of any explicit and contradictory treaty clauses. This link to treaties of commerce is encompassed in the indicative list annexed to the Draft Articles and also includes contemporary BITs.[60] As a third argument on the continuity of BITs, these often contain so called 'war-clauses' to regulate protection guarantees and resulting compensation claims in situations of armed conflict. Thus, their drafters envisaged their application during armed conflict. Art. 4 Draft Articles supports this argument.

General treaty law as well as the BITs themselves anticipate their application during conflict and occupation. One can further subsume those BITs under the bulk of 'laws in force' in the country as regulated by IHL under Art. 43 Hague Regulations and 64 GC IV as referred to above. Several peace treaties signed between the defeated States and the US in the aftermath of the Second World War act as examples of State practice on continuity: The Agreement on Reparation from Germany of 1946 and the Treaty of Peace with Japan of 1951 exemplify such an approach.[61] Returning to the aforementioned primary IHL guidance on laws in force in the country, Art. 43 Hague Regulations ensures respect for the laws of the occupied State territory, including its laws on contracts, which 'prohibits the occupying power to nullify or suspend any legitimate State contracts …

---

58 ILC, 'Draft articles on the effects of armed conflict on treaties, with commentaries' (2011) UN Doc A/66/10 <http://legal.un.org/ilc/texts/instruments/english/commentaries/1_10_2011.pdf> accessed 14 October 2017 (Draft Articles).

59 Ibid, Art. 2, para 4-9.

60 Ibid, Art. 3.

61 Agreement on Reparation from Germany, on the Establishment of an Inter-Allied Reparation Agency and on the Restitution of Monetary Gold (opened for signature 14 January 1946, entered into force 24 January 1946) 55 UNTS 69 and Treaty of Peace with Japan (opened for signature 8 September 1951, entered into force 28 April 1952) 136 UNTS 45.

by amending … laws or by issuing a legislative declaration to that effect'[62]. Art. 64 GC IV also works with the presumption of continuity by stating that

> [t]he penal laws of the occupied territory shall remain in force, with the exception that they may be repealed or suspended by the Occupying Power in cases where they constitute a threat to its security or an obstacle to the application of the present Convention.[63]

Moreover, the commentary reiterates that '[t]he idea of continuity of the legal system applies to the whole of the law (civil and penal law) in the occupied territory'[64].

Following this assumption, the occupant must uphold the interests of the ousted government, which include, as *Benvenisti* states, obligations towards foreign nationals including their investments.[65] *Meron* equally argues that the occupant is bound by the treaties that were in force prior to the occupation, albeit he emphasises that this concerns treaties addressing the maintenance of public order and civil life.[66] By analogy, *Burke* asserts that the same applies to multilateral treaties: 'A multilateral treaty that has been ratified by the occupied State is certainly a "law in force in the country"',[67] or 'there is no a priori reason why multilateral conventions on other matter should not be applicable to occupied territory'.[68] *Mayorga* phrases this new link between the occupant and the pre-existing treaty as one of indirect or derivative consent, which transfers obligations to the occupying power both regarding substantive obligations and procedures of dispute settlement.[69]

---

62 Pieter Bekker, 'The Legal Status of Foreign Economic Interests in Occupied Iraq' (*Asil Insights,* 18 July 2003) <https://www.asil.org/insights/volume/8/issue/20/legal-status-foreign-economic-interests-occupied-iraq> accessed 10 October 2017.

63 Naomi Burke 'A Change in Perspective: Looking at Occupation through the Lens of the Law of Treaties' (2008) 41 New York University Journal of International Law and Politics 103, 115 (hereafter Burke, 'Change in Perspective').

64 Pictet, *Commentary* (n 6) 335 on Art. 64.

65 Benvenisti, *Law of Occupation* (n 9) 18.

66 Theodor Meron, 'Applicability of Multilateral Conventions to Occupied Territories' (1978) 72 AJIL 542, 550.

67 For a debate on the suspension of treaties, see Burke, 'Change in Perspective' (n 63) 115.

68 Adam Roberts, 'Transformative Military Occupation: Applying the Laws of War and Human Rights' (2006) 100 AJIL 580, 589.

69 Mayorga, 'Occupants, Beware of BITs: Applicability of Investment Treaties to Occupied Territories' (n 1) 33.

The matter of dispute settlement and compensation claims is the second matter which suffers from legal uncertainty, both regarding IHL and the application of BITs during occupation. As BITs are applicable during times of occupation, their exact scope influences the arising protection obligations and potentially resulting compensation claims. If BITs contain full protection and security clauses as well as guarantees of national treatment or most-favoured-nation treatment, this changes the standard of due diligence which the host State of the BIT must provide – a standard that must take into account the restrictions of the host State. The widest limitation on the protection of investment surely arises during the occupation and takeover of factual control over the territory in question. To successfully bring forward a compensation claim, the violation of an obligation must firstly be established. Secondly, circumstances precluding wrongfulness must be excluded. The specific situation of occupation, however, might easily offer such recourse when damages have been caused by third actors or were conducted out of military necessity.[70] Thus, one must analyse these steps in a case-by-case examination and under the respective BIT in question.

II. The Case of Ukraine as an Illustration of the Uncertain Co-Application of Laws

The territorial dispute over parts of Ukraine, most prominently the Crimean Peninsula and eastern Ukraine, as well as the protection of investment between Ukraine, Russia and private investors serves as an illustrative example of the continued dispute over the application of treaties and the interaction of different fields of law.[71] Since early 2014, the Russian grasp of parts of Ukrainian territory, including the takeover of military and political control over Crimea, as well as the partly open, partly covert incursion of Russian forces and equipment in Eastern Ukraine, have given rise to a political and legal outcry of the international community. Yet, discordant reactions by States and diverging argumentation by international lawyers have left private investors in Ukraine struggling. Ukraine possesses

70 Eric de Brabandere, 'Host State's Due Diligence Obligations in International Investment Law' (2015) 42 Syracuse Journal of International Law and Commerce 320.

71 Territorial disputes following an unlawful transfer of territory, for example in Western Sahara, the Palestinian territories or the current tensions surrounding the South China Sea, provide further examples of such disputes.

several different investment treaties with other countries, including Russia, the UK, the US or Germany, obliging the State to protect foreign investment on its territory – some of them include provisions addressing the outbreak of hostilities or insurrections and some incorporate provisions on essential security interests of Ukraine, releasing the State of certain protective duties when pursuing its own legitimate military objectives.

Since 2014, Russia has started imposing Russian laws and legislated new regulation for Crimea in various sectors, such as the financial sector, army services or pension payments.[72] These alterations need to be analysed in detail for their validity under the laws of occupation – a matter which is highly problematic, given that Russia does not acknowledge its status as an occupying force and therefore denies the applicability of the laws of occupation.

A similar question arises with regard to the BITs in force. Which BITs should be applied to settle arising disputes: those between Ukraine and the foreign investors' country or those between Russia and the foreign investors' country? The Ukrainian case is one in which these matters have been or are currently being brought to international attention with regard to compensation claims in investor State arbitrations. Moreover, these ongoing developments pose a conflict between the different legal regimes.

Since mid-2016, numerous investment arbitration claims have been raised against Russia under the UNCITRAL Arbitration Rules pursuant to the Russia-Ukraine BIT. These disputes surround the alleged Russian expropriation of investments of Ukrainian investors in Crimea.[73] Different legal issues concerning the interpretation of certain terms, most notably 'investment' and 'territory', have arisen. While 'investment' covers a broad array of subjects, the investments in question were made prior to the Russian takeover in 2014 and therewith were Ukrainian investments in *de jure* Ukrainian territory rather than Ukrainian investments in factually

---

72 Laura Brank, Danial Gal, Timothy Lindsay et al, 'The Imposition of Russian Law in Crimea: What Does this Mean for Foreign Banks and Companies?' (2014) 19 Westlaw Journal 1.

73 Among others, *Stabil LLC and Others v the Russian Federation* (International Investment Agreement) [2015] PCA Case No 2015-35; *LLC Lugzor and Others v the Russian Federation* (Investment Arbitration) [2015] PCA Case No 2015-29; *Privatbank and Finance Company Finilion LLC v The Russian Federation* (Investment Arbitration) [2015] PCA Case No 2015-21; *Aeroport Belbek LLC and Mr. Kolomoisky v the Russian Federation* (Investment Arbitration) [2015] PCA Case No 2015-07.

Russian-controlled territory. Thus, the tribunals must elaborate on the notion of foreign investment. Secondly, Art. 1 of the BIT interprets 'territory' to be the territory of Russia and Ukraine respectively, as defined in conformity with international law. The takeover of Crimea by Russian forces, however, is broadly considered an unlawful annexation.[74] The latter provides an additional obstacle to the recognition of any arbitral award delivered in this regard, as it might be considered a recognition of the alteration of the status of Crimea.[75] If unchallenged, it further reinforces the factual consolidation of Russia's control over the peninsula. Initial decisions delivered in February 2017 shrank back from actually discussing the lawfulness of the Russian control over Crimea and stated that Russia's obligation under the Russia-Ukraine BIT was triggered following 21 March 2014: the signing date for the decree on the inclusion of Crimea into the Russian Federation signed by President *Vladimir Putin*.[76] These decisions represent a conflict between the general *ex iniuria jus non oritur* rule and the Stimson Doctrine of non-recognition of unlawful territorial changes.[77] To not further consolidate the annexation of Ukrainian territory, compensation claims against the regular host State, Ukraine, would comprise the correct, albeit potentially ineffective channel.

---

74 Sergeis Dilevka, 'Arbitration Claims by Ukrainian Investors under the Russia-Ukraine BIT: Between Crimea and a Hard Place?' (*CIS Arbitration Forum*, 17 February 2016) <http://www.cisarbitration.com/2016/02/17/arbitration-claims-by-ukrainian-investors-under-the-russia-ukraine-bit-between-crimea-and-a-hard-place/> accessed 10 October 2017; UN GA Res 68/262 (27 March 2014) UN Doc S/A/68/262, 'The General Assembly, ... [c]alls upon all States, international organizations and specialized agencies not to recognize any alteration of the status of the Autonomous Republic of Crimea and the city of Sevastopol on the basis of the above-mentioned referendum'.

75 Convention on the Recognition and Enforcement of Foreign Arbitral Award (opened for signature 10 June 1958, entered into force 7 June 1959) 330 UNTS 38, Art. V (1) (c) on the recognition and enforcement of awards.

76 'Russia is Obliged to Protect the Ukrainian Investors in Crimea after the annexation – IA Reporter' (*Ukrainian Hot News*, 10 March 2010) <https://ukrhotnews.com/2017/03/10/russia-is-obliged-to-protect-the-ukraini-an-investors-in-crimea-after-the-annexation-ia-reporter/> accessed 10 October 2017.

77 Benvenisti, *Law of Occupation* (n 9) 142.

D. Concluding Remarks

The contemporary regime of a belligerent occupation establishes the occupant as the temporary administrator of a foreign State's territory. Under this premise, the occupant has to safeguard both public order and the welfare of the affected population. The primary rules concerning the protection of (foreign) property under IHL offer a first fundamental protection, while the regulations concerning the introduction or alteration of the laws in force in the occupied territory prevent the occupant from transforming the territory, including its economy:

> The idea of the law of occupation was to prevent the occupying power from modelling the governmental structure of that territory according to its own needs disregarding the cultural, religious or ethnic background of the society of the occupied territory.[78]

The example of occupied Iraq, however, has shown how discretionary arguments concerning the welfare of the population and resulting necessary changes can be. In particular, the reaction of the international community and its States are of utmost importance to control the occupant's rule in the territory. For the occupant to solely act as an administrator and not as conqueror of new territory, States must hold the State in question accountable to the law of occupation and refuse to acknowledge measures going beyond its scope.

Traditionally, damages resulting from armed conflict were integrated into negotiations for a peace treaty, which left the compensation for losses dependent on the discretion of the negotiating parties, primarily the former occupying power and the victim's home State. The evolution of international law has produced other channels to pursue compensation, such as by means of diplomatic protection via the investor's home State or potentially through regional human rights courts.[79] Investment law, however, offers a much more promising and direct way to claim compensation by the affected investor against the State. Yet, it equally triggers new debates over the interaction of IHL and investment law. The ongoing investment arbitration in Ukraine illustrates the arising dilemma: On the one hand, the arbitrations against Russia, the occupant, but not the original BIT host State, acknowledge and therewith strengthen the occupant's claim over the territory, as they are based on the idea of the

78 Dörmann, 'International Humanitarian Law' (n 54) 308.

79 Robert Kolb, *Advanced Introduction to International Humanitarian Law* (Elgar Publishing 2014) 195.

transfer of treaty obligations to the occupying State. As such, they are an instrument of recognition of transfer of territory and might impede the notion of occupation as a temporary, but not inherent change of power. On the other hand, they could be considered as a means to hold the occupant accountable for violations and therewith also enforce adherence to primary obligations. The recent cases again highlight the importance of the interaction between the different fields of international law. A narrow analysis of each single field of law without recognising its broader effects in other fields will not simplify, but rather hamper the protection of investments during occupation.

Concluding Observations: how International Humanitarian Law is Shaped to Meet the Challenges Arising from Areas of Limited Statehood – Theoretical Problems in Practice

Björnstjern Baade, Linus Mührel and Anton O. Petrov

A. Introduction

The vast majority of armed conflicts since World War II have been non-international in character.[1] In addition to the traditional civil war between a territorial State and a rebel faction, many of these recent conflicts have been and are being fought between a State and various actors, or indeed between non-State actors themselves.[2] Often, outside involvement internationalises and therefore further complicates the situation. These conflicts take place in, contribute to, and indeed create areas of limited statehood in which the territorial State can no longer ensure the implementation of its own law.

1 Michael Clodfelter, *Warfare and Armed Conflicts: A Statistical Reference to Casualty and Other Figures, 1500-2000* (2nd edn, McFarlan & Co. 2002) 593-94; see also the contribution by Vincent Widdig, 'Detention by Organised Armed Groups in Non-International Armed Conflicts – The Role of Non-State Actors in a State-Centred International Legal System' in this volume 124 (hereafter Widdig, 'Detention by Organised Armed Groups'). For an explanation of the decline in inter-State warfare, see recently: Oona A. Hathaway and Scott J. Shapiro, *The Internationalists: How a Radical Plan to Outlaw War Remade the World* (Simon & Schuster 2017).

2 In fact, most conflicts in recent years were fought between non-State actors, and the number of fatalities in these conflicts was only slightly lower than in conflicts with State-involvement according to the available statistical data: Marie Allanson, Erik Melander and Lotta Themnér, 'Organized violence, 1989–2016' (2017) 54 JPR 574, 575-79, for all data of the Uppsala Conflict Data Program see <http://ucdp.uu.se/> accessed 20 November 2017; see also: Heike Krieger, 'Where States Fail, Non-State Actors Rise? Inducing Compliance with International Humanitarian Law in Areas of Limited Statehood' in Heike Krieger (ed), *Inducing Compliance with International Humanitarian Law: Lessons from the African Great Lakes Region* (CUP 2014) 504 (hereafter Krieger, 'Where States Fail, Non-State Actors Rise?').

As exemplified by the contributions to this volume, the challenges posed to IHL and its subsequent implementation by such conflicts are manifold. The increase in armed activities by non-State actors is widely, and rightly so, regarded as a dangerous phenomenon, which might require adaptations to IHL.[3] This volume endeavoured to examine if and how such a development in the law has taken or could take place. Can the rules and principles of IHL be adapted to the challenges of modern armed conflict in a legitimate manner, or are they too rigid, frozen in a state that seems unreasonable under contemporary conditions?

B. The Research so far

This volume sought to expand upon the insights that the research of Collaborative Research Centre 700 'Governance in areas of limited statehood' (*Sonderforschungsbereich* – SFB) generated, in particular the groundwork laid by Project C8 on 'Security Governance' and 'Legitimacy and Law-Making' in IHL.[4]

Ensuring compliance with IHL has always been challenging. The need for international criminal tribunals, the International Criminal Court, and potentially a regional African court,[5] which prosecute at least the main perpetrators of grave international crimes, is testament to this. In areas in which a State's actual power to enforce its law and provide security for the population is fragile or even non-existent, ensuring compliance with IHL by all actors involved becomes even more of a challenge.[6]

---

3 See eg Antonio Cassese, 'States: Rise and Decline of the Primary Subjects of the International Community' in Bardo Fassbender and Anne Peters (eds), *The Oxford Handbook of the History of International Law* (OUP 2014) 49, 69.

4 This research took place in the first funding period from 2010 to 2013 on 'Security Governance and International Law: Humanitarian Governance in Areas of Limited Statehood' and in the second period from 2014 to 2017 on 'Legitimacy and Law-Making in International Humanitarian Law'.

5 See Balingene Kahombo, *Africa within the Justice System of the International Criminal Court: the Need for a Reform* (KFG Working Paper Series No. 2, 2016).

6 Cf also Robert Kolb, *Ius in Bello: Le droit international des conflits armés*, (2nd edn, Helbing Lichtenhahn 2009) 494-96 (hereafter Kolb, *Ius in Bello*).

Traditionally, States considered armed non-State actors within their borders an entirely domestic affair, i.e. rebels to be dealt with as traitors.[7] While States' internal law still regards them as such, their number, persistence and influence has risen starkly,[8] which indicates that responses beyond repressive (military) action by States and beyond (international) criminal prosecution for breaches of IHL[9] may be necessary from an IHL point of view.[10] Project C8 focused in particular on the Great Lakes Region of Africa, which in part exhibits the traits of an area of limited statehood, in order to explore whether IHL is effective in such areas and how its implementation could be enhanced.[11] A central result of this project and the SFB's research more generally was that a rule's prospects for compliance improve significantly if the rule is regarded as legitimate.[12] Even non-State actors who seemingly engage in casual violence against civilians can usually be understood as rational actors.[13] To remain legitimate, and thus effective, the law might therefore have to develop to meet new challenges.[14]

---

7 Lassa F. L. Oppenheim, *International Law: A Treatise*, vol. II: *War and Neutrality* (3rd edn, Longmans, Green and co. 1921) 76, para 59; for the caution exercised by States when drafting CA 3 and AP II see Raphael Schäfer, 'A History of Division(s): A Critical Assessment of the Law of Non-International Armed Conflict' in this volume 43.

8 Cf Sven Chojnacki and Zeljko Branovic, 'New Modes of Security: The Violent Making and Unmaking of Governance in War-Torn Areas of Limited Statehood' in Thomas Risse (ed), *Governance Without a State? Policies and Politics in Areas of Limited Statehood* (Columbia University Press 2011) 89.

9 Reed M. Wood, 'Understanding strategic motives for violence against civilians during civil conflict' in Heike Krieger (ed), *Inducing Compliance with International Humanitarian Law: Lessons from the African Great Lakes Region* (CUP 2014) 13, 41 (hereafter Wood, 'Understanding strategic motives for violence'); Krieger, 'Where States Fail, Non-State Actors Rise?' (n 2) 535-40.

10 This is not to say that the threat of repressive action, such as criminal prosecution, serves no purpose. It may be one of the reasons that induces a party to an armed conflict to comply: Krieger, 'Where States Fail, Non-State Actors Rise?' (n 2) 550-51: non-coercive instruments may work best under a 'shadow of hierarchy'.

11 Heike Krieger, 'Introduction' in Heike Krieger (ed), *Inducing Compliance with International Humanitarian Law: Lessons from the African Great Lakes Region* (CUP 2014) 1.

12 Krieger, 'Where States Fail, Non-State Actors Rise?' (n 2) 504.

13 Ibid, 518-20; Wood, 'Understanding strategic motives for violence' (n 9) 43.

14 Concerning the challenges posed by asymmetrical warfare, cf: Heike Krieger, 'Deutschland im asymmetrischen Konflikt: Grenzen der Anwendung militärischer Gewalt gegen Talibankämpfer in Afghanistan' in Dieter

C. The Development of Law in Theory and Practice

In order to scrutinise the need for and the possibilities of a development of IHL with regard to areas of limited statehood, in particular two topical subjects were discussed in this volume. First, it was debated whether IHL provides for a legal basis for detention in NIACs,[15] and, secondly, it was discussed how IIL reacts to risks to investments emanating from armed conflicts. The contributions strove to shed light on these practical legal issues in a manner that is also historically and theoretically informed.

I. Detention in Non-International Armed Conflicts

IHL does not provide for an express authorisation for detention in NIACs. Seemingly unimpressed by this state of affairs, in practice, detention in NIACs is commonplace.[16] How IHL deals with that phenomenon is therefore of considerable importance and was the subject of various contributions. Must and can existing rules and principles be legitimately developed through interpretation? Do new rules have to be created *de lege ferenda* or is the law as it stands adequate? Does international law authorise detention or do States have to enact domestic legislation for that purpose in order to comply with the requirement for a legal basis imposed by IHRL? Do non-State actors enjoy the authority to detain?

What is to be done if a legal rule seems normatively necessary, but, at first glance at least, no relevant legal material can be located, is a general question of legal theory that is of particular importance for IHL. Often, such a situation is framed as the existence of a normative gap and it is suggested

---

Weingärtner (ed), *Die Bundeswehr als Armee im Einsatz: Entwicklungen im nationalen und internationalen Recht* (Nomos 2010) 39, 59.

15 For an overview of the issue, see: Marco Sassòli, 'Internment' in Frauke Lachenmann and Rüdiger Wolfrum (eds), *The Law of Armed Conflict and the Use of Force* (OUP 2017) 568, 574-75, paras 25-30.

16 Geneva Academy (ed), *Reactions to Norms: Armed Groups and the Protection of Civilians, Policy Briefing No. 1* (2014) 63-68 <https://www.geneva-academy.ch/joom-latools-files/docman-files/Publications/Policy%20Briefing/Geneva%20Academy%20Policy%20Briefing%201_Amed%20Groups%20and%20the%20Protection%20of%20Civilians_April%202014.pdf> accessed 20 November 2017.

that there is a need to fill it.[17] In addition to explicit analogies,[18] highly indeterminate treaty provisions like the Martens Clause in Art. 1 (2) AP I,[19] and general concepts or principles such as military necessity[20] may play a role in addressing such situations.[21]

Constructing a legal basis for detention in NIACs through existing treaty law, customary law or general principles appears to be far from easy. The existence of such a legal basis has been debated intensively in recent times.

---

17 Jörg Kammerhofer, 'Gaps, the *Nuclear Weapons* Advisory Opinion and the Structure of International Legal Argument between Theory and Practice, (2009) 80 BYIL 333, 354 et seq; Ulrich Fastenrath, *Lücken im Völkerrecht* (Duncker Humblot 1991) 15 et seq.

18 See Kevin J. Heller, 'The Use and Abuse of Analogy in IHL' in Jens D. Ohlin, *Theoretical Boundaries of Armed Conflict and Human Rights* (CUP 2016) 232 (hereafter Heller, 'Use and Abuse of Analogy').

19 See Katja Schöberl and Linus Mührel, 'Sunken Vessel or Blooming Flower? Lotus, Permission and Restrictions within International Humanitarian Law' in this volume 59 (hereafter Schöberl and Mührel, 'Sunken Vessel or Blooming Flowe?').

20 Arguing in favour of the principle as an independent constraint on military activities: ICRC, *Interpretive Guidance on the Notion of Direct Participation in Hostilities under International Humanitarian Law* (ICRC 2009), 78-82 (hereafter ICRC, *Direct Participation*); Etienne Henry, *Le Principe de nécessité militaire: Histoire et actualité d'une norme fondamentale du droit international humanitaire* (Pedone 2016), 623-80 (hereafter Henry, *Nécessité militaire*); for critique, see: W. Hays Parks, 'Part IX of the ICRC "Direct Participation in Hostilities" Study: No Mandate, No Expertise, and Legally Incorrect' (2010) 42 JILP 769, 829 (hereafter Parks, 'No Mandate'); in turn, for a defence see: Nils Melzer, 'Keeping the Balance Between Military Necessity and Humanity: A Response to Four Critiques of the ICRC's Interpretive Guidance on the Notion of Direct Participation in Hostilities', (2010) 42 JILP 831, 892 et seq (hereinafter Melzer, 'Keeping the Balance').

21 See Schöberl and Mührel, 'Sunken Vessel or Blooming Flower' (n 19), who find insufficient support for military necessity as an independent principle, but consider the Martens Clause to provide that something which is not explicitly prohibited by IHL is not *ipso facto* permitted.

In contrast to some scholars,[22] but also States[23] and the ICRC,[24] *Manuel Brunner, Vincent Widdig,* and *Matthias Lippold*[25] – whose contribution unfortunately is not a part of this volume –[26], found that the most persuasive arguments speak in favour of the conclusion that IHL currently does not authorise detention in NIACs.[27] *Katja Schöberl* and *Linus Mührel* found this to be the currently prevailing view in international legal discourse.

For States and international organisations that are bound to human rights requiring a legal basis, this finding (only) leads to the need for them to create a legal basis. This basis can either be found in their domestic law, or – as *Matthias Lippold* considered,[28] in accordance with the UK Supreme

22 See most recently: Daragh Murray, 'Non-State Armed Groups, Detention Authority in Non-International Armed Conflict, and the Coherence of International Law: Searching for a Way Forward' (2017) 30 LJIL 435, 446-49 (hereafter Murray, 'Detention in NIAC').

23 For the Obama Administration's position, which derives authority to detain, *inter alia*, from CA 3, see: Naz K. Modirzadeh, 'Folk International Law: 9/11 Lawyering and the Transformation of the Law of Armed Conflict to Human Rights Policy and Human Rights Law to War Governance' in Jens D. Ohlin (ed), *Theoretical Boundaries of Armed Conflict and Human Rights* (CUP 2016) 193, 217, fn 53 (hereafter Modirzadeh, 'Folk International Law'); but cf Lawrence Hill-Cawthorne, *Detention in Non-International Armed Conflict* (OUP 2016) 72 considering US practice to be ambiguous (hereafter Hill-Cawthorne, *Detention in NIAC*).

24 ICRC, *Internment in Armed Conflict: Basic Rules and Challenges* (Opinion Paper 2014) 7-8 <https://www.icrc.org/en/download/file/3223/security-detention-position-paper-icrc-11-2014.pdf> accessed 20 November 2017 (hereafter ICRC, *Internment in Armed Conflict*).

25 LLM (NYU), Doctoral Researcher at the Institute for Public International and European Law of the Georg-August-University Göttingen.

26 See Matthias Lippold, 'Between Humanization and Humanitarization? Detention in Armed Conflicts and the European Convention on Human Rights' (2016) 76 ZaöRV 53, 92-93 (hereafter Lippold, 'Between Humanization and Humanitarization?').

27 See in the same vein: Hill-Cawthorne, *Detention in NIAC* (n 23) 71 et seq, while taking into account the UK Government's recent expression of opinio juris in the case of *Serdar Mohammed.*

28 See on this: Lippold, 'Between Humanization and Humanitarization?' (n 26) 80, 91 et seq.

Court's judgment in *Serdar Mohammed*[29] and the ICRC[30] – in Security Council resolutions explicitly or implicitly authorising detention. Further specifications concerning the conditions and limits of detention might then be supplied by applicable IHRL.[31] Non-State actors, who are not bound by human rights enshrined in treaties, are thereby either left unbound, or, if considered bound to a customary rule prohibiting arbitrary detention,[32] unable to comply with that rule's requirement to detain only when there is a legal basis.[33] But binding non-State actors in some manner would seem desirable to further IHL's aim of protecting the individual.[34]

II. The Protection of Investment in Times of Armed Conflict

Dorota Banaszewska – whose contribution unfortunately is not a part of this volume –[35] drew attention to the fact that not only the relationship between IHL and IHRL can pose a challenge, but also the one between IHL and IIL, which may seem strained by the need to apply in situations of armed conflict. Due diligence obligations, for example under a 'full protection and security' standard, may require a State to do everything feasible to protect investments. A pivotal question in that regard is which role IHL should play in determining the protection and security owed to the investor. IHL might seem better suited for supplying standards appropriate to the situation of armed conflict, but it should not allow States to discard their IIL obligations at will.

Ira Ryk-Lakhman Aharonovich complemented this analysis by shedding light on the categorisation of tangible investments as military objectives.

---

29 *Abd Ali Hameed Al-Waheed (Appellant) v Ministry of Defence (Respondent) and Serdar Mohammed (Respondent) v Ministry of Defence (Appellant)* [2017] UKSC 2, Lord Sumption (with whom Lady Hale agrees), paras 18-30 (hereafter *Serdar Mohammed*).

30 ICRC, *Internment in Armed Conflict* (n 24) 8.

31 Cf *Serdar Mohammed* (n 29), paras 90 et seq.

32 On this controversy, see: Andrew Clapham, 'Focusing on Armed Non-State Actors' in Andrew Clapham and Paola Gaeta (eds), *The Oxford Handbook of International Law in Armed Conflict* (OUP 2014) 766, 786 et seq (hereafter Clapham, 'Focusing on Armed NSAs'); as well as the contribution by Widdig, 'Detention by Organised Armed Groups' (n 1).

33 Hill-Cawthorne, *Detention in NIAC* (n 23) 217-22.

34 For a proposal, see: Hill-Cawthorne, *Detention in NIAC* (n 23) 225 et seq; see also Widdig, 'Detention by Organised Armed Groups' (n 1).

35 Legal advisor working for the Council of Europe in Paris.

Dual-use and revenue-generating targets proved to be the most contentious. The due diligence duty imposed by IIL may at times be at odds with the requirements of IHL in this regard. Any norm conflict would have to be resolved by the *lex specialis* rule on a case-by-case basis.

Charlotte Lülf analysed the protection provided by IHL in situations of occupation, in particular with regard to the occupations of parts of Ukraine in 2014 and of Iraq in 2003. Art. 43 Hague Regulations and Art. 64 GC IV generally require the occupying power to respect the laws of the occupied territory, and BITs of the occupied State may be interpreted to constitute such laws. Under certain conditions, the occupying power may, however, make necessary changes to these laws, mainly in order to safeguard its own security and the well-being of the population in the occupied territory. While the impetus of IHL can insofar be understood to be 'conservationist' – protecting the status quo as far as possible –, the exception clauses have, in the past, been interpreted in a manner that may qualify as very liberal, for example when the US initiated major changes to Iraq's economy.

D. The 'Nature' of International Humanitarian Law

In the discussion of these practical issues, the more theoretical question concerning the permissive or restrictive 'nature' of IHL proved to be of considerable significance. The question whether the effect, or purpose, of IHL is to restrict States' options, or to permit them to make use of additional ones, is frequently termed as pertaining to the 'nature' of IHL. It is often understood to have an influence on how gaps may or may not be filled. *Pia Hesse* observed that the *Lotus* case – the classical starting point for a discussion of the 'nature' of international law in general – might be ill-suited for answering this question, since it rather coordinates States' exercise of jurisdiction, and has no direct impact on a characterisation or interpretation of IHL. Like *Anton O. Petrov*, *Katja Schöberl* and *Linus Mührel* found IHL to be generally restrictive, serving to restrict States' freedom in times of armed conflict.

The terms 'restrictive' and 'permissive' themselves are relative in nature. The categorisation of IHL may accordingly depend on the perspective taken, and might therefore offer more than one answer. IHL may in fact both enable and restrict States' conduct.[36]

---

36 Cf Jens D. Ohlin, 'Introduction: The Inescapble Collision' in Jens D. Ohlin (ed), *Theoretical Boundaries of Armed Conflict and Human Rights* (CUP 2016) 1, 1.

IHL and the institutional practice surrounding it can be understood as governance. According to the definition developed in the SFB, governance denotes 'institutionalized modes of social coordination to produce and implement collectively binding rules, and/or to provide collective goods'.[37] The contributions of this volume have shown that IHL's governance function, the social coordination that IHL is meant to make possible and the collective good modern IHL is meant to provide, serves two purposes.

On the one hand, by producing and implementing binding rules, IHL seeks to provide security to individuals, combatants and civilians alike – but of course to different degrees. It aims to protect them from the consequences of armed conflict that are not militarily necessary.[38] This is the humanitarian aspect of IHL, which is clearly reflected in its historical origins.[39]

On the other hand, bearing in mind that IHL allows for encroaching on individuals' interests in ways otherwise inconceivable under IHRL,[40] its function can also be understood as enabling States' armed forces to conduct warfare in an effective manner.[41] The legal prohibition of Art. 2 (4) UN-Charter embodies the aspiration that inter-State war should not break out.

---

37 Tanja Börzel et al, 'Governance in Areas of Limited Statehood: Conceptual Clarifications and Major Contributions of the Handbook' in Tanja Börzel et al (eds), *The Oxford Handbook of Governance and Limited Statehood* (OUP 2018) 6.

38 For the shift of the purpose of the laws of war from honour and chivalry to humanitarian concerns, see: Robert Kolb, 'The Protection of the Individual in Times of War and Peace' in Bardo Fassbender and Anne Peters (eds), *The Oxford Handbook of the History of International Law* (OUP 2014) 317 at 321 et seq (hereafter Kolb, 'Protection of the Individual'); compare Silja Vöneky, 'Francis Lieber (1798 – 1872)' in Bardo Fassbender and Anne Peters (eds), *The Oxford Handbook of the History of International Law* (OUP 2014) 1137, 1139-40, who would already ascribe it to *Lieber*; for an even later date (after AP I and in the 1990s), see Amanda Alexander, 'A Short History of International Humanitarian Law' (2015) 26 EJIL 109 (hereafter Alexander, 'Short History of IHL').

39 See eg Frits Karlshoven, 'History of international humanitarian law treaty-making' in Rain Liivoja and Tim McCormack (eds), Routledge Handbook of the Law of Armed Conflict (Routledge 2016) 33, 34 et seq.

40 For example, collateral damage under Art. 57 (5) (b) AP I.

41 Cf *Raphael Schäfer's* contribution for the war-legitimising effect of IHL; also concerning the disciplinary effect of IHL: Eyal Benvenisti and Amichai Cohen, 'War is Governance: Explaining the Logic of the Laws of War From a Principal-Agent Perspective' (2014) 112 Michigan Law Review 1363, 1367 et seq.

Likewise, the domestic law of States prohibits internal strife.[42] IHL embodies the realisation that peace may collapse despite our best efforts at preserving it.

The *jus in bello* thus cannot become a *jus contra bellum* by rendering the conduct of hostilities impossible. Once an armed conflict exists, IHL allows States to fight it effectively to a degree that would not be possible under IHRL, but that is limited nonetheless. To speak in *Lotus* terms, restrictions on States' sovereign independence, which is in itself a principle of international law,[43] are not presumed, but based on the positive provisions of IHRL.[44] IHL in turn offers States greater freedom to wage war. Non-State actors have so far not been understood as beneficiaries of that function.

E. How to Approach Non-State Actors

Since the involvement of non-State actors forms a significant part of modern armed conflict, particularly in areas of limited statehood, IHL needs to respond and maybe adapt to this situation.[45] To this end, two aspects should be taken into account when considering (the need for) a development of IHL: military necessity and capacity from non-State actors' point of view (1.) as well as their self-interest in complying with IHL. The latter can be engaged by creating incentives for compliance by non-State actors as groups (2.) and by individual fighters (3.).

42 A *jus contra bellum internum* does not exist (yet) as a distinct rule of international law: Claus Kreß, 'Review Essay on Emily Crawford, The Treatment of Combatants and Insurgents under the Law of Armed Conflict/Anthony Cullen, The Concept of Non-International Armed Conflict in International Humanitarian Law/Noam Lubell, Extraterritorial Use of Force against Non-State Actors/Sandesh Sivakumaran, The Law of Non-International Armed Conflict' (2012) 83 BYIL 145, 159.

43 Samantha Besson, 'Sovereignty' in Rüdiger Wolfrum (ed), MPEPIL, vol. IX (OUP 2012) 366, 378 et seq, paras 85-89, 114-17.

44 Hill-Cawthorne, *Detention in NIAC* (n 23) 66-67; Heller, 'Use and Abuse of Analogy' (n 18) 285.

45 Murray, 'Detention in NIAC' (n 22) 456.

I. Take into Account their Situation, in Particular their Military Necessities

As with States' armed forces, rules that seek to attract compliance by non-State actors must also take into account the non-State actors' situation; in particular, their capacity to comply with certain rules.[46] This may mean taking into account the resources available to a specific non-State actor,[47] but also military necessity seen from the non-State actor's point of view. An example from the law of IAC may illustrate this: interpreting a rule like Article 4 A (2) GC III so as to require an irregular fighter (belonging to an IAC party) to be exceedingly easy to spot from afar will certainly not attract compliance, as it does not sufficiently take into account the operational pressures exerted on this specific aspect of warfare.[48] This was recognised in Art. 44 AP I, which, 'owing to the nature of the hostilities', adjusts the obligation and requires only to openly carry one's arms.[49] IHL likewise does not require non-State actors to wear a uniform.[50]

Similarly, as noted by *Vincent Widdig*, the lack of a basis for non-State actors to detain might have adverse consequences for individuals, combatants and civilians alike, who might not be captured, but killed or treated inhumanely.[51] By giving non-State actors no practical choice but to violate the law, IHL loses relevance to them.[52] This is mirrored by the emphasis IIL puts on due diligence obligations for States in armed conflict, which acknowledges that even the capacity of States to ensure certain results can be limited.

---

46 Anton Petrov, 'Non-State Actors and Law of Armed Conflict Revisited: Enforcing International Law through Domestic Engagement' (2014) 19 JCSL 279, 281, 293-94 (hereafter Petrov, 'NSAs and LOAC').

47 Cf Art. 5 AP II: 'within the limits of their capabilities'; Sandesh Sivakumaran, *The Law of Non-International Armed Conflict* (OUP 2012) 295-96 (hereafter Sivakumaran, *Law of NIAC*).

48 For such an interpretation in the British Military Manual of 1958, see: Emily Crawford, 'From Inter-state and Symmetric to Intra-state and Asymmetric: Changing Methods of Warfare and the Law of Armed Conflict in the 100 Years Since World War One' (2014) 17 YbIHL 95, 104-6 (hereafter Crawford, 'LOAC since WWI').

49 Ibid.

50 Petrov, 'NSAs and LOAC' (n 46) 290, 292-93.

51 Cf Murray, 'Detention in NIAC' (n 22) 450-451; Anthea Roberts and Sandesh Sivakumaran, 'Lawmaking by Nonstate Actors: Engaging Armed Groups in the Creation of International Humanitarian Law' (2012) 38 Yale J. Int'l L. 107.

52 Cf Clapham, 'Focusing on Armed NSAs' (n 32) 769.

Finally, in terms of capacity, it should not be forgotten that knowledge of the law is a precondition for compliance.[53] Providing training in IHL for non-State actors, as done by the ICRC and Geneva Call,[54] is therefore of considerable importance.

Taking into account such considerations, of course, does not mean that they will prevail in determining what the law provides for or ought to provide for.[55] Taking into account the military necessities of parties to the conflict must not lead to an unreflected race to the point where 'anything goes'. A case in point is the temptation to compensate military inferiority by actions violating IHL that exploit the other side's adherence to this body of law, which may at times be observed in some non-State actors.[56] Taking operational needs into account cannot mean a return to the doctrine of *Kriegsraison*, which allows for any and all action required by military necessity.

As many rules of modern IHL show, military necessity is and will remain an important aspect of the law of armed conflict, but so will humanitarian concerns. Being too 'responsive' to the needs of non-State actors in particular might dilute established standards without actually improving compliance,[57] and might thus also damage IHL's legitimacy. For example, a group's capacity to control the actions of its fighters might often be problematic in practice.[58] But this cannot absolve the group and its leaders from responsibility for crimes committed, or lower legal standards. After all, asymmetry has always been a hallmark of NIAC.[59]

Likewise, when considering taking into account non-State actor views and practices, it should not be forgotten that, especially in areas of limited statehood, non-State actors may thrive which endanger human rights. They

---

53 Petrov, 'NSAs and LOAC' (n 46) 281.

54 For the ICRC see: Steven R. Ratner, 'Law Promotion Beyond Law Talk: The Red Cross, Persuasion, and the Laws of War' (2011) 22 EJIL 459.

55 Cf Sandesh Sivakumaran, 'How to Improve upon the Faulty Legal Regime of Internal Armed Conflict' in Antonio Cassese (ed), *Realizing Utopia: The Future of International Law* (OUP 2012) 525, 534.

56 Crawford, 'LOAC since WWI' (n 48) 108-9; Petrov, 'NSAs and LOAC' (n 46) 289-90; Robin Geiß, 'Asymmetric conflict structures' (2006) 88 IRRC 757, 758.

57 Cf James T. Johnson, 'The Ethics of Insurgency' (2017) 31 Ethics & International Affairs 367, 381-82 (hereafter Johnson, 'The Ethics of Insurgency'); Petrov, 'NSAs and LOAC' (n 46) 303.

58 Johnson, 'The Ethics of Insurgency' (n 57) 372; Krieger, 'Where States Fail, Non-State Actors Rise?' (n 2) 509.

59 Petrov, 'NSAs and LOAC' (n 46) 290.

may fill a governance gap left by the territorial State and disregard well-established human rights standards or turn against other States and their populations – effective governance by actors willing and able is a vital precondition for human rights protection after all.[60]

II. Create Incentives for the Non-State Actor as a Group

Historically and in addition to general humanitarian motives, a principal reason for the development of and compliance with IHL has been self-interest.[61] Reciprocity, the mutual abstention from violations which benefits both sides' protected persons, has long been recognised as one of the driving forces behind compliance.[62] Not alienating the enemy more than necessary to ensure a more sustainable peace, better operational effectiveness, or simply an interest in not destroying more than necessary the spoils of war, have proven to be other factors of self-interest of warring parties which lead to better protection for the individual.[63] In addition to such self-interest, which still serves as a meaningful rationale to justify IHL,[64] IHL may by

60 Cf John C. Dehn, 'Whither International Martial Law? Human Rights as Sword and Shield in Ineffectively Governed Territory' in Jens D. Ohlin (ed), *Theoretical Boundaries of Armed Conflict and Human Rights* (CUP 2016) 315, 315, 340-42, 347.

61 However, it should be noted that self-interest can only be one factor in explaining States' and other entities' decision-making processes, cf: Andrea Bianchi, 'Law, Time, and Change: The Self-Regulatory Function of Subsequent Practice' in Georg Nolte (ed), *Treaties and Subsequent Practice* (OUP 2013) 133, 137; Thomas Forster, 'International humanitarian law's old questions and new perspectives: On what law has got to do with armed conflict' (2017) 98 IRRC 995 (hereafter: Forster, 'IHL's old questions and new perspectives').

62 For this, as well as the separate legal question of belligerent reprisals, see: Shane Darcy, 'Reciprocity and reprisals' in Rain Liivoja and Tim McCormack (eds), *Routledge Handbook of the Law of Armed Conflict* (Routledge 2016) 492, 492 et seq; Petrov, 'NSAs and LOAC' (n 46) 285-86, 304-5; see generally: Bruno Simma, 'Reciprocity' in Rüdiger Wolfrum (ed), MPEPIL, vol. XIII (OUP 2012) 651.

63 Kolb, 'Protection of the Individual' (n 38) 322.

64 Morten Bergsmo and Tianying Song, 'Ensuring Accountability for Core International Crimes in Armed Forces: Obligations and Self-Interest' in Morten Bergsmo and Tianying Song (eds), *Military Self-Interest in Accountability for Core International Crimes* (Torkel Opsahl 2015) 1, 14 et seq, enumerating in a non-exhaustive manner *inter alia* domestic legitimacy, accomplishment of

now be so entrenched in States' militaries as to be effective qua internalisation.[65] For many non-State actors, compliance cannot be expected in that manner.

As *Lars Müller* and *Vincent Widdig* emphasised, improving IHL's input legitimacy for non-State actors by involving them in the law-making process in some form could be a method to encourage compliance.[66] This has been actively pursued by the NGO Geneva Call, which has successfully been engaging with non-State actors, encouraging them to sign 'Deeds of Commitment' to IHL, providing support to comply with them, and monitoring compliance.[67] Here, just like with States, self-interest can further compliance with IHL.[68] Recently, the Brussels Court of Appeal took note of the Deed of Commitment signed by the PKK and their intent to abide by IHL; this happened in the context of determining whether the group had the necessary degree of organisation to be a party to a NIAC in the sense of the *Tadic* test, and, thus, not count as 'terrorists' under Belgian domestic law.[69] Shared self-interest might also be used to conclude 'special agreements' in the sense of CA 3 between States and non-State actors that clarify and reinforce the applicable legal framework.[70]

By committing to the observance of IHL in one form or another, non-State actors may seek to benefit from others' reciprocal commitments – for example, if connected to a certain population that is in its interest to protect – or, just like States, they might seek political legitimacy and

---

counter-insurgency and peace-building, internal morale, order and discipline, i.e. operational effectiveness. See the other contributions in that volume, too.

65 Cf eg Harold H. Koh, 'Internalization Through Socialization' (2004-2005) 54 Duke Law Journal 975; Forster, 'IHL's old questions and new perspectives' (n 61).

66 Krieger, 'Where States Fail, Non-State Actors Rise?' (n 2) 531-34; Crawford, 'LOAC since WWI' (n 48) 114; Petrov, 'NSAs and LOAC' (n 46) 298 et seq; cf Jean d'Aspremont, 'Non-State Actors and the Formation of International Customary Law: Unlearning Some Common Tropes' in Iain Scobbie and Sufyan Droubi (eds), *Non-State Actors and the Formation of Customary International Law* (Manchester University Press 2018, forthcoming) (hereafter d'Aspremont, 'Non-State Actors and the Formation of International Customary Law').

67 Clapham, 'Focusing on Armed NSAs' (n 32) 802-5; Sivakumaran, *Law of NIAC* (n 47) 107 et seq (on their legal nature) and 538-41 (on Geneva Call in particular); see also the contribution by *Vincent Widdig* in this volume 124.

68 Krieger, 'Where States Fail, Non-State Actors Rise?' (n 2) 520-31.

69 Cour d'appel de Bruxelles, Arrêt à charge de X et al, No. 2017/2911 (14 September 2017).

70 Petrov, 'NSAs and LOAC' (n 46) 298, 312.

operational effectiveness by complying with IHL.[71] In this context, symbolic validation is an important feature. Deeds of Commitment, signed in Geneva City Hall's Alabama Hall (where the First GC was signed in 1864), and with the Government of the Republic and Canton of Geneva acting as custodian of the Deeds, might do more to improve a group's compliance with IHL than a direct change in the law-making process, which States are bound to vigorously oppose in any case.[72]

Nonetheless, exploring the practice of non-State actors in armed conflict, to a certain extent mirroring the ICRC customary law study, might be a worthwhile endeavour.[73] Besides the already mentioned risk of hereby diluting IHL standards,[74] it remains to be seen if one non-State actor would feel bound to the practice of another.[75]

III. Create Incentives for Individual Fighters

Another important idea to improve compliance by non-State actors is to grant their fighters some form of immunity for their participation in the hostilities equivalent to combatant immunity.[76] However, the gains in compliance that may be achieved from this might be more than offset by

71 Krieger, 'Where States Fail, Non-State Actors Rise?' (n 2); Clapham, 'Focusing on Armed NSAs' (n 32) 803-4; see also: David Kennedy, 'Lawfare and warfare' in James Crawford and Martti Koskenniemi (eds), *The Cambridge Companion to International Law* (CUP 2012) 158, 162-64, 179-80.

72 See for this process established by Geneva Call: Geneva Call, *Engaging Armed Non-State Actors in a Landmine Ban: The Geneva Call Progress Report (2000-2007)* (Geneva Call 2007) <https://www.files.ethz.ch/isn/100311/gc-progress-report-07.pdf> accessed 20 November 2017.

73 Annyssa Bellal, *From Words to Deeds: Exploring the Practice of Armed Non-State Actors and its Impact on the Implementation of International Law*, Geneva Academy Project in partnership with Geneva Call, <https://www.geneva-academy.ch/our-projects/our-projects/detail/55-from-words-to-deeds-exploring-the-practice-of-armed-non-state-actors-and-its-impact-on-the-implementation-of-international-law> accessed 20 November 2017.

74 Petrov, 'NSAs and LOAC' (n 46) 305-6.

75 Ibid, 303, 308. In favour of customary law created by and for non-State actors, see d'Aspremont, 'Non-State Actors and the Formation of International Customary Law' (n 66).

76 Cf Sivakumaran, *Law of NIAC* (n 47) 514-20; Emily Crawford, *The Treatment of Combatants and Insurgents Under the Law of Armed Conflict* (OUP 2010) 153 et seq.

the loss in incentive not to take up arms in the first place.[77] In any case, a customary rule granting combatant immunity to fighters of well-organised armed groups complying with IHL certainly does not exist yet.[78] When considering granting non-State actors' fighters such immunity to improve compliance with IHL, it may be a separate issue whether this immunity should be extended to the leadership. Similar to a prosecution for the crime of aggression for a serious violation of the prohibition of using inter-State force,[79] it could – depending on the particular circumstances – be advisable to retain the possibility to sanction the persons primarily responsible for breaking the internal peace of a State.[80] Under the law as it stands, amnesties are a policy choice that States can and should consider.[81] Art. 6 (5) AP II encourages States to grant amnesties, as should the toll the civilian population is likely to bear if the conflict continues, because there is no incentive for non-State actors to stop it[82]. Considering compliance with IHL as a mitigating factor in treason charges might be another option.[83]

The peace process in Columbia, which at the time of writing is still ongoing, is an example of amnesties being part of a settlement.[84] But, it also highlights that many details need to be worked out for such amnesties to be

77 Petrov, 'NSAs and LOAC' (n 46) 310 et seq; Claus Kress, 'Der Bürgerkrieg und das Völkerrecht: Zwei Entwicklungslinien und eine Zukunftsfrage' (2014) 69 JZ 365, 370 (hereafter Kress, 'Bürgerkrieg und Völkerrecht').

78 Considering it to be *in statu nascendi*: Antonio Cassese, 'Should Rebels be Treated as Criminals? Some Modest Proposals for Rendering Internal Armed Conflicts Less Inhumane' in Antonio Cassese (ed), *Realizing Utopia: The Future of International Law* (OUP 2012) 519, 523-24 (hereafter Cassese, 'Rebels as Criminals?').

79 Art. 8 bis ICC-Statute.

80 For the discussion of a very restricted right to resistance in the case of the worst human rights violations, see: Kress, 'Bürgerkrieg und Völkerrecht' (n 77) 371.

81 See in detail, including doubts regarding the effectiveness of amnesties as an incentive for compliance with IHL, Petrov, 'NSAs and LOAC' (n 46) 305; Frédéric Mégret, 'Should Rebels Be Amnestied?' in Carsten Stahn et al (eds), *Jus Post Bellum: Mapping the Normative Foundations* (OUP 2014) 519, 539-40.

82 See Wood, 'Understanding strategic motives for violence' (n 9) 41-43.

83 Kolb, *Ius in Bello* (n 6) 495.

84 'Columbia: President Santos grants Farc members amnesty' *BBC* (11 July 2017) <http://www.bbc.com/news/world-latin-america-40564577> accessed 30 November 2017.

perceived as legitimate.[85] Grave breaches of IHL certainly constitute a legal red line.

F. States, Courts, Scholars and the Development of International Humanitarian Law

Both, detention and the protection of investment in armed conflicts, are far from being abstract academic subjects. *Dorota Banaszewska's*, *Charlotte Lülf's* and *Ira Ryk-Lakhman Aharonovitch's* contributions showed this concerning the topic of investment protection. *Hannah Dönges'*[86] contribution, which unfortunately could not become a part of this volume, exemplified this most clearly for the subject of detention: even peacekeeping operations detain persons who can be directly affected by the legal constraints, or a lack thereof. The reality on the ground tends to spawn challenges that had not been conceived of when the rules were initially devised. The attempt to establish a detention regime that conforms to rule-of-law standards can meet severe difficulties in practice. However, such challenges may also exert pressure on the law and relevant actors to step up to the occasion and develop a framework which allows for reasonable solutions to the practical problems that arise.

As *Raphael Schäfer* found in his contribution, legal development, in particular changes in the laws of armed conflict, has generally been gradual and evolutionary in the past, not abrupt and revolutionary. While in some instances, States have proactively regulated warfare – the treaty prohibitions of asphyxiating or deleterious gases[87] and the prohibition of laser weapons[88] seem to be the only examples so far –, most changes in IHL

85 Alexandra V. Huneeus and Rene Uruena, 'Introduction to Symposium on the Columbian Peace Talks and International Law (November 3, 2016)' (2016) 110 AJIL Unbound 161.

86 Doctoral Researcher at the Centre on Conflict, Development & Peacebuilding (Graduate Institute Geneva) and a PhD Candidate in International Relations/Political Science at the Graduate Institute of International and Development Studies.

87 Declaration concerning the prohibition of the use of projectiles with the sole object to spread asphyxiating poisonous gases 1899 and Art. 23 lit. a HR, which of course were woefully ineffective in WWI and also fraught with some interpretative uncertainty: Thilo Marauhn, 'The Prohibition to Use Chemical Weapons' (2014) 17 YbIHL 25, 28 et seq.

88 See Kolb, *Ius in Bello* (n 6) 298.

have been reactive, attempting to adapt the law to 'the new realities of warfare'.[89]

Since 9/11, many proposed adaptations to the restrictions imposed on States by IHL as well as IHRL, have aimed at granting States greater freedom to meet new challenges.[90] As noted above, legitimate interpretations need to take into account all legally relevant reasons, including the will and practice of States. Overemphasising deference to States, though, may in certain situations lead to the creation of mere 'folk international humanitarian law', i.e. 'a set of concepts spoken and interpreted by a broad range of actors to provide a loose moral restraint on the organized use of lethal force'.[91] The approach of US administrations to IHL since 9/11 at least in part seems to resemble such a categorisation. As *Charlotte Lülf* notes in her contribution, in addition to international courts and tribunals, as far as they have jurisdiction, the responsibility to effectively hold States to reasonable interpretations of their competences and obligations under IHL falls first and foremost to other States in the international community, which should choose not to recognise excessive claims. The work of scholars may likewise play a role in this discourse.

If the discourse on how to interpret and apply IHL were left solely to military institutions, the demands of military necessity would likely be given too much weight at times.[92] While auto-interpretation by States is sure to remain a decisive part of IHL in the near future, the contestation of their

---

89 Crawford, 'LOAC since WWI' (n 48) 106; Robin Geiß and Andreas Zimmermann, 'The International Committee of the Red Cross: A Unique Actor in the Field of International Humanitarian Law Creation and Progressive Development' in Robin Geiß et al (eds), *Humanizing the Laws of War: The Red Cross and the Development of International Humanitarian Law* (CUP 2017) 215, 226-27 (hereafter Geiß and Zimmermann, 'The ICRC: A Unique Actor').

90 Modirzadeh, 'Folk International Law' (n 23) 196 et seq.

91 Ibid, 224.

92 Cf Robert Cryer, 'The International Committee of the Red Cross' "Interpretive Guidance on the Notion of Direct Participation in Hostilities": See a Little Light' in Robin Geiß et al (eds), *Humanizing the Laws of War: The Red Cross and the Development of International Humanitarian Law* (CUP 2017) 113, 135-36 (hereafter Cryer, 'ICRC and Direct Participation'); Chris af Jochnick and Roger Normand, 'The Legitimation of Violence: A Critical History of the Laws of War' (1994) 35 Harv. Int'l L. J. 49, 74; Raphael Schäfer, 'Anwendung humanitärvölkerrechtlicher Normen in asymmetrischen Konflikten: Extensive Auslegung oder "Lawfare"-Methode?' (*Völkerrechtsblog*, 23 December 2015) <http://voelkerrechtsblog.org/anwendung-humanitarvolkerrechtlicher-normen-in-asymmetrischen-konflikten/> accessed 20 November 2017.

interpretations by other States and scholars is likewise an important feature of international law as a decentralised legal order.[93] Indeed, interpretations advanced by scholars can contribute to adapting established IHL rules to specific situations;[94] the issuance of expert manuals that seek to restate the *lex lata* for the contingencies of naval, air, cyber, and soon, space warfare,[95] or the ICRC's customary law study,[96] speak to the relevance attached to such an enterprise.

The exact requirements of the law will, of course, remain subject to controversial debate in many cases. But it is certainly advisable to adhere to the methodological standards established in international law; even though, their nature and requirements may in themselves be subject to controversy. One should avoid the urge to fill perceived *lacunae* in the law using a methodology that could be wielded too freely, since in different hands it might produce vastly diverging results.[97] For example, the use of analogy, a methodological device well-known to many domestic legal orders, is rarely advanced or accepted in international law as an argument. Most recently, its post-9/11 use to seek an expansion of the legal options of

93 Alexander, 'Short History of IHL' (n 38) 130 et seq, and in particular 136-37; cf Anton Petrov, 'Lawfare? We need the states to interpret international humanitarian law' (*Völkerrechtsblog*, 28 December 2015) <http://voelkerrechtsblog.org/lawfare-we-need-the-states-to-interpret-international-humanitarian-law/> accessed 20 November 2017.

94 Crawford, 'LOAC since WWI' (n 48) 113.

95 Louise Doswald-Beck (ed), *San Remo Manual on International Law Applicable to Armed Conflict at Sea* (CUP 1994); Humanitarian Policy and Conflict Research (HPCR), *Manual on International Law Applicable to Air and Missile Warfare* (CUP 2013); Michael N. Schmitt (ed), *Tallinn Manual on the International Law applicable to Cyber Warfare* (2013); Michael N. Schmitt (ed), *Tallinn Manual 2.0 on the International Law Applicable to Cyber Operations* (CUP 2017); the forthcoming Manual on International Law Applicable to Military Uses of Outer Space (MILAMOS), for further information see: <https://www.mcgill.ca/milamos/> accessed 20 November 2017.

96 For its impact, and the function of custom to adapt to new challenges, see: Jean-Marie Henckaerts, 'The International Committee of the Red Cross and Customary International Law' in Robin Geiß et al (eds), *Humanizing the Laws of War: The Red Cross and the Development of International Humanitarian Law* (CUP 2017) 83, 92, 96 et seq (Henckaerts, 'ICRC and Custom').

97 Cf Cryer, 'ICRC and Direct Participation' (n 92) 136.

the US in its 'War on Terror', also as regards detention in NIACs, showed clearly the potential implications of such a development.[98]

Since questions of methodology are always questions of competence, anyone interpreting and applying IHL must take into account his or her position in the law-making process. An interpretation too detached from the interpretative constraints of State will and practice might be rejected in practice. The resistance to the Interpretive Guidance on the Notion of Direct Participation in Hostilities under International Humanitarian Law advanced by the ICRC in 2009[99] and even its customary law study[100] is a case in point. Regarding the latter, the theoretical question of what counts as State practice and *opinio juris*, and how such material should be evaluated formed a decisive part of the critique by States and scholars.[101]

It has also been noted that interpreters should be wary of too uncritically equating an expansion of the law with progress.[102] Scholarly attempts at

---

98 Heller, 'Use and Abuse of Analogy' (n 18) 234, 275 et seq, rejecting such analogies as unlawful under international law.

99 ICRC, *Direct Participation* (n 20); Kenneth Watkin, 'Opportunity Lost: Organized Armed Groups and the ICRC "Direct Participation in Hostilities" Interpretive Guidance' (2010) 42 JILP 641, 693-94: '... certainly not a re-statement of existing law ... does not reflect either the nature of warfare or the historical and contemporary scope of armed conflict ... bias against State armed forces ...'; Parks, 'No Mandate (n 20). For a defence, see: Melzer, 'Keeping the Balance' (n 20).

100 Jean-Marie Henckaerts and Louise Doswald-Beck, *Customary International Humanitarian Law*, vol. I: Rules (CUP 2005).

101 See 'Letter from John Bellinger III, Legal Adviser, U.S. Dept of State, and William J. Haynes, General Counsel, U.S. Depart. of Defense, to Dr. Jacob Kellenberger, President, International Committee of the Red Cross, Regarding Customary International Law Study, November 3, 2006' reprinted in (2007) 46 ILM 514, 515-16, calling for a 'more rigorous' approach to the ascertainment of State practice and *opinio juris*; confirmed in Department of Defense, *Law of War Manual* (2015) 1075; likewise Daniel Bethlehem, 'The Methodological framework of the Study' in Elizabeth Wilmshurst and Susan Breau (eds), *Perspectives on the ICRC Study on Customary International Humanitarian Law* (CUP 2007) 3, 4 et seq; Iain Scobbie, 'The approach to customary international law in the Study' in Elizabeth Wilmshurst and Susan Breau (eds), *Perspectives on the ICRC Study on Customary International Humanitarian Law* (CUP 2007) 15, 27: 'less stringent [than the ICJ in the *North Sea Continental Shelf* case]'.

102 See, maybe somewhat too critical in his appraisal of International Criminal Law: Jean d'Aspremont, 'The Two Cultures of International Criminal Law' in Kevin J. Heller et al (eds), *Oxford Handbook of International Criminal Law* (OUP 2018, forthcoming), Working Paper available <https://ssrn.com/abstract=2910295> accessed 20 November 2017.

'pushing' for certain rules to rapidly become accepted as custom despite clear resistance by States[103] seem unlikely to be successful. However, clinging to a very restrictive interpretation of States' will in spite of a glaring need to interpret the law in a manner that allows for resolving issues that arise in practice might similarly delegitimise the law. Legitimate interpretations that provide reasonable solutions to legal problems require taking into account all interpretative aspects provided for in the VCLT, such as a rule's object and purpose, its effectiveness and systematic considerations. However, legal practice shows that certain marks of authority may compensate for a lack of adherence to the rules of interpretation reflected in the VCLT. For example, the Pictet Commentaries to the four 1949 Geneva Conventions, written a decade prior to the adoption of the VCLT, emphasized subjective aspects of interpretation rather than objective ones, i.e. they relied heavily on the *travaux préparatoires* and the circumstances of the treaties' conclusion (the 'spirit of the time'). Nevertheless, the commentaries were widely taken into account in legal practice by reference to their authority[104] and established a basis for many concepts which are widely accepted today in IHL as well as in international criminal law.[105]

When reflecting on their profession, and in particular when attempting to apply indeterminate legal concepts to the challenges of contemporary times, lawyers should bear in mind not only their own role in the law-making process, but also the purpose and limits of the law they interpret. The increased input-legitimacy of being mandated to study State practice or

103 Explicitly so, envisioning to recruit the ICRC and the UN GA as 'midwives', Cassese, 'Rebels as Criminals?' (n 78) 524.

104 See eg *Prosecutor v Milutinovic et al* (Judgment Volume 4 of 4) IT-05-87-T (26 February 2009) Annex B; *Prosecutor v Stanisic and Zupljanin* (Judgment Volume 3 of 3) IT-08-91-T (27 March 2013) Annex III; *Prosecutor v Hadzihasanovic et al* (Decision on interlocutory appeal challenging jurisdiction in relation to command responsibility) IT-01-47-AR72 (16 July 2003) para 15; *Prosecutor v Tadic* (Judgment) IT-94-1-A (15 July 1999) para 93; Joint Separate Opinion of Judges Higgins, Kooijmans and Buergenthal in Arrest Warrant of 11 April 2000 (*Democratic Republic of the Congo v Belgium*) [2002] ICJ Rep 3, 63, para 31.

105 For further reading, see Linus Mührel, 'Die Kommentare des Internationalen Komitees vom Roten Kreuz, ihre Autorität und ihr Einfluss auf die Entwicklung des humanitären Völkerrechts im Wandel der Zeit' in Sebastian Wuschka et al (eds), *Zeit und Internationales Recht* (Mohr Siebeck 2018, forthcoming).

interpret the law – enjoyed to some degree by the ICRC –[106] increases the significance that a contribution might have in legal discourse, but is certainly not determinative of it.[107] States may yet reject its interpretations.[108] While certainly not free to devise new solutions from scratch – unless labelled *de lege ferenda* –, interpreters cannot be restricted to only that which has already been thought. If that were the case, no development save by treaty amendment or compellingly clear State practice would be possible. It is also legal scholars' task to devise possible solutions to new challenges by employing legal methodology.[109] Maybe it is one of the enduring lessons of *Lotus* that, in doing so, the burden of argumentation rests on them. Yet, the existence of abstract terms and general clauses in IHL treaties, in particular the Martens Clause,[110] and the existence of diverse aspects relevant for interpretation in the VCLT, show that the law is meant to regulate even situations unthought-of before, as well as respond to new challenges.

Interpretive proposals *de lege lata* as well as proposals *de lege ferenda* which aim to adapt the law to new challenges, must take into account not only humanitarian concerns, but also the demands of effective warfare if they seek to make an impact.[111] This also includes the need for obtaining as

---

106 See in general: Geiß and Zimmermann, 'The ICRC: A Unique Actor' (n 89) 215; Kelisiana Thynne 'The role of the International Committee of the Red Cross' in Rain Liivoja and Tim McCormack (eds), *Routledge Handbook of the Law of Armed Conflict* (Routledge 2016) 477, 481, 486-90; for the customary law study: Henckaerts, 'ICRC and Custom' (n 96) 96 et seq.

107 For the critical reactions to the ICRC's Interpretive Guidance on Direct Participation, see: Cryer, 'ICRC and Direct Participation' (n 92) 132 et seq.

108 Geiß and Zimmermann, 'The ICRC: A Unique Actor' (n 89) 237.

109 See Anne Peters, 'The Rise and Decline of the International Rule of Law and the Job of Scholars' in Heike Krieger et al (eds), *The International Rule of Law: Rise or Decline?* (forthcoming), Working Paper available <https://ssrn.com/abstract=3029462> accessed 20 November 2017.

110 Cf Kolb, *Ius in* Bello (n 6) 122-26.

111 Most clearly: Geoffrey S. Corn et. al, 'Belligerent Targeting and the Invalidity of a Least Harmful Means Rule' (2013) 89 International Law Studies 536, 541: '… LOAC must, as it has historically, remain rationally grounded in the realities of warfare', and *in concreto* 610 et seq; see also on this Cryer, 'ICRC and Direct Participation' (n 92) 132 et seq; Jochnick and Normand, 'The Legitimation of Violence' (n 92) 83-84, although *in concreto* too critical of the practicality of the 1923 Hague Rules of Air Warfare, for whose (partly) customary law status see: Michael N. Schmitt, 'Air Warfare' in Andrew Clapham and Paola Gaeta (eds), *The Oxford Handbook of International Law in Armed Conflict* (OUP 2014) 118, 121-22.

much legal certainty as possible. Members of armed forces, who manage high levels of factual uncertainty in fulfilling their tasks,[112] have a keen interest in knowing precisely what the law requires from them so as not to become liable to disciplinary sanctions or criminal prosecution.[113] Considering the dynamic nature of warfare, military personnel applying the law will often, and legitimately so, enjoy discretion in making *bona fide* decisions on the ground.[114] These are structural cornerstones of IHL that cannot be spirited away: IHL is not only intended to protect the individual, but also to enable States to wage armed conflicts effectively. Any expectations that IHL will abolish suffering completely and at the same time attract perfect compliance will necessarily be disappointed. But attempts to interpret IHL in a manner that would unreasonably relax existing restrictions on warfare to the detriment of the protection of individuals should likewise be disappointed.

During the first conference of the SFB Project C8 in 2011, *Robert Cryer*[115] aptly described this state of affairs and the sometimes seemingly excessive expectations towards IHL in the following manner: 'International Law isn't Mommy. It's not going to make everything all right'. But the aspiration that the law can make a contribution, and lead to reasonable solutions legitimately adapted to new challenges, should not be abandoned.[116] It is our hope that this volume makes a small contribution to that endeavour.

---

112 See eg Barry R. Posen, 'Foreword: Military doctrine and the management of uncertainty', 39 (2016) Journal of Strategic Studies 159.

113 Amichai Cohen, 'Legal Operational Advice in the Israeli Defense Forces' (2011) 26 Connecticut Journal of International Law 367, 384; Jeremy J. Marsh and Scott L. Glabe, 'Time for the United States to Directly Participate' (2011) 1 VJIL 13.

114 Cf Henry, *Nécessité militaire* (n 20) 686.

115 Professor of International and Criminal Law, University of Birmingham (United Kingdom).

116 Cf Cryer, 'ICRC and Direct Participation' (n 92) 133-34.

Index

Table of Cases

International Case Law

European Court of Human Rights

A and Others v the United Kingdom, Application No. 3455/05, Judgment (19 February 2009)
Aksoy v Turkey, Application No. 21987/93, Judgment (18 December 1996)
Al Dulimi and Montana Management v Switzerland, Application No. 5809/08, Judgment (21 June 2016)
Al-Jedda v the United Kingdom, Application No. 27021/08, Judgment (7 July 2011)
Al-Sadoon and Mufhdi v the United Kingdom, Application No. 61498/08, Decision on Admissibility (3 July 2009)
Al-Skeini and Others v the United Kingdom, Application No. 55721/07, Judgment (7 July 2011)
Bankovic and Others v Belgium and Others, Application No. 52207/99, Decision of Admissibility (12 December 2001)
Brannigan and McBride v the United Kingdom, Applications No. 14553/89 and 14554/89, Judgment (26 May 1993)
Chagos Islanders v the United Kingdom, Application No. 35622/04, Decision of Admissibility (11 December 2012)
Hassan v the United Kingdom, Application No. 29750/09, Judgment (16 September 2014)
Issa and Others v Turkey, Application No. 31821/96, Judgment (16 November 2004)
Lawless v Ireland, Application No. 332/57, Judgment (1 July 1961)
Loizidou v Turkey, Application No. 15318/89, Judgment (18 December 1996)
Markovic and Others v Italy, Application No. 1398/03, Judgment (14 December 2006)
Medvedyev and Others v France, Application No. 3394/03, Judgment (29 March 2010)
Öcalan v Turkey, Application No. 46221/99, Judgment (12 May 2005)
Pisari v the Republic of Moldova and Russia, Application No. 42139/12, Judgment (21 April 2015)

International Arbitral Tribunals

Abed El Jaouni and Imperial Holding SAL v Lebanese Republic (pending) ICSID Case No. ARB/15/3

Administration of Lighthouses Arbitration (France v Greece) (Award) (1956) RIAA 155

Aeroport Belbek LLC and Mr. Kolomoisky v the Russian Federation (Investment Arbitration) [2015] PCA Case No. 2015-07

Alps Finance and Trade v Slovakia (Award) (2011) UNCITRAL, IIC 489

American Manufacturing & Trading, Inc. v Republic of Zaire (Award) (1997) ICSID Case No ARB/93/1

Amlyn Holding v Republic of Croatia (pending) ICSID Case No. ARB/16/28

Ampal-American Israel Corporation and others v Arab Republic of Egypt (Decision on Liability) (2017) ICSID Case No. ARB/12/11

Asian Agricultural Products Ltd v Sri Lanka (Final Award) (1991) ICSID Case No. ARB/87/3 30 ILM 580

Bayindir v Pakistan (Decision on Jurisdiction) (2005) ICSID Case No. ARB/03/29

Beijing Urban Construction v Yemen (Desicion on Jurisdiction) (2017) ICSID Case No. ARB/14/30

Cessation of Vessels and Tugs for Navigation on the Danube River (Award) (1921) 1 RIAA 97

CME Czech Republic B.V. v Czech Republic (Final Award and Separate Opinion) (2006) 9 ICSID Rep 264

Fedax NV v Venezuela (Award on Jurisdiction) (1997) ICSID Case No. ARB/96/03

Joy Mining v Egypt (Award) (2004) ICSID Case No. ARB/03/11

Joseph Houben v Republic of Burundi (Award) (2016) ICSID Case No. ARB/13/7

LESI SpA v Algeria (Decision on Jurisdiction) (2006) ICSID Case No. ARB/05/3

LLC Lugzor and Others v the Russian Federation (Investment Arbitration) [2015] PCA Case No. 2015-29

Malaysian Historical Salvors v Malaysia (Award on Jurisdiction) (2007) ICSID Case No. ARB/05/10

Malaysian Historical Salvors v Malaysia (Decision on the Application for Annulment) (2009) ICSID Case No. ARB/05/10

MCI v Ecuador (Award) (2007) ICSID Case No. ARB/03/6

Mitchell v Democratic Republic of the Congo (Award) (2004) ICSID Case No. ARB/99/7

Pantechniki S.A. Contractors & Engineers v Republic of Albania (Award) (2007) ICSID Case No. ARB/07/21
Petrobart Limited v The Kyrgyz Republic (Award) (2005) SCC Case No. 126/2003
Privatbank and Finance Company Finilion LLC v The Russian Federation (Investment Arbitration) [2015] PCA Case No. 2015-21
PSEG Global Inc. v Turkey (Award) (2007) ICSID case No ARB/02/5
Romak SA v The Republic of Uzbekistan (Award) (2009) UNCITRAL, PCA Case No. AA280
Ronald S. Lauder v Czech Republic (Final Award) (2001) UNICITRAL, IIC 205
RREEF Infrastructure Limited et al v Spain (Decision on Jurisdiction) (2016) ICSID Case No. ARB/13/30
Saluka Investments B.V. v The Czech Republic (Partial Award) (2006) UNCITRAL
Stabil LLC and Others v the Russian Federation (International Investment Agreement) [2015] PCA Case No. 2015-35
Técnicas Medioambientales Tecmed, S.A. v The United Mexican States, ICSID Case No. ARB (AF)/00/2

International Court of Justice

Accordance with International Law of the Unilateral Declaration of Independence in Respect of Kosovo (Advisory Opinion) [2010] ICJ Reports 403
Application of the Convention on the Prevention and Punishment of Genocide (Bosnia and Herzegovina v Serbia and Montenegro) (Judgment) [2007] ICJ Reports 43
Arrest Warrant of 11 April 2000 (Democratic Republic of the Congo v Belgium) (Judgment) [2002] ICJ Reports 3
Legal Consequences of the Construction of a Wall in the Occupied Palestinian Territory (Advisory Opinion) [2004] ICJ Reports 3
Legality of the Threat or Use of Nuclear Weapons (Advisory Opinion) [1996] ICJ Reports 226
North Sea Continental Shelf (Federal Republic of Germany v Denmark; Federal Republic of Germany v Netherlands) (Judgment) [1969] ICJ Reports 3
Nuclear Tests (Australia v France) (Judgment) [1974] ICJ Reports 253
Nuclear Tests (New Zealand v France) (Judgment) [1974] ICJ Reports 457
Reparation for Injuries Suffered in the Service of the United Nations (Advisory Opinion) [1949] ICJ Reports 174

International Criminal Tribunal for Rwanda

Prosecutor v Akayesu (Judgment) ICTR-96-4-T (2 September 1998)

International Criminal Tribunal for the former Yugoslavia

Prosecutor v Aleksovski (Judgment) IT-95-14/1-T (25 June 1999)

Prosecutor v Boskoski et al (Judgment) IT-04-82 (10 July 2008)

Prosecutor v Hadzihasanovic et al (Decision on interlocutory appeal challenging jurisdiction in relation to command responsibility) IT-01-47-AR72 (16 July 2003)

The Prosecutor v Kupreskic et al (Judgment) IT-95-16-T-14 (14 January 2000)

Prosecutor v Limaj et al. (Judgment) IT-03-66 (30 November 2005)

Prosecutor v Milutinovic et al (Judgment Volume 4 of 4) IT-05-87-T (26 February 2009)

Prosecutor v Stanišić and Zupljanin (Judgment Volume 3 of 3) IT-08-91-T (27 March 2013)

Prosecutor v Tadic (Judgment) IT-94-1-T (7 May 1997)

Prosecutor v Tadic (Decision on the Defence Motion for Interlocutory Appeal on Jurisdiction) IT-94-1 (2 October 1995)

Permanent Court of International Justice

S.S. Lotus (France v Turkey) [1927] PCIJ Series A No. 10

Lighthouses Case between France and Greece (France v Greece) [1934] PCIJ Series A/B No. 62

UN Human Rights Committee

General Comment No. 26: Continuity of Obligations (8 December 1997) UN Doc CCPR/C/21/Rev.1/Add.8/Rev.1

National Case Law

Belgium

Cour d'appel de Bruxelles, Arrêt à charge de X et al, No. 2017/2911 (14 September 2017)

Bochart v Committee of Supplies of Corneux (1920) No. 327, AD 1919-1922

City of Malines v Societe Centrale pour L'Exploitation du Gaz (1925) No. 362, AD 1925-26

Germany

Federal Prosecutor General (Germany), Targeted Killing in Pakistan Case, Case No 3 BJs 7/12-4, 157 ILR 722

Singapore

N.V. de Bataafsche Petroleum Maatschappij and Others v The War Damage Commission (1956) 23 ILR 810

United Kingdom

Abd Ali Hameed Al-Waheed v Ministry of Defence [2017] UKSC 2
Al-Jedda v Secretary of State for Defence [2008] 1 AC 332
Serdar Mohammed v Ministry of Defence [2014] EWHC 1369 (QB); [2014] CN 1019
Serdar Mohammed v Ministry of Defence [2015] EWCA Civ 843; [2015] WLR (D) 354
Serdar Mohammed v Ministry of Defence [2017] UKSC 2

United States

Mohamad et al v Palestinian Authority et al, 556 US 494 (2012)
Tel-Oren et al v Libyan Arab Republic et al, (1984) 726 F.2d 774, 233 U.S.App.D.C. 384
The United States of America v Wilhelm List, et al (1948) Law Reports of Trials of War Criminals selected and prepared by the United Nations War Crimes Commission, Volume VIII, 66